the series on school reform

Patricia A. Wasley
Coalition of
Essential Schools

Ann Lieberman
NCREST

SERIES EDITORS

Joseph P. McDonald
Annenberg Institute
for School Reform

The Work of Restructuring Schools:
Building from the Ground Up
ANN LIEBERMAN, Editor

Stirring the Chalkdust:
Tales of Teachers Changing Classroom Practice
PATRICIA A. WASLEY

Incorporating the following books from the
PROFESSIONAL DEVELOPMENT AND PRACTICE SERIES

D0095936

The Work of Restructuring Schools

BUILDING FROM THE GROUND UP

EDITED BY
Ann Lieberman

FOREWORD BY
Seymour B. Sarason

Teachers College
Columbia University
New York and London

Published by Teachers College Press, 1234 Amsterdam Avenue, New York, NY 10027

Library of Congress Cataloging-in-Publication Data

The work of restructuring schools : building from the ground up /
  edited by Ann Lieberman.
      p.   cm.—(The series on school reform)
   Includes bibliographical references and index.
   ISBN 0-8077-3404-7 (cloth : acid-free paper).—ISBN
0-8077-3403-9 (paper : acid-free paper)
     1. Elementary school administration—United States—Case studies.
  2. Middle schools—United States—Administration—Case studies.
  3. Educational change—United States—Case stuides. I. Lieberman,
Ann. II. Series.
LB2822.5.W67   1995
372.12′00973—dc20   94-24898

ISBN 0-8077-3403-9 (paper)
ISBN 0-8077-3404-7 (cloth)

Printed on acid-free paper

Manufactured in the United States of America

02   01   00   99   98   97   8   7   6   5   4   3   2

Contents

Foreword

It is one of the virtues of this book that its title contains the word *work*. Today, we hear the word *restructuring* daily in regard to schools and the private sector. What gets conjured up by re-"structuring" is some executive who is rearranging "forms" with the result that the "bottom line"—be it in the form of money or test scores—will improve. Just like that! The public knows in regard to the private sector that restructuring means that some people will be out of work. When the word *restructuring* is used in regard to schools, people are not (usually) thrown out of work, and the public is led to assume that some rearrangement of "form" will take place to achieve better educational outcomes. What the public is not told is the work that will be required to achieve those outcomes. I am not, of course, referring to instances where someone on high dictates the restructuring and the peons below have to accommodate, like it or not. That kind of restructuring is a form of game playing, a charade, a rearrangement that gives the appearance that the nature of work will change whereas the reality is that it will not, unless for the worst.

The contribution of this case book is that it realistically describes the quality and quantity of work required by the personnel of a school who have come to see that the regularities characterizing their school need to be altered. And they quickly learn that it is hard work, very hard work, because they are not seeking to change forms but themselves and their colleagues. I say "quickly learn" because the decision to undertake change more often than not is accompanied by a kind of optimism and rosy view of the future that, temporarily at least, obscures the predictable turmoil ahead. But that turmoil cannot be avoided and how well it is coped with separates the boys from the men, the girls from the women. It is, as these cases well depict, rough stuff.

This is not a book propagandizing for a particular methodology or ideology and claiming unexcelled successes. It is a book that does justice to its intent and title: restructuring schools is very hard work, it cannot be programmed by the calendar, it is problem producing as well as problem resolving, it has no end point, it is a continuous process, there are breakthroughs but also brick walls, and it is indisputably worthwhile. This is a realistic book that should be read and pondered by those who do not comprehend the demanding personal involvement and work—usually beyond the usual school day—the process re-quires. The work of restructuring is not for the faint hearted. It is for those who seek a redefinition of their professional lives, for those who want to put *their* imprimatur on *their* school. To someone like me who does not get encourage-ment from observing the educational scene, this book was inspiring. There are educators "out there" who are fighting the good fight and by writing about it honestly remind us that it is a very worthwhile personal–educational–intellectual endeavor. I am personally grateful to Ann Lieberman for her leadership role in encouraging the writers of this book to do what they did and to write about it. As the writers make clear: salvation for our schools will not come from without but from within. That is a message I wish more members of our profession would take seriously.

Seymour B. Sarason

The Work of Restructuring Schools

BUILDING FROM THE GROUND UP

Restructuring Schools: The Dynamics of Changing Practice, Structure, and Culture

Ann Lieberman

Since 1983, when *A Nation at Risk* was first published, talk about reforming American schools has continued unabated. But as understanding of what it takes to fundamentally change schools has grown, so has the nature of the discussion (Darling-Hammond, 1993; Fullan, 1992; Hargreaves, 1991; Little, 1993; McLaughlin & Talbert, 1993; Sarason, 1990; Tyack, 1990). Reform has come to be seen as involving systemic change, taking place in specific contexts and over longer periods of time. Many ideas, like teacher development, which encourages "growth in practice," and involvement in the adoption, adaptation, and construction of curriculum (approaches to practice that are defined by democratic values, enabling state and district policies that support local invention) are becoming a part of the changing paradigm for restructuring schools. These ideas suggest a view of reform that requires the combined participation of those who study schools, those who work in schools, and those who support schools. This collaboration is crucial to understanding how and in what ways deep changes take place over time, and how to surmount the inevitable obstacles that must be faced along the way.

The case studies in this volume were commissioned by the National Center for Restructuring Education, Schools, and Teaching (NCREST) at Teachers College, Columbia University, which was founded in 1990 to support the creation of schools that are learner-centered, enriched by teachers' learning opportunities, and supported by assessment practices that inspire continuous improvement. This collection focuses specifically on elementary and middle schools. Much of the recent literature on restructuring has been about secondary schools. Elementary schools are clearly different. They often do not have natural groups like departments, but increasingly elementary schools are figuring out unique ways to bring faculty together to work on restructuring. It was to better illuminate how such schools go about organizing people, ideas, and practices that we undertook this volume. Authors were invited to document schools where the faculty had been working on restructuring efforts that were of long enough duration to have made some substantial changes, and where those involved have looked to change and improve the whole school rather than seeing their efforts as one more unconnected project. One case study, Smylie and Tuermer's, was originally part of a group of studies documenting the changing role of teacher unions. The data was so rich, the authors consented to write a version of their work to fit the specifications of this volume. From this collection, it is therefore hoped that readers can gain perspective on what "systemic change" means to different schools—both from within the school and at the district level.

THE CONTEXTS BEING STUDIED

The six case studies in this book are drawn from five different states: Kentucky, Florida, Indiana, South Carolina, and Maine. Five of the studies are of elementary schools and one is of a middle school. Brooksville Elementary School and Fredericks Middle School in Florida (Chapters 4 and 3 respectively) are part of a long-term shared decision making (SDM) contract between the Live Oak Teachers Union and the County School Board that began in 1989. Wheeler Elementary (Chapter 2) is now seen as one of the exemplars for the Kentucky Education Reform Act, although the school turned to multi-age grouping and teaming before the passage of this legislation as part of the first cohort of schools in the Gheens Academy—a local network formed within the Louisville School District by Phil Schlechty and designed to support schools in the process of change. Keels Elementary (Chapter 6) is part of a 12-school project in South Carolina supported by a large state reform effort. Hammond, Indiana (Chapter 5), has long been known for its stable and cooperative labor relations and its collaborative work in improving schools. (In this case, we see how important the history is to the context of "restructuring schools" and how enlightened leadership at school, district, and union levels succeeds in eventually building a cooperative relationship). New Suncook (Chapter 7), although situated in rural Maine, with a potential for great isolation, is connected to the national reform effort through its association with the Southern Maine partnership—a school-university partnership between the University of Southern Maine and a group of schools in the area. All of these schools are still cultures in the making, yet five of the six have gone a long way toward reinventing the cultures of their schools.

UNIVERSAL YET PARTICULAR KNOWLEDGE

The intent of the studies commissioned by NCREST was to have each case be true to its own context but, at the same time, adhere to a broad outline that enabled comparable information to be collected. (See the appendix at the end of the chapter for the outline provided to the case study researchers.) In this way, we hoped to be able to view themes at greater levels of generalization than that afforded by the specifics of the stories being told. This was problematic, for although similar information was sought in all the case studies, the schools differed in so many ways: in the ways the state and local contexts supported school reform, in their history and changing demographics, in the dynamics of individual school and district cultures, in the role of leadership, and so on.

It is sometimes true that the essential elements of school life are missing from case studies of schools and, in their absence, we often fail to see the critical missing components that may serve as barriers to *or* supports for sustaining lasting change. In some ways, good case studies, like good mysteries, do not leave out details that help to illuminate the case. Yet unless these details are attached to larger conceptual ideas, we are in danger of drowning in a welter of unrelated anecdotal material that obscures what is really happening and what lessons can be learned. In trying to achieve a balanced view, each case study here attempts to get at the important ideas that emerge from close observation of the school itself while seeing it in its district, state, and/or network context. This chapter, in like fashion, searches for the universal themes while making manifest the particulars of each context.

THE RESEARCHERS AND THE RESEARCHED: RETHINKING THE TRADITIONAL RESEARCH PARADIGM

Accurate and inclusive documentation of efforts to restructure schools has become an important challenge for researchers; understanding the work of restructuring demands a rethinking of the relationships between the researchers and the researched (Lieberman, 1992). Getting closer to school people who are changing their practices presents greater opportunities for understanding the change process—closeness allows for greater depth of understanding of practice, particularly if the researcher is there over time.

Those involved in the dailiness of classroom life must act and react on the basis of the immediate need to resolve problems and dilemmas and respond to individual and group demands. Researchers can play the role of "critical friends" who are there but, because they are not doing the work themselves, have a measure of distance and time to interpret what they see. Personal relationships, shared understandings of deeply held values, and openness to the process by which organizational knowledge gets built helps research-based educators connect *with* school-based educators who are experiencing change. This closeness does not come without problems.

Schools and classrooms are embedded in a larger context that may or may not be supportive of the change process. Reports or case studies that put a spotlight on individuals make them vulnerable—sometimes to their peers as well as to their supervisors. Researchers must be concerned about the effects of their writing on those whom they are researching as well as about the comprehensiveness and accuracy of their observations. *What* is written as well as *how* it is written becomes important. Protecting people who are struggling to make substantial changes while, at the same time, writing truthfully about the uneven and difficult change process becomes a major challenge. Researchers who are rewarded for written work must be sensitive to the fact that such writing creates an authority of its own that can be used to enhance or deepen understandings about schools but can also be used to disclose or punish schools.

It is important to recognize that these studies result from a negotiation between the outsiders and the insiders, the researchers and the researched. Since there is no one way to develop a common language and a collective sense of purpose for those who innovate and those who study them (Brown, 1991), researchers and school-based educators are building a variety of forms of collaborative relationships: several of them are represented in this volume (see also Miller & O'Shea, forthcoming).

Goldsberry (Chapter 7) started as a "friendly observer," a faculty member of a college who had been active in a school-university partnership. New Suncook was one of the original schools in the University of Southern Maine partnership, so it was easy and natural for Goldsberry to become accepted by the school. Chapter 7 was written by several teachers, the principal, and Goldsberry, a university educator who sees himself as the "weaver" of the many pieces of the story. Since this was a retrospective, it is not surprising that individuals' memories were different, and that there was much discussion about the differing perceptions of the history of this 7-year evolution during the process of constructing a coherent story. This case study now serves as an outline history for the school, documenting its organizational learning and helping to preserve institutional memory of the school's progress.

In several of these case studies, university-based researchers had reputations for being innovative and supportive of school restructuring. Their involvement in writing case studies in the past gave them entrée to the schools through the personal relationships that they had developed over the years. (This is particularly true in Whitford's writing of Chapter 2. She has long been known as a researcher who works sensitively with schools.) In these cases, researchers checked their descriptions of the school with members of the school faculty for accuracy of data and interpretation. Berry used the case study of Keels Elementary (Chapter 6) for an occasion to hold a week-long institute where the case study was critiqued and also used for the development of future plans for the school. Smylie and Tuermer wrote their case study (Chapter 5) as part of a larger project on the changing relationships between labor and management (see Kerchner & Koppich, 1993).

Bondy (Chapter 3) and Ross and Webb (Chapter 4) have tracked a district-wide, shared decision making project in the Live Oak district since its inception in 1989. Working out of the R and D Center for School Improvement at the University of Florida, researchers and school-based educators have worked together, providing twice yearly "formative evaluations" from the university to the district that have served as status reports. In addition, a year-end report is given to the school board and the teachers' union. Having worked together over a long period of time, these researchers have made friends with their school partners, negotiating both the "telling of the stories" and the terms of their ongoing relationship. They have recognized that building knowledge about change can place both university and school people in positions where they are more vulnerable, demanding greater sensitivity to the social and political contexts of which they are a part.

INITIATION AND SUPPORT FOR CHANGE

The Roles of Principals and a Core Group of Teachers

Both Wheeler and New Suncook started their reform effort with principals who were involved in a restructuring network. Wheeler's principal was one of the original members of the Gheens Academy in Kentucky. New Suncook's principal was part of the Southern Maine Partnership. In each of these cases, the principal and a small group of teachers came together in a core group to think about reinventing their schools. Although New Suncook is a rural school and Wheeler more suburban, the actual work they were doing was similar. Each built a shared vision (in writing) of what they thought their school should be. (Work on this vision was supported by the reform networks of which they were members.) Both elementary schools sought to use ideas of multi-age groups and team teaching as a way of expanding their work to include a broader view of student learning, and to develop a structure for teacher participation.

These two case studies show how, eventually, the early resistance of some teachers gave way to developing norms of innovation and optimism (see Webb, 1994). Each shows the power of the authentic bottom-up participation of teachers: starting with a few, slowly building their commitment by encouraging and engaging them in discussion, supporting a vision, then acting on that vision and inventing ways to make it a reality.

The similar role that the principals played in both of these case studies (one male, one female) provides some valuable lessons in leadership. Each started small—always bringing teachers to meetings and having many conversations, both private and public. Recognizing that it was important to provide structures for continuing discussion and eventual action, the principals held retreats, secured small state grants to work on problems in-depth, and created teams and team leaders. Both schools linked the idea of student success to teacher participation and development, planning to enrich the learning environment for students by creating that same rich environment for teachers.

The Role of the District in Enabling Reform

Sometimes the pressure to change comes from district leadership. In three of these case studies the district generated the most important thrust for reform. Both Fredericks Middle School and Brookville Elementary are part of the Live Oak district. Live Oak initiated shared decision making (SDM) by teachers and administrators as an important means to help schools restructure. The case studies of Fredericks (Chapter 3) and Brookville (Chapter 4) are especially interesting as they contrast with one another, confounding our common sense notions about predictions for success. Fredericks had a long history in the district as being a "special, progressive" school. This seemed like a perfect place for SDM to take hold because collaborative relationships had long been a hallmark of the school. Brookville, on the other hand, had long been known for its troubled administrator-teacher relationships and appeared to be a poor bet to succeed. (However, as Stinchcombe [1965] reminded us over 25 years ago, change upsets the strength of stable ties.) Contrary to expectations, Fredericks struggled with shared decision making, which upset its informal structure and settled ways of working. At Brookville, on the other hand, this innovative decision-making structure provided a newfound voice for teachers and a new forum for change. Facile explanations of readiness for reform need to be informed by the context as seen not only by the reformers, but by the participants as well. Those who are in the culture may experience it far differently than those who observe it.

The case study of Hammond, Indiana (Chapter 5), is a story of the growth of "collaborative labor relations, community support, administrator-board relations, and a system mindful of the need for capacity building." This is a case of stable and enlightened union and school leadership that worked through several crises, eventually learning how to involve the total community in restructuring its schools. Because the case covers a long period of time, we see how the stakes have increased from "improving" schools to "restructuring" them to creating systemic change.

The Role of State Reform

Keels Elementary in Columbia, South Carolina (Chapter 6), in an upper-middle-class suburban district, is the one school in the district situated on the "other side of the tracks." In contrast to Hammond, Keels lost its old community through shifting demographics and had to start again with a new community. As one of the schools helped by the Education Improvement Act of 1984 (the school reform bill for South Carolina that gave schools incentive money when it raised test scores), Keels provides an example of a school where the principal (and her predecessor) helped to empower a cadre of teachers who worked especially hard to enable their students to achieve. Teachers at Keels became known throughout the state for their growing expertise in the areas of technology, reading, and quality child care. Using the resources that the principal was able to provide, the school helped to expand teacher capacities, to change the teacher-student relationship from "passive to active," and to blur the lines between curricular and extracurricular activities.

LEARNING ABOUT THE "WORK" OF RESTRUCTURING SCHOOLS

While the major focus of this book is on the actual work involved at the school or district site that goes into making progress toward a learner-centered agenda for reform, other important factors are not ignored: state policies, union rules and regulations, forward- or backward-looking leadership, committed teachers, district- and statewide change efforts that promote or impede change, incentives that encourage work in a particular area of concern, newly formed networks that provide norms for change beyond those provided by the formal system. State, district and local policies as Linda Darling-Hammond shows in Chapter 8, are often ignored, misunderstood or contradictory to new practices. However, these policies play a significant role in enabling schools to initiate and sustain important changes in practice.

By demonstrating a variety of ways that progress can take place, the case studies in this book seek to get closer to the school without sacrificing the need to understand how supports outside the school matter. "Work" is defined not only as what teachers and students do, but also as what principals, practices, and policies enable them to do in different settings over time.

What has often been missing from the documentation of schools attempting important changes is the web of interpersonal relationships that often dominate the change process; the interpretations that teachers and principals make of reformers' ideas and the consequent actions they take while learning about and creating their own ideas. Also missing has been an understanding of the critical importance of the kind of massive and continuous support needed to cope with the inevitable tensions that come with the change process. This kind of information might help us to understand why it is that some schools can suffer tremendous conflict and yet strengthen their resolve to change, whereas others experience one small incident that topples their good intentions. We enrich our understanding of conflict and how it plays out in different school cultures as it becomes one of the defining characteristics of change.

Learning from Experience—Turning Problems into Possibilities for Change

Part of the answer to this question may be found in the process of how schools as organizations learn from experience (Darling-Hammond, 1993; Murphy & Hallinger, 1993). Schools that attempt to change inevitably experience conflict—some of it serious. Often this is reason enough for going back to old ways of working, simply because old ways are comfortable and because those involved cannot imagine any other choices (Fine, 1994). But some people and some organizations, by learning from their mistakes, use what they learn to create new structures and new levels of participation, in some cases determining what immediate steps to take and how people can be mobilized to support them. This process is dramatically illustrated in the Hammond case study (Chapter 5). In the first round of improvement efforts in the 1970s, a negotiated agreement between the district and the teachers' union created school improvement teams. At one point, the work of two teams was questioned by a district review committee, which charged that the schools did not have approval for their innovative plans. (The significance of this incident, a constant dynamic when fundamental change is taking place, is that issues of power and control are juxtaposed against issues of trust, support, and commitment.) As decision making appeared to be moving from the district to the local school, the school board reversed the teams' decisions—causing great tension and turmoil. This breach between district and schools clouded the atmosphere of trust that had been built up over the years. Eventually, understanding what they had done, the district set up a new structure, the strategic planning committee, to review the existing school improvement process and to make recommendations. Although this was not easily accomplished, the new committee, which was broadly representative, created a firmer basis for collaboration and deepened the agenda for more fundamental reform.

New Suncook (Chapter 7) offers another example of learning from experience. In this small rural school, the process unfolded as a series of opportunities for change that evolved from pressure to deal with new needs; taking advantage of these opportunities raised the magnitude and complexity of the reform effort while, at the same time, deepening the knowledge and understanding of practice by a group of involved teachers. It was as if the school used a set of building blocks, with each block providing some needed learning by the teachers, and each leading to a broader and more enlightened agenda for school change. A small initial grant of $2,000 to create a research into practice (RIP) team (a group of six teachers studying research, visiting each other's classrooms, and establishing a dialogue between teachers) paid off in larger and broader exposure to other reform efforts as the members of the team grew in sophistication through these small experiences. Each meeting, visitation, and discussion taught them more so that they, with the help of another team, eventually came to link broad-based ideas to the daily practice of change in their school. The narrative shows us how the staff made each organizational experience work toward developing the process of the school's education and, eventually, toward its transformation. Naturally these experiences are always bumpy, stressful, and messy, but to get to this kind of rethinking takes this kind of long-term work. These kinds of experiences provide the basis for new configurations of work, new ways of talking with one another, and new ways of seeing students more actively engaged in work. Such experiences in elementary schools must be supported and nurtured by the principal.

Shaping a New Relationship: Teachers in Foreground, Principals in Background

In four of these case studies, the authors explore the roles of the principals in relation to small groups of teachers, giving us a sense of what it means to rethink the role of leadership in restructuring schools. The "effective schools" of the 1980s placed the principal at the head of school improvement efforts. It was his or her job to be an "instructional leader," which meant that the principal was responsible for directing and overseeing teachers' work with students; one primary task of the principal was to get teachers to work cooperatively. An important focus for improvement was to "align" the curriculum throughout the grades, which was supposed to provide a major incentive for teachers to cooperate.

The 1990s view of leadership is related to rethinking the goals of the school. This involves moving toward a curriculum that encourages students to deal with real-world problems and teaches them to think conceptually in integrated ways, to work cooperatively where possible, and to use broad-based means of assessing their knowledge and abilities. Achieving these goals may indeed require a transformation of past approaches to the problems of leadership (Derrington, 1988). These case studies show principals acting as partners with teachers, involved in a collaborative quest to examine school practices to see how they can improve what the school is doing for all of its students. Principals do not control but, rather, support teachers, helping to create opportunities for them to grow and develop. At Wheeler and New Suncook the principals intentionally built a core group of teachers that provided leadership for the staff; at Keels and Brooksville, the principals learned that power and control are antithetical to trust and risk taking on the part of teachers. In all cases, how faculty and principal work to shape each other's role is seen as a process: eventually teachers are empowered to decide and ask for what they need, while principals learn to find ways to provide them with consistent support and continuous opportunities to grow and expand their repertoire.

Building Shared Meaning through Action and Reflection

Until teachers are willing to talk to one another about what they are doing in their own classrooms, it is difficult to initiate meaningful conversations about school change. But how does this actually happen? At Wheeler (Chapter 2), teachers initially said "tell us what to do and we'll do great." But when no one came forward to tell them what to do, several teachers finally realized that they would have to take responsibility to initiate something. The Gheens Academy gave release time to several teachers just to read and to talk. This eventually led to two changes: the teachers developed a shared vision for the school and established multi-age teams—the former a design for the future and the latter a practical step toward getting there.

At New Suncook, (Chapter 7) a state grant, written by the principal and a teacher, created the initial impetus for change. The grant provided money for a team of six teachers to learn about current educational issues, to observe one another, to have time to talk with one another, and to create an environment that encouraged teachers to reflect on their teaching.

At both of these schools, the most powerful impediment to reform—the isolation of teachers—was being transformed. Teachers were being given time to read and learn and to talk about their learning and together think through what they might envision as a future for their school. They were initially skeptical, but soon became engaged in thinking about how to make use of what they were reading and finding out about. Both schools embraced some of the same key ideas, including active student involvement in making decisions, which led to more student choice in how they were to learn; the concept of "multiple intelligences," which led to a variety of changed instructional strategies such as Wheeler's multi-age groups and a set of activities called "learning connections"; and New Suncook's multi-age teams.

It is apparent, from these and other case studies, that teachers need support to legitimatize time spent getting together with each other to read, talk, and discuss different viewpoints in order to gain a broader perspective so that they can see themselves as participants in a nationwide movement to transform schools. Initial reluctance is to be expected; years of being told what to do breeds dependence on other people's ideas and a sense that teachers' knowledge is not important. Sooner or later, however, the talk must produce activities; teachers must see for themselves that students can learn from one another and that activity-based curriculum increases students' involvement. These activities subsequently become a fertile source for teachers' discussions, expanding their thinking about their own and their students' roles in the classroom.

Tension and Conflict: Inside and Outside the School

Each of the case studies reveals different areas of conflict both in and outside the school. There is district and local school conflict over who controls what decisions, and concern at the district when one school looks different than its neighbor. There is conflict among teachers as they change from dependence to independence while moving from "congenial" to "collegial" relationships (Bill Johnson, personal communication, October 12, 1993). New structures put teachers and principals in different relationships to one another, changing expectations as power relationships are reconfigured. Working in unfamiliar groups and in unfamiliar ways with students breeds insecurity and defensiveness among teachers. While teaching always carries with it a measure of tension, learning new ways of working increases that tension. Conflict increases as the changing school culture begins to shift from superficial conversations to serious discourse about learning, teaching styles, modes of organizing the curriculum, and so on (Little, 1993). But this is to be expected; reforms such as these touch deeply on people's values and worldviews about knowledge, the purpose of schools, and the roles of teacher and student—all very contentious issues in American society. It is not so much a question of whether or not conflict will arise, but how this conflict is handled. When viewed as productive conflict—a natural and inevitable part of the change process—teachers learn that it is all right to hold differing views and to argue for them, that it is a part of working toward building a norm of inquiry in the school, so that ideas about improving teaching and learning become the basis of ongoing discussion. These norms do not come easily, since most of us who teach have not had opportunities to publicly debate and discuss the complexities of teaching and learning as ideas, separate from our own styles and ways of working.

At Keels (Chapter 6), the teachers find a way to tell the principal and vice principal that they are not sensitive to the context of the school. In Hammond (Chapter 5), there is major turmoil over the district's lack of trust of local school decision making. Eventually, a new committee is created to deal with the conflict that has arisen. At New Suncook (Chapter 7), the RIP team, forgetting to involve special education teachers in the proposed changes, must later deal with their concerns. In all the case studies, there is initial resistance to change (and with some people it is constant), particularly when some teachers become progressively more involved and forge ahead of their peers. Time, persistence, increased openness, and, often, the creation of new structures (e.g., teams, school site committees) to handle dissent may help, but the pressures inherent in learning to do things differently create an inevitable and ubiquitous tension in the school that must be expected and handled.

Using and Making New Structures Work for Reform Purposes

All of these case studies show new structures being created that help to transform the schools. These schools and districts demonstrate that one important way to change the "regularities" of schooling is to intentionally create new mechanisms for reform (see Sarason, 1972). But they also reveal that these mechanisms must fit the particulars of the context and the perceived problems and needs that arise.

For Hammond, there was the creation of the professional development academy, a place that honors the idea of learning and development as a continuous form of inquiry into practice. It formed as a result of the experiences of the enlarged collaborative group that was in charge of restructuring Hammond's schools. For New Suncook and Wheeler, there were the formation of teacher teams, and multi-age groups of students; these were formed when the teachers realized that they needed to think differently about student grouping, as well as about how they themselves could come together naturally to talk about students, curriculum, and pedagogy. There were also retreats, where time away from school was used to discuss long-term plans, as well as to work on the inevitable problems that needed fuller discussion and alternative solutions. There were core planning teams in Hammond, and clubs at Keels. At Brookville and Fredericks shared decision making (SDM) teams were created. There were also team leaders and Research into Practice Teams of teachers. All of these are examples of different structures that were built as a result of activities to encourage the process of change in schools and districts.

Sometimes a mechanism can be created before any restructuring has taken place, as in New Suncook. Here the RIP team served as the initiator of change. In Live Oak, the district supported shared decision making teams in Fredericks and Brooksville. But often, "form follows function," as at Wheeler, where teams and multi-age groups were formed by faculty as a result of reading and discussion about how the school could deal with the idea of multiple intelligences and the diversity of its student body. Keels created clubs as a result of their newfound understanding that curricular and extra-curricular activities need not be separated. In these situations, the schools discovered that they could encourage new ways of working with new support structures. These organizational forms then became parts of the whole of what is meant by "restructuring schools."

Student Work: The Agenda for Teacher Work

Two strong and related seminal themes in all of these case studies are: changing the work of students and providing ways for teachers to talk publicly about that work. The focus on students mobilizes teachers to commit themselves to making major changes in how they—as well as their students—participate in school, though the specifics of the process differ depending on the context of each of these case studies. But there is no question that providing the means for students to participate more actively in school becomes an unshackling experience for teachers. By relinquishing total control of how students learn, teachers are enabled to see their students more fully engaged in learning activities, giving concrete meaning to the theory of "active student learning."

Wheeler's case study (Chapter 2) documents movement from a school with "traditional, top-down management"—an orderly and strict environment in which teachers rely on heavy use of drill-and-practice worksheets—to a school organized around three primary and two intermediate multiage, heterogeneous teams of 88 to 120 students and 4 to 5 teachers. All of the teams were nongraded, giving students a longer time to develop and demonstrate their skills and abilities. Students often worked in groups and had debates; some learned to prepare and deliver daily newscasts utilizing closed circuit TV. Teachers made use of parent volunteers who, among other things, helped organize students' video portfolios. Since the focus of the school was on student success, the energy, motivation, and commitment of the teachers were directed toward rethinking how students actively engaged in work, and time was provided for teachers to talk about and learn more about their students.

The Hammond case study (Chapter 5), while a documentation of long-term district-union collaboration that gives much attention to organizational structures and processes, is also very much about the continuous focus of this district on student learning. Smylie and Tuermer maintain that emphasis on students is what has remained at the center of the school improvement process, driving the restructuring of schools in the district even during times of crisis and conflict.

The dramatic story of those at Keels Elementary (Chapter 6), who built a whole new culture, saw the focus change from blaming the students to figuring out how to find ways to support student success. The leadership of two successive innovative principals and a core group of teachers inspired a "can do" attitude in the school. While the major focus was on curriculum change, "fueled by an infusion of technology," virtually every part of the organization of the school was included in the process of change. Starting with language arts in the primary grades, the school has moved toward examining all aspects of the curriculum, supported by methodological change that includes longer time blocks, cooperative learning, and innovative use of computers.

The faculty at New Suncook (Chapter 7) began by reading research. As at Wheeler, they progressed to multiage grouping, observing and learning from students while building a professional community through teamwork and continuous schoolwide discussion about learning. At New Suncook, as at the other schools, the focus on students was central to the change process. Teachers learn about themselves by seeing their students work and learn in different ways. Providing experiences that change the way students work is as important to teacher learning as it is to student learning.

Creating a Professional Community

Perhaps the most significant and critical understanding we gain from these cases is how professional communities develop among teachers and their principals, communities that "encourage and enable [teachers] to transform their teaching" (McLaughlin & Talbert, 1993, p. 7). Such communities are built as teachers, unpacking the baggage of years of unexamined attitudes, beliefs, and practices, come to trust one another enough to participate in group discussions.

Although discussions are often of an abstract nature at first, teachers come to share moving experiences, observations of changes in students' motivations to learn, excitement about coming to school, involvement in project work, and enthusiasm for learning. A community of teachers like this raises the work of teaching to new levels of complexity, where it is treated as an unfinished task with dilemmas to be weighed and curricula to be crafted and where students are at the center of teacher learning. At the same time, it develops ways of providing the stimulation that is needed to consistently deepen teachers' practice.

These communities are built in different ways in different places. At Wheeler, over time the principal patiently persuaded two groups of teachers to pilot multiage teams—without getting discouraged when initially no one volunteered. At Fredericks, the imposition of formal shared decision making, decades after there had been informal working teams, upset a community ethos that had long been established; while at Brookville, an SDM team became a forum for discussing school change where nothing had existed before. At New Suncook, over several years, a group of teachers supported by the principal slowly began to talk and work together, first about research on reform and then, eventually, about their growing understanding and expanding view of students' work.

For elementary school teachers there is no built-in structure, such as a high school department, and teachers, although loosely bound together by grade levels, do not often use this commonality as a basis for building community. What is noteworthy about the case studies presented here is that community was built around shared understanding of new theories of learning and intelligence, and around a search for ways to support student success at school, both within and across grade levels. The focus was on creating school cultures where students and adults lived and worked together in a community that was excited about learning—whether about children, research, or teaching. Colleagueship was built on shared struggles, changed practices, and much trial-and-error learning.

Although each of the case studies describes different starting points for change, and although each takes place in a different part of the country, all of them find that comprehensive change in the school as a whole requires focusing on issues of restructuring and transformation of *the school,* rather than on specific projects or innovations. Their concerns are less with "cooperative learning" and "whole language" (although these may be a part of school practice) than with building a school culture that "works" for the students and the adults. The visions and values that concern themselves with such ideas take root slowly, but the changes they make possible distinguish these schools from others. These individuals' understanding that changing schools demands changing practices, and that structures must be built to support these changed practices, leads them toward cultures of colleagueship, continuous inquiry, and collaborative work that may well mark the organizational path to the schools of the future.

APPENDIX: CASE STUDY FORMAT

We would like to provide you with a general outline to help in the writing of the cases on restructuring schools and professional development schools. These categories should allow enough room for your own styles of writing and data collection. It is our hope that they won't inhibit the basic "story" that you want to tell.

   I. Introduction and background
      What is the larger context of your school?
      What are the state policies that enable or inhibit change
      Describe the local context.
      Is the school embedded in a larger network or coalition? Describe the school's connection to it.
  II. The context and description of the school
      How would you describe the school, its students, neighborhood, faculty, parent body, and so on?
 III. What is the school trying to do?
      What is the school's vision? What are its values?
      What is or continues to be the focus of work at the school?

What characterizes the school as special, innovative, and/or visionary?

IV. How has the school gone about making change? What structures, new roles, responsibilities, ways of working have changed? How?

How would you describe the way the school has gone about changing?

What roles, responsibilities, groups, or committees have been formed to rethink what the school is doing and how those at the school can achieve their vision?

V. What programmatic changes or teaching/learning strategies have been made?

What teaching strategies are being used? Changed curricular ideas? Instructional innovations? Student-oriented formats? New approaches to curriculum (e.g., cooperative learning, teaching to themes, process-oriented teaching [e.g., writing, etc.])?

VI. What have been the barriers and/or tensions that have impeded progress? What has facilitated the changes?

VII. What kind of personal and organizational learning has taken place?

VIII. What is your analysis of this school?

What are the lessons to be learned about policy, practice, technical assistance, teacher learning, development, change, and so on?

REFERENCES

Brown, J. S. (1991). Research that reinvents the corporation. *Harvard Business Review,* January/February, 102–117.

Darling-Hammond, L. (1993). Reframing the school reform agenda: Developing capacity for school transformation. *Kappan, 74*(10), 753–761.

Derrington, M. L. (1988). *The role of the principal: Tradition, transition and transformation, an ethnographic study of two high school principals.* Unpublished doctoral dissertation, University of Washington, Seattle.

Fine, M. (1994). (Ed.). *Chartering urban school reform: Reflections on public high schools in the midst of change.* New York: Teachers College Press.

Fullan, M., with S. Stiegelbauer. (1992). *The new meaning of educational change.* New York: Teachers College Press.

Hargreaves, A. (1991, April). *Restructuring restructuring: Postmodernity and the prospects for educational change.* Paper delivered at the annual meeting of the American Educational Research Association, Chicago.

Kerchner, C. T., & Koppich, J. E. (1993). *A union of professionals: Labor relations and educational reform.* New York: Teachers College Press.

Lieberman, A. (1992). The meaning of scholarly activity and the building of community. *Educational Researchers, 21*(6), 5–17.

Little, J. W. (1993). Teachers' professional development in a climate of educational reform. *Educational Evaluation and Policy Analysis, 15*(2), 129–151.

McLaughlin, M., & Talbert, J. (1993). *Contexts that matter for teaching and learning.* Stan-
ford, CA: Center for Research on the Context of Secondary School Teaching.

Miller, L., & O'Shea, C. (forthcoming). *Partnership: Getting deeper, getting broader.* New
York: Teachers College, Columbia University, National Center for Restructuring
Education, Schools, and Teaching.

Murphy, J., & Hallinger, P. (Eds.). (1993). *Restructuring schooling: Learning from ongoing
efforts.* Newbury Park, CA: Corwin Press.

Sarason, S. (1972). *The culture of the school and the problem of change.* Boston: Allyn & Bacon.

Sarason, S. (1990). *The predictable failure of educational reform: Can we change course before it's
too late?* San Francisco: Jossey-Bass.

Stinchcombe, A. (1965). *Social structure and organization.* In J. March (Ed.), *Handbook of
Organizations* (pp. 142–193). Chicago: Rand McNally.

Tyack, D. (1990). "Restructuring" in historical perspective: Tinkering towards utopia.
Teachers College Record, 92(2), 170–191.

Webb, R. B. (1994). *Shared decision-making and school restructuring in Live Oak County.*
New York: Teachers College, Columbia University, National Center for Restructuring Education, Schools, and Teaching.

Chapter 2 _____

With a Little Help from Their Friends: Teachers Making Change at Wheeler School

Betty Lou Whitford
Donna M. Gaus

It is early June of 1991, and school is over for the summer. The parking lot of Wheeler Elementary School is virtually empty, and the near windowless building gives few clues about how best to enter. The brick, multisided structure looks more like a small fortress than a suburban school, oddly cut off from the adjacent subdivision of small ranch and split-level houses with neat lawns. The principal has not yet arrived for what is to become the first of many long conversations about the school. There is time, then, to take a look around.

In striking contrast to the cold, impersonal exterior, the lobby of Wheeler Elementary School is ablaze with color. An enormous blue and yellow doormat lies just inside the double doors of the main entrance. In the center of the doormat is an old fashioned red schoolhouse framed across the top by the words "Expecting the Best, Producing Success," and at the bottom by "Wheeler School—For Kids" in black block letters. Half hidden behind a silk ficus is a modest paper sign that reads, "National Model School."

On the bright yellow walls, posters are displayed at child level, advising "Reading is Cool" and "Be Kind." Another poster, "Wheeler Expectations for Students," is illustrated with icons and lists four rules—positively stated—about walking quietly in the hallways and respecting other people and their space and property. The last rule, illustrated with an image of a child's hand atop an adult's, reads, "All adults in this building are dedicated to making students successful. I will respect and respond to those adults."

The right side of a glass-encased directory lists the names of teachers on six instructional teams—Bears, Peanuts, Mickeys, Mustangs, Falcons, and Weebles. The left side lists the names of administrators; the office, cafeteria, and custodial staff; the PTA president; and over 20 other personnel for art, music, speech, Spanish, band, orchestra, physical education, and something called "strategy."

Posted low on the large glass panel separating the office from the lobby is a lengthy quote attributed to Dr. Martin Luther King, Jr. about being the best at whatever one does. Another wall displays a school dedication plaque dated 1969, a color-coded bus schedule indicating eight routes, the rainbow logo of the school system, an American flag, and several large baskets of red silk tulips.

Just off the lobby is a gym; next to it is a large multi-purpose room with a stage along one side. Brightly painted on the walls of this room are separate renderings of the twin towers of Churchill Downs, roses, horses, the paddle wheel steamer "Belle of Louisville," several hot air balloons, and a fleur de lis— symbols that leave no doubt about the school's Louisville, Kentucky location. Furnished with round tables and child-sized chairs, the room brings to mind meetings in other elementary school cafeterias, where adults would sit awkwardly in the too-small chairs, their knees angled above their waists.

Back in the office, a staff member—the counselor perhaps—explains the school's multi-age, nongraded team arrangements to a youngster whose mother is transferring her to Wheeler from a private school. She concludes, "So you'll be an intermediate student here rather than a fourth grader. Isn't that neat? You'll like that!" Later, this staff member is introduced as the school secretary.

TWO FOCUSES OF CHANGE

This introduction to Wheeler only hints at what the school is about.[1] Since 1986, the staff has persisted with the hard, time-consuming work of transforming the school by focusing on two major changes. The first change, and the more challenging of the two, has been continually developing a learning environment in which children experience and build on success and at the same time enjoy being at school. The second change, reducing teacher isolation, is in part a strategy used to address the first. But it is also about teacher learning and professional enhancement.

What specifically has changed? According to the principal, Charlene Bush, when she arrived in 1985, the school enjoyed a good reputation. She recalls friends commenting on her promotion from counselor to principal with, "Oh, you got Wheeler—you're lucky. That's a good school."

What she found was the traditional top-down management; an orderly, strict environment; respectable test scores; and an experienced staff. Teachers worked diligently in self-contained classrooms at each of the K–5 grade levels, relying heavily on basal readers, detailed curriculum guides, and drill-and-practice worksheets. There were few complaints.

Now the school is organized around three primary and two intermediate multi-age, heterogeneous teams of 88 to 120 students and 4 to 5 teachers. On the primary teams are children whose ages would traditionally place them in Grades K–3; the intermediate teams are composed of those students once grouped as fourth and fifth graders. Children generally remain on a primary team for 4 years and on an intermediate team for 2 years. One result of this nongraded way of organizing children is that yearly retention or "failing a grade" has been eliminated. Instead, children are given longer spans of time to develop and to demonstrate the abilities needed to progress from the primary to the intermediate program and from intermediate to middle school.

Within the teams, teachers use flexible grouping; that is, they group students in a variety of ways in addition to by demonstrated ability. By not relying exclusively on ability grouping, students have opportunities to work, play, and learn with and from many different youngsters.

The adults in the building are interacting in new ways as well. Teachers on the same team have a common planning time daily. They also send representatives to the school's Participatory Management (PM) Committee, established by a vote of the faculty as a result of a contract agreement between the National Education Association (NEA)-affiliated Jefferson County Teachers Association and the school board. Many decisions, including those about the budget, are made at the school through a consensus-building approach on the teams and through the PM Committee.

What children are given opportunities to do is also different. For example, youngsters often work in groups critiquing each other's writing or debating responses to teacher-posed questions rather than individually filling in right-answer driven worksheets, taking spelling tests, and reciting the multiplication tables. To facilitate these ways of working, round tables and chairs have replaced individual student desks. To illustrate the kinds of changes teachers at Wheeler are working toward, here is a composite description of activities on one team, developed from observations on different days.

Student Change: A Multi-Age Primary Team

It is this team's turn to broadcast "Wheeler's World," the daily opening-of-school news show. Assembled in the library are five or six children who every day for a week are responsible for the telecast received in each room over closed circuit TV. Children operate the cameras and serve as anchors—reporting news, sports, the weather, book reviews, and interviews.

This is only one of the activities that routinely takes place in what now is called the "Technology Information Center." Recent additions include two CD ROM machines and a teachers' workroom equipped for laminating, binding, and copying instructional materials. Providing these and other services has earned Wheeler's librarian several state awards.

During the next hour, in one classroom, 22 children of varying achievement levels are working together in groups on different tasks. Many of the children are 6 and 7 years old; a few are 5, 8, or 9. Their demonstrated abilities are wide-ranging, including, for example, nonreaders as well as children who are writing and publishing their own stories. The teacher, with previous experience in middle school science, handles the subject content for the team of 89 students and four teachers. Science is not the sole focus in this classroom, however. Because the teachers have worked during the summer to integrate their curriculum, reading, writing, art, and other subjects are often addressed concurrently.

As with most classrooms in the building, every available inch in this room is filled with shelves of books and stacks of boxes, bags, and cans brimming with the stuff of a hands-on curriculum. Small cups of rock candy crystals growing on strings are arranged on a card table in one corner. In another, a rocker is creaking as one of the youngest children in the room tells a story to several classmates sitting on the floor around him. While he appears to be prompted by notes on the piece of paper he holds, the sheet is actually blank except for seven or eight curly pencil marks.

In an aside, the teacher quietly explains that the rock candy, mentioned in a story the class is working with, is part of a science lab; the rocker is the author's chair; and the story-teller is, in the teacher's words, "presently a nonreader."

Other groups of children are sprawled on the floor or gathered at round tables. They are rarely still, alternately sitting, standing, or leaning across the tables toward each other as their engagement dictates. They appear to be quite at ease with each other. Their conversations are about the stories they are working on together. At one table, four children are discussing how to spell "caterpillar." A pair of children on the floor are working on their story, which has something to do with a high school monster. "We have been working on this for *weeks*," one explains dramatically, and continues, "We're almost *done!*" Her partner, proudly displaying the drawing he is finishing for the cover of the story, says, "Look, the high school is on fire!"

In a classroom just across the hall, the whole class is working with the teacher to write two limericks. The children call out suggestions and then count syllables together to see if they have the right number to fit the meter of the poem. And, at the teacher's prompting, they also think about the sense of the poem and consider whether it is limerick-clever or not. When the second limerick is complete, the teacher asks each student to choose one to put in his or her poetry notebook. As most of the children begin writing, the teacher asks one student to help her put the poem he has selected into his notebook. While doing this task together, she also questions him about the limerick and why he selected the one he did.

In a third nearby classroom, children are volunteering to read from their journals; many are eager to share. The teacher puzzles at this a bit, saying, "We usually don't have so many volunteers." Six or seven children read their entries, about dreams and recent events in the children's lives. A perusal of several journals reveals that the authors' later entries are longer than the earlier ones, and that they contain more complex sentence structures.

In the fourth classroom a group of children are estimating lapsed time by sitting still for what they guess to be 30 seconds, a minute, and other durations. They move from that exercise to work with clocks and calendars.

Teacher Change: Time Together

At lunchtime, the four teachers escort their classes to the cafeteria where parent volunteers supervise, leaving the teachers free to have lunch in the lounge with other adults. It is precious time to the teachers, who visibly relax and explain how grateful they are to have such help from parents. They do not leave their work behind, however; the conversations about home and families intermingle with talk of teaching materials, unit themes, and the needs of particular students.

These teachers have yet another time together during the day. It is their common planning time, unusual for elementary schools. During the first part of their meeting in the team leader's room, the four teachers discuss plans that call for parent volunteers to tape the next entries on each child's video portfolio. They also review the latest version of a new report card they will pilot for the school district, in which grades from A to F have been replaced with three categories: progressing with help, steady progress, and rapid progress. Subject areas have been replaced with statements about specific performance expectations. Some are those traditionally evaluated in elementary schools, such as "uses correct sentence structure" or "forms letters correctly," while others reflect new expectations for young children, such as "composes own stories" and "utilizes computer programs." Science is part of the primary program, and progress in five specific areas is reported to parents: observes, classifies, predicts, seeks solution, and participates in class activities.

At Wheeler, such time together, believed by most teachers to be essential to their work, is made possible because of the resource staff. While this team of teachers meets for planning, their students go to music, physical education, the computer lab, the science lab, or the strategy room. Throughout Wheeler's curriculum, but most explicitly during this resource time, the children work on what the faculty calls "MI," meaning multiple intelligences, a concept developed by Howard Gardner (1985). The faculty sees Gardner's ideas about seven different intelligences as an exciting theoretical justification for their focus on student success. By providing activities for children in each of the seven areas— spatial, musical, kinesthetic, linguistic, logical-mathematical, interpersonal, and intrapersonal—teachers have broadened the curriculum. This approach, they argue, enhances students' opportunities for experiencing success daily. When children are successful, they are happier and they enjoy coming to school.

Another recent addition to the curriculum is called "learning connections." On special days, once a week for 6 weeks (and sometimes in the evenings for parents and children), the children go to one of several learning connections activities. During this time, children might learn how to batik, create wall hangings, use the CD ROM equipment, or play chess, activities made possible in part through artist-in-residence grants or other adults volunteering to work with groups in special interest areas.

These changes—the ungraded program, flexible grouping, teaming, children actively engaged in a variety of learning experiences—have not come about easily or overnight. Rather, the staff has gradually taken on innovations, proceeding at a pace that has been comfortable for most. After 6 years, the changes are schoolwide. How has such change come about in a traditional school with an experienced staff and respectable test scores? Why did this seasoned faculty in a school that "wasn't broken" agree to try so many new approaches? What has come of their efforts to date? These questions are the focus of the remainder of this chapter.

CHANGE IN CONTEXT: SCHOOL AND DISTRICT POLICY

Wheeler Elementary School is located in the southeastern corner of Jefferson County, Kentucky, in a subdivision of ranches, split-levels, and a few apartment buildings. Some of the area around the subdivisions is rural. Almost 80% of the students are white, and most live in the immediate neighborhood. Just under 20% are African American students whose parents have chosen to send them to Wheeler even though other elementary schools are closer to their homes. A majority of the students are from moderate and middle-income families, although almost 30% are eligible for free or reduced-price lunch. Many have working parents, so some children take a different bus in the afternoon, one that will deliver them to a baby-sitter or other caregiver.

Wheeler is staffed with a principal, a counselor, 20 full-time teachers, a librarian, 6 resource and subject specialists, 5 paraprofessionals, 4 clerical staff, and 7 cafeteria and custodial personnel, some of whom are part-time employees. One of 87 elementary schools in a district serving 92,000 students, Wheeler's enrollment is at capacity with 545 students.

Initiating Change: The District

The changes taking place inside Wheeler were initiated at the district level. In the mid-1980s, the Jefferson County Public Schools established the Gheens

Professional Development Academy.[2] The first major reform effort directed by the academy was the planning associated with establishing professional development schools (PDS). Initial thinking about the local version of PDS focused on two goals to be taken on by a subset of the district's 160 schools. These schools would work on the dual mission of becoming exemplars of practice and centers for professional development. Beginning in 1986, the schools began a process of restructuring that over time has significantly altered the way some of the schools are organized and how staff and students interact. Wheeler is one of the schools that began making significant changes as a result of PDS planning sessions.

These sessions began during the winter of 1986, when approximately 100 elementary, middle, and high school principals and teachers met in seven day-long seminars at the Gheens Academy. Joined by central office administrators and university professors, the groups read and discussed an extensive bibliography focused on the nature of the problems facing educational reformers and what might be done to address them. Many lively and sometimes intense conversations occurred in small groups that were structured to include representatives of all participating roles.

Early discussions focused on the social and organizational structures of schools and the teaching occupation, the conditions of teaching and learning in schools, and the barriers to desired conditions. In later discussions groups worked toward consensus on beliefs about schooling, learning, and professional practice, as well as on how to create the conditions that would support change—ideas about which were drawn from readings and discussions about schools as cultures, professionalizing teaching, linking theory and practice, and a vision of schooling that promotes students as active, successful "knowledge workers," teachers as leaders, and principals as leaders of leaders.[3]

A constant theme throughout these sessions emphasized the need for those expected to implement educational change to be involved in its design. This meant that local schools would need to create their own responses consistent with the beliefs agreed to jointly by the faculties of the 24 schools involved. As Whitford (1994) explains, this expectation from the Gheens leadership was contrary to the normal top-down mandates of the past and as such was uncomfortable and confusing for most school faculties, that of Wheeler among them. Over time, however, the Wheeler PDS planners began to initiate change with the support of the professional network provided by the Gheens Academy.

The School Change Process at Wheeler

Wheeler's participation in PDS planning sessions in 1986 came about largely through the efforts of Charlene Bush, the school's principal. A veteran elementary counselor, Bush has worked in nine district elementary schools during her

27 years in public education. During her first year as a principal, 1985–1986, all district schools were invited to participate in PDS. She wanted Wheeler to be involved, but the faculty was hesitant and skeptical. She explained:

> Morale was not good across the building. I'd been hearing a lot about "teachers aren't well thought of" and such. When I asked them couldn't we please do this, they said, "Well, you know, we've seen things come and we've seen things go . . . and why do we want to do this? Is this going to be more work?"

She also remembers other principals advising her to "stand back and wait to see how things go with this restructuring business. You are crazy to do this in your first year." She recalled her own thinking on the issue:

> I know they were trying to give me good advice. They did not want me to be young and rash. They were very sincere, and I listened to them and then did absolutely the opposite! I thought about it long and hard and I agreed with them, but my heart wasn't there so I couldn't. I thought what's to lose if we try something and don't make any changes that are meritorious for children. At least we would have tried. I remember telling the faculty, when we all sit in the old teachers' and principals' home, we can say we tried. I don't ever want to go down without at least trying.

Bush is both persuasive and a risk taker. She is a strong leader, impossible to ignore and difficult to refuse. She knows how to "work the system" and can wheedle and cajole central office resources out of the most seasoned bureaucrats. Sometimes they give in just to stop her from calling, but usually it is because she has convinced them—just in case they did not already know—that Wheeler is doing wonderful, exciting things for children, and desperately needs whatever she is calling them about.

During that first year, Bush spent a lot of time talking with teachers about getting involved with restructuring. As a result, two teachers finally volunteered to attend the PDS sessions. Yet, as most teachers remained skeptical despite the principal's encouragement, restructuring did not begin with great enthusiasm on the part of the faculty. One teacher recalled:

> We were supposed to vote on two teachers [to participate in PDS planning], but we didn't have people jumping at this. We're really not much into voting around here. We just sort of said, okay, who wants to do this?

Several teachers recalled being frustrated during the planning sessions. One remembered, "We did a lot of talking, but it seemed all pie-in-the-sky, apple pie and motherhood and all that. No one would tell us what we were supposed to be doing."

Bush remembers having lots of conversations in the halls—with one or two teachers at a time—during the first 2 years of their restructuring effort:

> We had many what I call powerful conversations. I found I was more effective in the hall talking to one or two than I was in front of thirty— there was lots more dialogue. The first year, we agreed to do it, but the next 2 years was when the change really started taking place, and we started seeing ourselves differently.

Asked to elaborate, Bush explained:

> During that first year, I remember thinking, if they'd just tell us what to do, I know we'd do a great job. But they never did tell us. We finally realized that it was up to us. We'd been given an opportunity, but we had to initiate something. It became something we believed in, something we internalized, rather than something someone else believed in.

In the summer of 1991, Bush leaned back in her chair, her hands folded in front of her, and mused:

> This conversation is like rolling the film backwards. We've really come a long way from "please just tell us what to do." And, you know, teachers-as-change-agents is really, really important. The principal has to be one, too, and we could not have done this without the superintendent's support, but you need teachers willing. Then it's sort of like forming a line. First it's by twos and then threes and fours and suddenly everybody's in line.

As one teacher expressed it, "Our principal pushed us into change. She brought it into the building. At the same time, she didn't tell us, 'This is the way you are going to teach.' She let us have the leadership role."

TEACHERS MAKING CHANGE

During the 1986–1987 school year, the second year of their involvement in restructuring, Bush and several Wheeler teachers came to understand that they were expected to invent their own responses to the Gheens Academy's call for change. As they began to develop their ideas, Gheens supported them by providing the space and released time to meet, articles to read, the encouragement to dream, and the support to take risks. Wheeler staff met often at Gheens during 1986–1987, and Gheens staff members visited the school to work with the entire faculty.

Their study and conversations resulted in two initial changes that have had lasting influence in the school—developing a shared vision for the school and establishing multi-age teams. The conversations of the faculty about a shared vision resulted, with assistance from the Gheens staff, in their coining the motto "Expecting the Best, Producing Success" as a way of capturing Wheeler's decision to be explicit about focusing on student success. This phrase is prominent in the school, appearing frequently on T-shirts, mugs, and banners; in reports and letters to parents; and most recently, on cards that hang from most door knobs in the school. It is also often repeated by teachers when they are asked what Wheeler is trying to do with children.

Many Wheeler teachers also cite the importance of their annual faculty retreats in relation to maintaining a focus on student success while trying a variety of approaches to getting there. One teacher explained:

> Through the retreat, we meet together as a school and talk about our goals for the year and how we are going to meet them. But just because they are set or because we meet certain goals doesn't mean they stay exactly that way during the year or that we rest on our laurels for the rest of the year. We are constantly revamping and restructuring them. We are never really there; we are always updating and modifying. The retreat is an important activity because once school starts, you are thrown into a tailspin. Those things that happen daily get in the way of the goals that you have set. The retreat lays the foundation that guides the school the whole year long. The vision is implemented by Ms. Bush empowering the teachers to make decisions on a daily basis, things like schedules, rules, field trips, curriculum. The major decisions about these issues are made during the retreat.

Establishing the teams proved much more difficult than deciding that Wheeler's focus would be on student success. While Bush and many on the faculty had talked a lot about what they might try, Bush was pushing for this change more than anyone on the faculty. She commented:

> When we first decided to pilot the teams, we just talked about multi-aging—not being nongraded the way we are now. The purpose was to see if we couldn't provide more student success and eliminate the isolation for those teachers. So when I got up in front of a faculty meeting

and asked, "Who wants to do this?" and said, "We all agree that this is something we want to do" . . . no one volunteered. There was one of those long pregnant silences that I deliberately held, waiting for someone to say, "I will." But no one did.

That faculty meeting ended with Bush asking the faculty to think about it and come talk with her when some of them had decided to try being a team. Also, Bush started recruiting. She commented, "I talked with people I felt had a good shot at making this work. As they passed my door on their way to check their mail and sign out, I'd call them in and we'd talk." Asked about the characteristics of the people she talked with, Bush explained:

> Some people are just more flexible than others. I can see it in their teaching and in their ability to see themselves and me in different roles. I tended to think about people who, as we'd worked together and talked about what could happen here, would forget that I was the principal and they were the teachers and would just talk about some good things.

Eventually, the principal persuaded two groups of teachers to pilot multiage teams in 1987. Those who tried the intermediate team were already on the faculty. For the primary team, Bush recruited two Wheeler teachers who were best friends and had taught across the hall from each other for 19 years. The other two members of that team came to Wheeler after the start of the 1987–1988 school year. They were recruited specifically for the pilot primary team. One of these teachers had several years experience as a middle school team leader and accepted that same position on the primary team at Wheeler. The fourth member was a novice by Wheeler standards. Beginning her third year of teaching and "not set in her ways," according to Bush, she brought youth and enthusiasm to the venture.

These two teams experienced a lot of success during that first year, according to Bush. They in turn convinced the rest of the teachers and the parents of the merit of multi-age teams. The next year, 1988–1989, multi-age teams were established throughout the building.

Not only did these teachers begin to work together as teams with a team leader, they also began adopting new ways of working with children. Gradually, more and more teachers tried using manipulatives to teach math, organizing children into cooperative learning groups, and shifting to literature-based reading. As Bush recalled, "They got away from those awful dittos and things that had been a comfort level for years. Now we stress a developmentally appropriate, activity-based curriculum." One member of the original primary pilot team remembered:

For a while, even though I wasn't using the basals with reading anymore, I still would check the children's skill levels with those tests just so I could be sure in my own mind that they were really learning what I thought they should know.

This comment captures an approach to change that has been common in the building. For the most part, Wheeler teachers have experimented at their own pace. While some jumped out in front, trying a lot of new strategies at once, others have gradually tried new approaches that then altered their routine teaching practices. Many teachers attributed this approach directly to the principal's leadership. For example, one teacher explained:

The principal is supportive of progress at any speed. She acknowledges success and finds positive solutions when things are unsuccessful. If you need materials, she will get them. We're also encouraged to write grants.

Another teacher commented:

The one big plus behind Wheeler is our principal. She supports everything we do. She expects a lot and she gets it. She doesn't spend a lot of time checking up on teachers, yet she gets quality performance. That takes a lot of leadership.

Another way of working that was common among the faculty is expressed by this teacher:

We kind of tested the water first. Change doesn't come naturally. You've got to work very hard. You've got to change virtually everything you used to do. In going to a reform situation, it's going to test all your abilities, all your resources, but most of the pressure comes from inside you. It's the pressure you put on yourself to make a better program, rather than from the outside.

A few Wheeler teachers remain skeptical of some of the changes, particularly the state's mandate to fully include kindergarten children in the primary program. Other skeptics have left. Since the mid-1980s, about one-third of the staff has moved on. Some left teaching, but most transferred to other schools— and most of these left because of conflicts about the direction in which the school was heading or because they found the new working conditions uncomfortable. Most of the teachers who remained at Wheeler, and those who have transferred into the school since the mid-1980s, are enthusiastic about what they are doing. They have all expressed a willingness to try new ideas even when they may be a bit unsure of how to proceed or what the effects might turn out to be.

Another critical element in the approach to change of those at Wheeler has been their willingness to abandon ideas they found they did not like. As one teacher commented, "Each year we've changed what didn't work and tried something else." A former Gheens staff member made this observation:

> I think the reason Wheeler teachers may have difficulty talking about barriers is that they've immediately changed something that hasn't worked. If something's a barrier they discard it and try something else. Things that don't work aren't kept around long enough to be barriers.

Teacher Perspectives on Student Success

Restructuring has directly affected the entire school for about 5 years. It is only now that most teachers are able to express confidence about what they are doing, knowing from experience that they can change what they do not like and improve what they do like.

Creating a motto and displaying it prominently around the school is one way to draw attention to the goal of student success. And a majority of those interviewed actually used the words, "expecting the best, producing success," in the course of explaining what is of most importance in the school. But what do these words mean in the daily life of Wheeler?

A focus on student needs is part of the answer to that question. In interviews, many teachers talked about how the principal tries to balance the needs of teachers and students, but most feel that student needs are the priority. For example, one teacher said, "We always put the children first. Mrs. Bush really helps keep us focused on this. She'll say, 'Well, what is this going to do for the children?'" And another teacher reported, "Mrs. Bush balances the needs of children and teachers. She cares for the children and her teachers. She wants her school to go someplace." A third said, "It really is like being a good parent, putting the child's needs in front of your own." Another teacher expressed the student orientation this way:

> The ideal we hold ourselves together with is we expect the best, produce success, and yet we are realistic. Not all children will experience the same level of success in the same things. Children are all different. And, we don't let our needs get in the way of the needs of children. Mrs. Bush, probably a thousand times in my career, has said, "Now wait, what's best for the children?" It's only natural in any profession that that will come up—the conflict between the needs of teachers and kids. But

our primary focus is the children's needs and that every child feels successful at something every day.

In discussing student needs, one teacher's succinct response was, "What do the
children need for us to do so that they can learn—that's our vision."
     Another part of the answer concerns what children are given opportunities
to learn and do. In this regard, teachers talked about how the curriculum and
their instruction is "developmentally appropriate." That is, because they use
multi-age, nongraded grouping, Wheeler teachers must also create a curriculum that allows for differences in the points where children, regardless of chro-
nological age, "take off," jumping to new plateaus in their learning. These comments from three teachers illustrate these points:

> Our vision was to be teamed and ungraded because we wanted to ad-
> dress the whole child. We did this through multi-age grouping, coopera-
> tive learning, and going to literature-based reading.

> Our changes have been for the success of children. The teams keep kids
> from being held back because of poor performance in one area. This has
> eliminated retention totally, which increases self-esteem. It also provides
> each student the opportunity to be a leader in his or her own right. I
> have totally changed as a teacher.

> When you teach like this, they are all going to progress, so they are all
> going to succeed. The idea of multi-age is that kids take off at different
> points. Two children on my team just took off last summer. Last year,
> they made steady but slow progress. They were just trudging along.
> Then suddenly when they came back this year, they are just reading
> everything in sight. That fits the idea behind multi-age grouping. You
> don't lose them before they get to that point of taking off.

Other teachers stressed Wheeler's support for children. For example, in
talking about a standing-room-only open house, one explained, "People love
their school. It's just so supportive of children."
     And another:

> These children love coming to school, I think because it's not a threat to
> anyone. Everyone at Wheeler succeeds in some way, and even though
> the kids know that so-and-so can read better than someone else, it
> doesn't matter because everyone is succeeding at something. Everyone is
> different and that's okay. Their self-worth as a person is not tied to suc-
> cess in reading or in math. They don't think about where they are com-

pared to other kids because we don't say first, second, and third graders in relation to achievement.

Others emphasized that because students are enthusiastic about and engaged in the classroom activities—not withdrawn or bored—they enjoy themselves. These comments from two teachers illustrate this point:

> These kids just love school. When we were off for election day, some didn't want to be off. And, we don't have as many behavior problems because we do so many things. They are constantly moving along. I think it's being thematic [in the curriculum], too, and connecting into current events.

> I guess the main difference I see is in the kids. The kids enjoy coming to school. They get intrinsic enjoyment from school. The intrinsic motivation to learn is very high at Wheeler. Kids are stopping me in the hall now and saying, "What are we going to learn in math today?" or it might be English. Part of it is meeting needs which have been created by society. Kids today are stimulated so much by television, video games, movies that they develop the expectation that things should be interesting. What we're doing is meeting that expectation. We can't sit children in desks today and expect them to just absorb what we say. They have to be involved in learning.

Teachers on Teachers

In addition to a strong and encouraging principal, the teachers give each other credit for sustaining a change orientation at Wheeler. Most described a supportive, sharing culture among the teachers. These comments from five teachers provide a sample of the interview data:

> What's really different and special about Wheeler is that all the teachers share. The first week I was at Wheeler another teacher on another team came up to me. I didn't know her and she said, "I know you've got a lot to do, so to get going, here are some materials you might find useful." Teachers here do that all the time. It's incredible. In my experience, teachers at other schools don't do that.

> Teachers look upon each other as a support system—especially on the teams. And, there's a lot of sharing between the teams.

There is a strong sharing atmosphere here. It's a bright school with a glad-to-see-you attitude from the people in it.

We are a close-knit group. Everyone works hard together. We wanted shared decision making and PM [participatory management].

We spend most of our planning time talking on the team about instructional issues. We're close here. We share ideas. Now everyone has an opinion, but we're a compromising group. And we like to try new ideas.

DIFFICULTIES ENCOUNTERED

Along with the successes and positive attitudes, the teachers at Wheeler have also encountered difficulties and tensions during the past 6 years. As they talked about these, their descriptions tended to be couched in terms of what they have learned rather than in trying to locate blame somewhere. Many attributed this positive approach by the faculty to the principal's style and expectations. For example, one teacher observed:

I've been around for a lot of years and I've been to a lot of schools, so I can probably help you in accounting for what's positive and what's negative at various schools. The positive really comes from the top. If you have a positive administrator, then you have a positive staff and positive students. It's like going down the stairs. I think the big thing here is that the principal has said, "Wheeler is for kids. We're all here for them." Negativism just isn't allowed here. When there's a problem or concern, then Mrs. Bush works on it in a positive way. That's where it all comes from—the top.

Teachers most often mentioned problems and tensions associated with (a) finding enough time, (b) hosting visitors, and (c) learning to work on multiage teams. Each of these areas is addressed in the next sections.

Time

Wheeler has attracted some additional resources that have helped them to design and provide children with multiage experiences both on the teams and in various resource areas. For example, teachers have written successful grant proposals, the principal is persistent and resourceful vis-à-vis central office support, and a number of parents are able and willing to serve as volunteers. All of these factors contribute to Wheeler's success at providing children with a wider variety of activities than would otherwise be possible.

These resources also provide teachers on teams with a common planning time each day. This time is valued highly and, in fact, is a rare occurrence in elementary schools. Despite these resources, many teachers expressed the need for more time in order to plan for and work effectively with their multi-age classes. Here are some illustrative comments:

> Change itself is difficult. It's stressful. Everyone reacts to stress differently. There is a great deal of stress in teaching in general, then when you add the stress of teaching this new way, there is much more planning time needed, so much more is involved in planning. It takes hours and hours.

> Customizing teaching to each child's level, believe me, is time consuming, much more so than teaching the traditional way. But once you try it and see how it works and how much more you enjoy teaching, you just accept it. You start thinking of teaching as a career and not just a job. If there is an exodus of teachers from the profession because of this, then maybe that's just a part of it that we have to accept. Maybe that's just part of the change.

Another teacher expressed the need for planning time this way, "Knowing where to go for materials . . . that's not really a barrier, but it's hard. We're writing the curriculum and soaking up ideas from other teachers, but we still need more time for planning." And another:

> It's the planning to orchestrate a class like this, with all the hands-on, the creativity it requires, thinking of ways to get the material across that is very time consuming. Every week I have to read or skim four or five books to see if they are reading and getting out of it what they should.

Some talked about improvements over time, as did this teacher when she commented, "The first year was terrible; the second year was better. You use a lot of trial and error to find out what works."

A few teachers expressed concern over the state's mandate to include kindergartners in the primary program. Wheeler is complying with it, but not without concerns. Some teachers believe that 5-year-olds need more play time than their older primary classmates. Others express concern over the fact that the state currently only funds kindergarten for a half-day program. Under these circumstances, including 5-year-olds with older children in the primary program who attend all day further confounds teachers' planning problems. Bush says, "It's a Solomon-like decision that must be made. Either leave the child with the mother or put them in school all day."

Visitors

Wheeler has been trying new approaches, including multi-age, nongraded instructional teams, since 1988. As Jefferson County gained national attention for innovative practices, several district schools—Wheeler among them—have hosted many visitors. In 1990, the state passed the Kentucky Education Reform Act (KERA), which includes a mandate for all public elementary schools to replace Grades K–3 with a primary program. As a result, Wheeler has attracted even more visitors. For example, between November 1990 and May 1991, 669 visitors from 23 states and 3 countries observed at Wheeler. One teacher explained:

> We were just beginning to try new ideas, and almost right away, because of all the attention from visitors, we felt pressured to be proficient or even distinguished with the new ways of working. That was very stressful. We now limit visitors to certain days. And we're all much more confident and comfortable with our new roles.

Hosting a lot of visitors in the early stages of attempting change is a strategy advocated by some of the district's principals as a way of "acting yourself into believing," as one administrator puts it. The idea is that when a school begins to claim the label "innovative," visitors will come; the school must then show these observers something innovative. That, in turn, puts additional pressure on teachers to change. It also allows those inside the school to hear each other explain their views of the changes underway.

Such attention to and opportunities to talk abut what they are creating has been exciting and stimulating for most of the faculty at Wheeler. It is also disruptive. They have tried several strategies to handle visitors better, including limiting the number in a group, using outside funding to hire a part-time "tour guide," and limiting visitors to certain days. The current strategy limits visits to 1 day a week. As one teacher explained, "One tension is all the visitors here. We now limit visitors to 1 day a week. It's heard to teach when they are asking you questions while you are teaching."

Teams

Teachers identified several aspects of teaming that have forced them into new ways of working. These include learning to share students, making decisions with other teachers, and dealing with competition. For example, one teacher commented:

> Something that was hard for me was that I was always used to the principal making all the decisions. You just went and griped to the other teachers in the lounge, but that's the way it was going to be. But you can't do that here because you are responsible for making decisions, and it's hard making decisions. You might spend 3 hours discussing something very difficult and still not resolve it. Also I can see where someone might take things personally. It hasn't happened here, but I could see where feelings could get hurt. Teachers are used to being told what to do.

Another teacher explained:

> With teaming, you are working not with 30 but with 100. You have to learn to do things for others as well as for yourself. You have to say it's *our* program not *my* program. That's major and takes some getting used to.

A third teacher reported:

> Sometimes it's hard to be a team player, but I've learned to do that. And, well, it's hard to share kids. It's hard to get used to not having ownership of the children; they belong to the whole team. And learning to make decisions—the whole thing is, has been, a learning experience for me.

One of the primary teams has consistently been willing to try new ideas for the longest period of time. As a result, they have hosted many of Wheeler's visitors. They have also received additional resources from successful grant proposals. Some of the other teachers in the building have resented these perceived inequities, causing tensions among the teams. However, as other teams have developed their own reputations, and as confidence in Wheeler's new ways of working has increased in the school as a whole, these ill feelings have abated. Most teachers claim there is now a high level of cooperation among the teams, with only occasional feelings of competition and resentment.

PERSONAL AND ORGANIZATIONAL LEARNING

During the conversations about problems encountered, several teachers talked about how they had avoided some potential problems. For example, they believe they prepared parents well for the changes. One said, "We used up quite a few trees because we gave parents copies of everything we were reading about primary programs. And we found they didn't have to have a master's in elementary education to understand." Another observed:

> Parents could be a barrier, but not for us. We haven't found that at Wheeler because we brought the parents along. We kept them informed and asked their input, so they didn't say, "Oh this is just one of those silly radical things." They understood what we expected to achieve from the change. It's amazing how far they'll go for you when they believe in you.

In discussing problems and tensions, many teachers also talked about the other things they have learned. They talked about what happens both in the classroom with students and during their planning with other teachers. These accomplishments include learning to use new teaching and organizational strategies, such as cooperative learning and math manipulatives, as well as new curricular approaches, such as literature-based reading. One teacher advised, "You better learn a lot of organizational skills!" Another related how the teams modeled valued ways of interacting for children:

> It's easier to make family happen in teams. Teaming creates bonding with each other and through the bonding, we model what we want to happen to the kids. We worked on eliminating competition between the kids. It can be so destructive. The kids see us as teams of teachers working together.

Some teachers, commenting on these types of changes, appear to be surprised at how much they have changed. For example, one teacher, relatively new to Wheeler, remarked:

> Oh, my goodness, have I learned! I did some but very little cooperative learning before I came here. I have learned to teach without a textbook, without a teacher's edition. I had always stuck with the teacher's edition because I knew that was what the kids were going to be tested on. I've learned to be a team player. I've learned to do that.

Another said, "I've learned that kids really do learn from each other in multi-age groups—yes, more so than in traditional groups."

The teachers also often mentioned how important working with other adults is for them. One commented, "I've learned a lot by being on a team and being able to share with other teachers. We can say to each other, 'Gosh, this was a total disaster, don't try it,' or 'This worked great, do it!'" Another observed, "In self-contained classrooms, people are sometimes afraid to show others [what's going on] because they might want to outdo you. With teams, there's more cooperation rather than competition. Now the competition is between the teams."

Other teachers talked about what they've come to believe about the process of change itself. For example, one said, "Change has to be ongoing." Another observed:

> We've learned that teaming works and we'll fight to keep it. That doesn't mean we'll keep it the same every year. We'll look for new ways to improve it. This is my fifth year [teaming] and I have not done it the same in any 2 years. Partly it's because the children are different, but also we've continued to learn by reading, from research and the workshops we're going to.

Another teacher echoed this notion of continuous change by saying, "Now, we don't think we've made it. We can't rest on our laurels and rely on the same thing year after year. For one thing the kids are different every year. They have different needs."

The teachers also offered advice about school restructuring based on their experiences. One warned, "You can't learn unless you make a mistake. You have to develop your own plan and you have to be patient with it. You have to be willing to put in lots of extra hours. You can't walk out of the door at 3:15. It takes much more time than that to change a school." Another teacher offered, "One thing I've learned is to make priority goals. But if you don't get to number 3, don't worry. If you don't focus on those number 1 and 2 goals, it all falls by the wayside." And a third recommended, "You have to create a plan as a school. Look at what you are and what you want to be and put a time line on it. And don't try to do it too quickly. You have to get a handle on what you want your school to do."

ANALYSIS

The transformation described here did not happen quickly; nor is it complete. It began in the context of district-initiated reform that invited but did not require schools to participate. Pushed and prodded by a strong, resourceful principal, Wheeler teachers decided to try two strategies. They would develop multi-age instructional programs aimed at improving learning for children, and they would organize themselves into teams to increase professional interaction among teachers. Once they decided on those directions and sought help, the local Gheens Academy staff responded with technical assistance on a variety of topics, such as child development, the mechanics of working on teams, developing thematic units, planning budgets, and writing grants. Early in their efforts, those at Wheeler also decided to focus on children and their success.

Since those initial steps, Wheeler teachers have selected and developed an array of additional approaches that they see as compatible with their increasingly clear vision of student success. Learning connections, the strategy room, authentic assessments, video portfolios, multiple intelligences theory, the bank and store that run on "Wheeler bucks," the science lab, field trips, overnight camps—the list goes on and on.

Significantly to those at Wheeler, much of their restructuring occurred before the state mandated similar changes through the Kentucky Education Reform Act of 1990 (KERA). With the exception of the composition of school councils,[4] Wheeler's direction is very compatible with the requirements of KERA. Still, many at Wheeler attribute their success with restructuring, and particularly with the development of their primary program, to the fact that Wheeler teachers chose this direction, within both the school district and state reform contexts. As one teacher pointed out, "Some schools are doing a primary program only because it was mandated. We believe in it; we bought into it. That in itself sets us apart from what's going on out there."

The educational reform legislation known as KERA requires schools to replace Grades K–3 with the multi-age primary program. However, neither the legislation nor the subsequent regulation speaks to how schools should be organized to accomplish this. In other words, as long as children are not grouped by age prior to age 9, schools may organize in a variety of ways. For example, they could continue using self-contained classrooms or, as Wheeler has done, form teams. The multi-age grouping of young children in self-contained classrooms changes whom those children interact with, but it leaves the sanctity—and professional loneliness—of a teacher's classroom intact. Wheeler's decision to organize both adults and children into teams has dramatically affected what decisions are made, how those decisions are made, and how teachers work together.

Wheeler teachers, as is the case with Kentucky teachers generally, have long developed units and selected teaching strategies within the mandates of a state curriculum that specified the number of minutes each teacher had to devote to each subject area. Within these mandates, teachers could decide how to address the content, but since teachers worked almost exclusively in self-contained classrooms with "their own" children, any cooperation among elementary teachers depended more on personal initiative than on any organizational incentive.

Teachers at Wheeler now make many more decisions about curriculum and instruction. Some new decisions have come about because the teachers have decided to try new student assessment techniques, such as video portfolios, and new approaches, such as literature-based reading, process writing, using math manipulatives, and cooperative learning strategies. And they now make these decisions as part of an instructional team of several teachers. That process involves disagreeing, reaching consensus, or compromising with others on the team. They also make these decisions about groups of children with whom they will work over a period of years.

In addition, because of the team arrangements, some of the decisions these teachers are now making are entirely new. Unlike working in self-contained classrooms, teachers now must devise student schedules, decide who will teach which parts of the curriculum, and work to integrate curricula with other teachers. As a result, the curriculum is more diverse, built by teachers around a combination of thematic units, skill development, and confidence-building opportunities. Children also have more choices—about what to read, what to write about, and who to work and play with.

Many teachers recognize that what they have accomplished at Wheeler goes beyond the implementation of "a program." As the principal often comments, "Restructuring is not a program, it is a way of conducting school business." They have not just added new opportunities for their students or substituted student engagement for passivity. As they have planned, implemented, discarded, and fine-tuned various projects, they have also changed how they work. As they have eliminated the isolation of self-contained classrooms, they have grown professionally and developed confidence about trying new ideas. Both children and adults have more opportunities to be creative, engaged learners, instead of passive listeners, rote memorizers, or compliant subordinates who spend most of their time following the directives of others.

These new ways of working should help teachers to continue to invent and improve learning opportunities for students as the new state accountability system begins to encourage teachers to focus not just on a specified curriculum but on performance outcomes. In the words of one state assessment specialist, "We expect all students to achieve at high levels, but KERA is not just about what students know. It is about what they can do with their knowledge." Never before has schooling produced high performance from all students. Thus, all educators—teachers especially—must be, as Schlechty (1991) says, leaders and inventors. He argues,

> On the one hand, teachers are called upon to invent knowledge work for students at which they will be successful and from which they will learn things that are valued by society and its leaders. On the other hand, teachers are called upon to get students to do knowledge work. And getting other people to do things is the art and science of leadership. Thus the argument regarding the teacher's role in curriculum leadership and instructional leadership becomes moot, for built into the school as a knowledge-work enterprise is the idea that teachers are leaders. (p. 43)

Wheeler teachers are clearly on the track argued for by Schlechty. At a December 1992 holiday gathering of the faculty at the principal's home, a small group came together in the den after the meal to work on a community survey. The teachers debated the content of the cover letter and discussed ways to attract more African-American students to Wheeler. During this work, one teacher described a plan that would both expand the science lab opportunities and give students real work experiences. The idea is to create several positions for lab assistants. Students would apply for the job, receive a salary paid in Wheeler bucks, earn vacation time, accumulate sick leave, and prepare written evaluations of their performance. (Students already operate a bank with checking and savings accounts, credit, and loans transacted in Wheeler bucks.) As Bush often says, "The ultimate school is a moving target."

Acknowledgements. We sincerely thank all of the staff and students of Wheeler Elementary School for allowing us to observe their work, even on many days that were not set aside for visitors. Each one was also unfailingly gracious and patient with our many questions as they openly shared their insights and experiences.

NOTES

1. This chapter draws on multiple sources of data collected as a result of the researchers' ongoing interest in understanding the process and effects of school change. Wheeler was particularly interesting because it had a reputation as a good school, yet it became an early leader among local elementary schools engaged in reform.

Whitford, a professor of secondary education, approached the research at Wheeler as a supportive outsider. She became acquainted with the principal and two Wheeler teachers in the mid-1980s as she worked with the Jefferson County Public Schools' Gheens Academy and about 100 school and university educators to plan 24 professional development schools (Whitford, 1994). Wheeler was one of the 24 participating schools. Though supportive, Whitford was largely an outsider in local elementary schools, having worked exclusively in middle and high schools.

Gaus, a doctoral candidate in evaluation, approached the teachers at Wheeler as a friendly skeptic, maintaining some distance throughout as an external researcher. She led a research team that interviewed the Wheeler staff annually between 1988 and 1992 as part of PDS research conducted by the Center for the Collaborative Advancement of the Teaching Profession (see, for example, Ruscoe & Whitford, 1991). The center is housed at the University of Louisville and is co-directed by educators from the Jefferson County Public Schools and the School of Education.

Gaus and Whitford observed on-site sporadically between 1988 and 1991, and routinely for 18 months between the summer of 1991 and December 1992. Gaus was interested primarily in the effects of the changes on the children, while Whitford's interests were focused on the adults—how and why they changed and with what effects. Because neither researcher saw herself as an expert in elementary education, both authentically asked those in the school to help them understand what they were seeing. Over time, as mutual respect developed, the Wheeler teachers seemed quite comfortable teaching the researchers.

2. For a report about the Gheens Academy, see Kyle, 1988. Also, many of the ideas addressed during the local PDS initiative are more fully developed in Schlechty, 1991.

3. The full text of the "Visions Beliefs and Standards for the Professional Development Schools in Jefferson County, Kentucky" is in Kyle, 1988; excerpts are in Whitford, 1994.

4. At present, there are approximately 130 Participatory Management (PM) Committees operating in Jefferson County schools. These PM Committees came about as a result of negotiations between the teachers' union and the school board in 1988 (Hite, 1992). While many of these committees include parents, the agreement does not require their participation. These arrangements are contrary to mandates in the Kentucky Education Reform Act of 1990, which require each school in the state to form school councils by 1996. Council makeup is based on a ratio of 3–2–1; that is, 3 teachers, 2 parents, and 1 administrator are required as members. Alternatives to this structure must provide for at least one-third parent membership. As of this writing, only 3 of Jefferson County's 160 schools have such councils in place.

REFERENCES

Gardner, H. (1985). *Frames of mind: The theory of multiple intelligences.* New York: Basic Books.

Hite, D. M. (1992). *Decision making in a participatory management school: A case study.* Unpublished doctoral dissertation, University of Louisville, Kentucky.

Kyle, R. M. J. (1988). Innovation in education: A progress report on the JCPS/Gheens Professional Development Academy. Louisville, KY: Gheens Foundation.

Ruscoe, G. C., & Whitford, B. L. (1991, April). *Quantitative and qualitative perspectives on teacher attitudes: The third year.* Paper presented at the annual meeting of the American Educational Research Association, Chicago.

Schlechty, P. C. (1991). *Schools for the twenty-first century: Leadership imperatives for educational reform.* San Francisco: Jossey-Bass.

Whitford, B. L. (1994). Permission, persistence and resistance: Linking high school restructuring with professional development and teacher education reform. In L. Darling-Hammond (Ed.), *Professional development schools: Schools for developing a profession* (pp. 74–97). New York: Teachers College Press.

Chapter 3

Fredericks Middle School and the Dynamics of School Reform

Elizabeth Bondy

In 1990, Fredericks Middle School appeared to be a high-readiness candidate for the Live Oak County Public School District's newly adopted shared decision making (SDM) project. People inside and outside the school expected that SDM would be implemented smoothly and that the school would quickly become a leader in school restructuring. On closer analysis, it became clear that there were a number of factors related to the school's history and culture that made swift progress difficult.

This is the story of the first 3 years of SDM in a middle school known for its institutional self-confidence, faculty-administration collaboration, teacher leadership, and organizational self-analysis. It is a story of teachers and administrators struggling to define a destination and a means of getting there. This case highlights the stumbling blocks in the path of restructuring and teachers' and administrators' attempts to remove those stumbling blocks.

THE FMS TRADITION IN CONTEXT

Fredericks Middle School (FMS) was established in 1963 as a research and development school in the Live Oak County Public School District. Over the years, the school has gained the reputation of being progressive and innovative. A number of teachers commented that the shared decision making project was a logical step for this school due to its long history of faculty-administration collaboration.

The FMS faculty organized themselves into interdisciplinary teaching teams in the early 1970s to improve the academic program and increase collaboration among teachers. Teachers report that they have worked collaboratively on numerous projects over the years. For example, teachers developed a notebook to provide parents with information about the middle school concept, the middle school child, special programs at FMS, and a variety of issues such as drug use and adolescent suicide.

In the 1980s, FMS investigated and applied for membership in the Coalition of Essential Schools, a process supported and supervised by the Live Oak County School District. Teachers and administrators collaborated to develop a pilot coalition project in one sixth-grade team. The pilot project was extended the following year to include the entire sixth grade and one interdisciplinary team of seventh graders. In the third year, application of coalition principles was encouraged but not required of all teachers at FMS.

School governance was affected by participation in the Coalition of Essential Schools. The teachers and administrators formed a 24-member steering committee when FMS joined the coalition in 1985. A former principal explained that the committee's purpose was "to begin to look as a school at what we were doing [and] what we were becoming. [The committee worked to] create a vision, create goals." Schoolwide concerns were discussed in the steering committee. Problems were studied and programs and plans were developed. The committee took proposals to the faculty for further discussion before taking final action.

In 1989, 96% of FMS teachers voted to apply for participation in the district's pilot project in shared decision making. The SDM project was part of the contract between the Live Oak Teachers Union and the school board. The agreement included a plan to establish SDM in 10 pilot schools. FMS applied and was accepted as a pilot SDM school.

Some teachers noted that the coalition project paved the way for the shared decision making project. The principal explained that "SDM is very much a part of the coalition idea." The former principal explained that "one of the major things [we learned] from the coalition was that we needed a process for . . . restructuring . . . the school. The process was SDM." Teachers expect to be a part of decisions at FMS. One teacher said, "There are people here, like myself, who will stand up and fuss and argue if we think things are being dictated or pushed on us. We want to be able to have some say in [things]." Another teacher explained,

> From its inception Fredericks has been very open to teachers' input. . . . We have always had a say in decision making here, and we have always planned our curriculum according to what the teachers felt was most important. So I don't feel we are getting [something new]; we are just building on what we had already started.

Many teachers agreed that the SDM project was a logical step for FMS. They said SDM formalized and systematized a philosophy that had guided Fredericks for years.

FMS IN FOCUS: HISTORY AND CULTURE

FMS is part of the Fredericks complex of schools, which includes two elementary schools, a middle school, and a high school. Students from throughout the district are eligible to attend the Fredericks schools. Parents are anxious for their children to attend and typically begin the application process early. Shortly after their child is born, parents put his or her name on the Fredericks school's waiting list, which currently has over 13,000 names. About 370 new students (students who have not attended one of the Fredericks elementary schools) are admitted to the sixth-grade class at FMS each year.

The school board requires that Fredericks's student population match the black-to-white ratio in Live Oak County. Until recently, 25% of the student body was African American. Because the county's African-American population increased to 29% this year, the school soon may be required to increase its admissions of black students.

FMS families come from all parts of Live Oak County. Despite transportation problems, parents are active in the affairs of the school. Parent Advisory Council meetings are held during the day and typically attract 35 to 40 people. Once a year, the principal holds evening meetings in different parts of the county. These meetings are well attended. During the spring of 1992, a parent meeting was held at the school. The topic was improving study skills, a goal of Fredericks's school improvement plan. Students were offered incentives to come to the meeting and bring their parents. Eight-hundred people attended the meeting. Parent involvement is so high at Fredericks that some teachers believe parent attention makes their work more difficult.

Parents of students enrolled in the multicultural program are very involved in school life. The coordinator of the multicultural program is the only teacher who speaks enthusiastically of the parent involvement her program enjoys.

Fifteen-hundred students attended FMS in 1991–1992. They are taught by a faculty of 78 teachers, 13.4% of whom are African American. (The district requires that at least 12% of every school's faculty be black.) Fredericks teachers are organized into three grade-level teams (sixth, seventh, and eighth). Grade-level teams are further divided into subgroups. Each subgroup has one or more teachers from each of four major subject areas (English, science, social studies, math). Teachers on each subgroup team teach the same students and have a common planning time. Teachers have been organized on teams since the 1972–1973 school year, though the team structure has evolved over time. The current organization, known as the Howard Plan, has a stable sixth-grade team of teachers. The seventh- and eighth-grade teachers stay with the same students for 2 years.

About half of the FMS teachers have received or are pursuing master's degrees. Two of the teachers have doctorates and several more teachers are enrolled in doctoral programs. Almost 20% of Fredericks's teachers have been at the school for a decade or more. At the end of the 1990–1991 school year only five teachers left the school. In previous years the turnover was higher, with 12 to 24 teachers leaving each year. The teachers who leave generally are newer teachers who, some speculate, are overwhelmed by the many demands and high expectations that come with teaching at FMS.

There are three special programs at FMS. One is the Coalition of Essential Schools, which the school joined in 1985. A second is a mathematics magnet program that began in 1989. Seventy-five to eighty sixth graders enter the Mathematics Education for Gifted Secondary School Students program each year. Students qualify by performing well on a general mathematics exam. Admission to the mathematics magnet program is handled separately from the FMS admissions procedures. The program has increased the school's student population by 150.

A third special program at FMS is the multicultural program, which also has separate admissions procedures. FMS has been named a center for exotic languages. Students are assessed at a district office and admitted to the program based on their English proficiency. Together, the multicultural students at FMS speak 32 languages and come from 52 countries. There are 317 students enrolled in the multicultural program, the largest multicultural program in the district.

Contextual Features

Several recent events at FMS have influenced the evolution of SDM at the school. During the spring of 1991, a long-awaited renovation project was begun on the Fredericks campus. The project had several goals: to further separate the middle and high school students; to increase the school's enrollment capacity; to modernize the facility; to provide separate gymnasiums for the two schools; and to build new science, media, and administration/guidance buildings at the middle school. When construction is completed, there will be six buildings on the FMS campus. Construction was extended into the spring of 1992, causing teachers inconvenience and distress and disrupting faculty cohesion. One teacher explained her sense of isolation like this:

> If your house was being renovated and you had to live in a place with holes all around you and gates up all over the place, and you couldn't go to places that you were used to going, and you didn't see your kid for 3 days, you'd be feeling pretty bad! Then suddenly you bump into somebody you used to see a lot, and you say, "Oh, do you still live here?"

Teachers who were relocated to temporary classrooms during construction had few opportunities to talk with colleagues about schoolwide concerns. In addition, some teachers were disgruntled over their new room assignments. They believed their desires were not given adequate attention.

A second event that influenced SDM at Fredericks was a change in administration. The principal left Fredericks in 1990 for a district-level position. She had been at Fredericks for 8 years and was popular with faculty, parents, and students. She was a strong advocate of SDM and was referred to as "Ms. SDM" by a district administrator. The principalship was filled by the school's assistant principal, Paul Logan.

Although teachers are fond of the new principal, it has been difficult for him and for some faculty to adjust to the fast-changing situation at Fredericks. Getting used to a new administration, an ambitious construction program, and a newly established governance structure all at the same time put great strains on everyone in the Fredericks community. Teachers and administrators have not yet defined the role of the principal in an SDM school. Differences of opinion exist on this issue that have not yet been fully aired or worked out. Some teachers assumed that the principal would bring all decisions to the faculty. They were angered when they heard about decisions in which they believed they had not had a voice. A frequent complaint from some Fredericks teachers this year was, "I thought we were supposed to be an SDM school! Nobody asked me about this!" One teacher commented recently, "I wouldn't want to be Paul Logan for anything. Now that we're an SDM school, there's more bitching than ever!"

One of Mr. Logan's early decisions as principal had considerable impact on the SDM project. Although the steering committee (which had played a key role in school decision making since 1985) disbanded when SDM was introduced in the fall of 1989, another long-standing committee was maintained. This committee, which had been called "team and content leaders," was given the new name "leadership group." The members of the leadership group also had been members of the steering committee. The leadership group included the three grade-level team leaders, all content-area leaders, administrators, and program-area heads (e.g., bilingual, guidance, advisor-advisee). Although Mr. Logan viewed the SDM Council and the leadership group as having distinct functions, with the council responsible for "vision" and school improvement and leadership group responsible for assisting in the day-to-day running of the school, some teachers were disturbed by the existence of the leadership group. The role of the leadership group and its relationship to the SDM Council became a source of confusion and resentment for some council members. They questioned Mr. Logan's commitment to SDM because they believed he relied heavily on the advice of the leadership group. As will be discussed later in this case study, considerable progress has been made toward resolving tension over this issue.

District-level events also influenced the evolution of SDM at Fredericks Middle School. For example, the prolonged contract dispute between the teachers' union and the school board lowered teacher morale. A tight budget made summer negotiations difficult. When negotiations dragged on into the fall, the teachers' union announced a "work-to-the-rule" order. Teachers were asked to confine their job activities to only those required by the contract. This had a direct impact on the school's SDM efforts by shortening SDM Council meetings. Whereas the council had been meeting from 8:00 until 9:00 a.m., it delayed meeting until 8:30 a.m. so as to comply with the contract work hours. By November, council members realized that they were accomplishing little in half-hour meetings. Explained one teacher:

> We tried to stick with the work-to-the-rule thing, but we couldn't. We've finally said, "Screw it! We're gonna meet at our regular time." We weren't getting anything accomplished in a half an hour. With so little time to meet, no wonder we kept feeling confused about what we were supposed to be doing.

FMS teachers have a tradition of hard work, innovation, and commitment to students. They were eager to participate in the SDM project. Their story is one of perseverance in the face of challenging conditions that were part of the context, history, and culture of the school. Before we examine these challenges in more detail, and the school's attempts to address them, we turn to FMS's goals for SDM.

PLANNING FOR RESTRUCTURING

Although an increasing number of teachers at FMS have come to under-stand SDM as a school-restructuring strategy, there are still teachers who see shared decision making as an end in itself. For the latter group, SDM is simply a way to give teachers a say in school decisions. Some Fredericks teachers and administrators believe that the name of the project—shared decision making—misfocused attention on the method of the project instead of on its goal: namely, school restructuring.

Even teachers who talk about SDM as a restructuring strategy do not share a long-term vision for SDM. Most teachers say that the purpose of SDM is to improve student achievement and teacher professionalism, but they have not developed a focus for these broad aims. Instead, short-term goals have been identified at the three times when written plans were required by the district.

The first plan (July 1990) was drawn up by the SDM Council, based on faculty input. The plan focused on involving teachers more directly in budget and staffing decisions, promoting the personal and social development of students, and improving parent-school communication. Committees of council and noncouncil members were formed to develop proposals in each of these three areas. Some committee members were unclear about their assignment and just how they were to work with the council. Nevertheless, proposals were produced by all four committees and were shared with the faculty. Perhaps due to the complex nature of their topic, the greatest confusion over direction and purpose existed in the personal and social development committee. As a result, the committee did not produce a clear action plan.

The SDM Council worked with the faculty to develop a second plan during the spring of 1991. The plan was based on the district's school-improvement plan, called "Live Oak 2000," which was developed in response to a mandated statewide school improvement effort. District schools were told that their specific school goals had to address districtwide goals, which were in turn related to the state's goals. The faculty decided they would try to improve students' study skills, faculty and student use of hypermedia, and teachers' research skills. The purpose of the latter goal was to enable teachers to study and document innovation efforts at Fredericks. Study skills and hypermedia committees planned and carried out activities during the fall of 1991. The faculty research goal appears to have faded from teachers' memories.

A third plan, again addressing Live Oak 2000 goals, was developed during the spring of 1992. Its objectives include implementing a schoolwide peer coaching program, exploring flexible scheduling options, and incorporating vocational and life skills into the curriculum. The faculty had mixed reactions to these goals. Some teachers liked the goals. Some said the goals were acceptable but unexciting. They had hoped for bigger changes and worry that Fredericks has not displayed the initiative, nerve, or imagination needed to make significant improvements. Several people commented that they wished more teachers were risk takers. One teacher said:

> I keep saying, "Let's think big, let's think big," and then I'm just kind
> of shut down. Some of these people are always saying, "We just can't do
> that. The county won't let us do that." Well, how do we know we can't
> do that? It's like a defeatist attitude.

Teachers' Reactions to School Goals

Some teachers worry that the three 1992–1993 goals will get so watered down that they will not really change anything. For example, although peer coaching has the potential to bring about fundamental curricular and instructional change, it may only reinforce the status quo if it becomes a socializing opportunity for friends who teach the same way. Another concern about the goals is that they will get "short-stopped." By this, one teacher meant that the goals will not be adopted schoolwide and will not be adequately assessed for their impact. Some say that this happened with last year's goals. Although some teachers focused on the 1991–1992 goals, the entire faculty never got behind them. They became the projects of a few teachers rather than a schoolwide effort.

Teachers have been involved in identifying school improvement goals and some have helped to write the action plans for goal implementation. A number of the goals have been partially implemented. For example, the media specialist offered training sessions to teachers in the use of hypermedia, and some language arts teachers implemented a study skills program. However, many teachers comment that SDM has not accomplished anything significant at FMS. Their belief can be explained by the "short-stopping" phenomenon referred to earlier. That is, because school improvement efforts have not been given schoolwide support, many teachers are not aware of them, do not buy into them, or do not recognize them as their own.

To this point, then, FMS has identified several school-improvement goals and implemented action plans somewhat haphazardly. The goals have not been united by a vision of what FMS wants to become.

Some teachers have said that SDM efforts should be directed by Coalition of Essential Schools principles. Said one coalition supporter, "I see SDM as a vehicle to further the principles of the Essential Schools Project." Although the school claims to be in the coalition, only a small number of teachers have ever mentioned the coalition or linked the coalition to the SDM project. These few teachers explain that the coalition's principles provide a framework for thinking about school improvement. However, they believe that the school has not sustained its commitment to the coalition. Next year, the school plans to engage in the coalition's affirmation process. Teachers will have the opportunity to revisit and rethink the coalition's principles and consider their implications for SDM and school improvement.

Some teachers commented that it is difficult for teachers to think about school restructuring because they have never been given the opportunity to make significant changes in their own schools. Change has always been planned by others and imposed on teachers. Change has always been someone else's responsibility. Furthermore, FMS teachers have had few opportunities to talk with one another about school-improvement issues this year because of contract and construction disruptions. For this reason, the principal has decided to call more frequent faculty meetings and to focus discussion on school-improvement issues. The council planned and ran shareholders' meetings during the spring of 1992. The meetings were designed to promote dialogue about change and to encourage teachers to see themselves as responsible change agents. (Share-holders' meetings will be discussed in more detail later in this case study.)

Establishing Shared Governance

When the SDM Project was introduced at FMS, teachers' attention was di-rected to procedural issues. The first procedural issue discussed was how to form an SDM Council. Teachers became embroiled in a lengthy debate over who would serve on the council. Several faculty and team meetings were held to determine how best to select council members. Several explanations were offered for the controversy. Some said teachers were unclear about the purpose and functions of the council and therefore did not know what criteria to apply to the selection of council members. Others believed that some of their col-leagues resisted changing the school's governance structure. Still others said that some teachers were worried about losing their formal and informal leadership roles. Explained a teacher, "People who have felt safe and comfortable in posi-tions have some concerns that their authority is being taken away from them."

The faculty decided to meet in teams and agreed that each team would propose a selection plan. The council would review the three proposals for points of agreement and disagreement and bring a single proposal back to the faculty for further discussion. A plan was agreed upon, but elections were post-poned until the faculty voted on whether they should vote across teams or only for those teachers on their team. The large majority of the faculty voted in favor of having the faculty vote across teams. One teacher explained the rationale for this kind of election:

> We were trying desperately to make this seem like a unified school.
> Although we do have the sixth-, seventh-, and eighth-grade teams, we
> would like to look at it as Fredericks Middle School. That was the
> biggest reason to go with the open school election. We are trying to
> become more unified and consistent in our programs across the board.

With the election of the council, facultywide conversation about SDM stopped. The council began its work by developing a plan for how it would operate. That work took over 15 hours of meeting time, including a full school day during which council members were excused from classes. A number of council members became annoyed at the slow pace of the work and wanted to begin to tackle school problems. Others thought it important that the council first agree on a clear plan of operation. By the end of the 1990 school year, the council had gathered data from faculty regarding priorities for school improve-ment. The council met during the summer to draw up the first school-improvement plan.

Designing a workable governance structure consumed teachers' attention in the first year of SDM. Teachers worried about who would sit on the council. Many called for "new blood" and, indeed, no team leaders were elected to the SDM council. The faculty was pleased with the results of the election. What did not take place during the early days of SDM at FMS was a discussion about the meaning and purpose of SDM. Often teachers said they were not sure what the council was supposed to do, or what SDM was all about. One teacher said, "They don't tell you what the council is supposed to do. That was part of the problem in developing a council. How do you ask people to participate in something when you don't know what it's going to do?" These concerns never became the focus of school discussion. When the school year began in the fall of 1990, the council invited teachers to drop their problems and concerns in SDM suggestion boxes located in team planning areas. This action helped define SDM as a mechanism for solving teachers' immediate problems, rather than a process for examining long-term school improvement issues.

By early 1992, the SDM Council recognized that something had to be done to pull the faculty together and focus its collective attention on school improvement. Council members understood that the faculty lacked a shared definition of SDM, that communication between the council and the rest of the faculty had been poor, and that non-council members were not involved in SDM. (Each of these problems will be discussed in the next section of the case study.)

Council members had become more sure of their roles. They viewed themselves as leading the school's "growth and visions" efforts. They also had become more sure of the role of non-council members. They saw their colleagues as responsible for school improvement. In short, they had come to see SDM as everyone's responsibility. They used the word "shareholders" to emphasize that every teacher had an investment in the school and a responsibility for its future. In shareholders' meetings held during the spring, facilitators worked to show teachers that SDM and the SDM Council were two different things. They emphasized that everyone at FMS was responsible for making SDM work. To this end, teachers were asked not only to suggest what problems the school should tackle the next year but to volunteer to serve on at least one school-improvement committee.

Another step the council took to clarify roles was to develop and present to the faculty a chart entitled "What is Shared Decision Making?" (See Figure 3.1.) The chart includes the district's and the school's definition of SDM.

According to the district, "Shared decision making is a democratic management style that involves teachers, parents, students, staff members, and administrators in the making of school-based decisions. Faculty and administrative energies are directed at designing, developing, and implementing strategies to improve instructional practices and to maximize student achievement."

For Fredericks Middle School, shared decision making is represented by

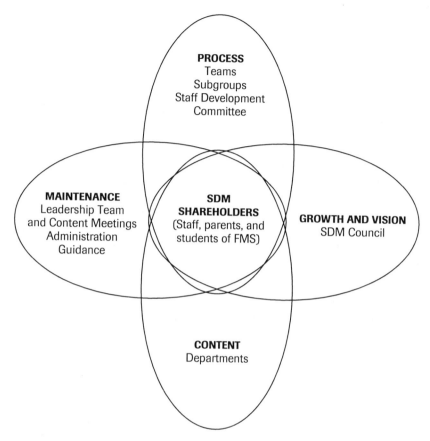

Figure 3.1 What is shared decision making?

the SDM Council, which through faculty input has been defined as the visionary vehicle for the school. It will, when given approval by the "shareholders," take a leadership role in the development of strategies designed to improve instruction, maximize student achievement, improve the school environment, and increase professionalism.

A diagram indicates the kinds of decisions to be addressed through SDM and the groups responsible for making those decisions. Council members hoped that teachers would begin to focus on the broader purposes of SDM rather than on the narrow procedures for decision making.

The council began to classify the issues the faculty brought to them as "maintenance issues," day-to-day issues that could be handled by existing committees, or "vision issues," long-term school-improvement issues that should be handled by the SDM Council. The council wanted to help the teachers see that standing committees should handle day-to-day maintenance issues and that the council should focus on developing new programs that would improve the quality of the workplace and student achievement. As many council members are aware, some teachers are concerned about this classification scheme because they fear that some maintenance issues may not get the attention they deserve if they are relegated to standing committees. One teacher said,

> I think the fact that we wanted to change some of those things was visionary. Now [those changes] won't happen because [the issues] became maintenance items. . . . [The issues] will just go [back] to the group that's been working on [them] all along. . . . I don't think anything new will come out of it. . . . We don't want things to be maintained in the same old way. There should be vision involved in those things that are ongoing.

Teachers expressed particular concern about two maintenance items, discipline and advisory. They want to see these areas examined carefully. As one teacher emphasized:

> If you really look at discipline [as something more than] M & M's and Titan Bolts . . . you have to get under the surface and eventually [in]to the curriculum. You have to ask, 'How might *we* be contributing to discipline problems? Are we really meeting the kids' needs?' To see the problem as simply needing a new discipline plan does not [examine] the depth of the issue. [That approach] will lead to just one more bandaid [solution] to discipline.

One council member said that the council must see to it that teachers' maintenance concerns "do not fade away." Judging by the degree of teacher interest in some of these matters, this is a good idea.

Fredericks Middle School has made important accomplishments in the areas of role definition and council-faculty communication as it has struggled to establish shared governance. The council has struggled to figure out what it should and should not be doing and has attempted to share these insights with the faculty. Perhaps it is premature to call these efforts "accomplishments"— their impact on the faculty and on school improvement remains to be seen. It is encouraging, however, to see a number of non-council members serving on committees and writing up Live Oak 2000 action plans.

CHALLENGES TO SDM PROGRESS

When SDM began at FMS it appeared that the school would move effortlessly into shared governance. No one at the school would say that progress toward SDM has been quick or easy. Many problems impeded the school's SDM efforts. In recent months, the council has taken steps to address these impediments. Let's take a look at those problems and the attempts to tackle them.

Establishing Shared Meaning

FMS teachers and administrators have not shared an understanding of what SDM means, what its purpose is, or how it should be conducted. Many non-council teachers developed the view that SDM meant that the council would solve the day-to-day problems teachers identified as important:

> Let's not get into these wish lists and dream fantasies that will never happen. The goals should be specific, realistic, and not farfetched. You have to work on the goals that are immediate and not try to be too broad.

Teachers expected to be consulted about proposals before the council took action but did not see themselves as responsible for developing or implementing solutions. In other words, many teachers have viewed their role in SDM as identifying problems to be solved and giving feedback about proposed solutions. They have viewed the SDM Council as responsible for solving the problems.

An explanation for this view may lie in the way the county introduced SDM to core teams, and core teams, in turn, introduced SDM to their respective schools. Because the first order of business of the SDM project was the formation of a council, the school focused on the *procedures* of SDM rather than its *purpose*. This early focus on establishing a council had two effects. First, it denied people the opportunity to consider the purposes of the project. Second, it served to pair the SDM project, with the SDM Council in the minds of many teachers. That is, teachers began to think of "council" and "SDM" as synonymous. They viewed anything beyond identifying problems to be solved as the responsibility of the elected council.

A contributing factor to teachers' confusion over the meaning of SDM is the project's title, "shared decision making." This title focuses attention on making decisions rather than on the nature of those decisions. Had the project been called "school restructuring," or "shared thinking," as one council member suggested, teachers might have interpreted its purpose and their role in the project quite differently. As it is, many teachers interpreted SDM simply as meaning that they should have a say in every school decision, that they have the right to be heard and the collective power of veto on decisions they do not like, but no individual or collective responsibility to design or implement SDM plans.

By the 1991–1992 school year, council members had taken a broader view of SDM and everyone's role in the project. As one council member explained, "We shifted the focus from 'What can we [the council] do for you?' to 'What efforts are *you* [the teachers] willing to make to improve this school?'" Council members became determined to show teachers that SDM was their responsibility. They planned small-group teacher meetings to promote this understanding. The meetings were called "shareholders' meetings" to emphasize teachers' ownership of the school and its future. Teachers were asked to sign up to work on committees before leaving the meeting. Noncouncil members volunteered to serve on writing committees to draw up action plans for the three Live Oak 2000 goals. These committees planned to reconvene during the summer of 1992 to develop plans and implement action steps.

Council members appear to agree about the purpose of SDM more now than they have in the past. Although some council members continue to say that SDM should address day-to-day school procedures and policies, the council has classified such topics as "maintenance" items and relegated them to other committees. The council has declared (in shareholders' meetings and by way of a written description of SDM) that the domain of SDM includes issues related to "growth and vision." As one teacher said, "SDM should help set the course and keep us on the right track."

Resolving Power-Related Issues

In 1990, when SDM was getting started, some faculty members believed a few leader teachers had special influence and power at FMS. When the faculty voted on SDM Council membership, they elected many teachers who had leadership potential but had not been part of the school's formal leadership structure. Council members had to learn more about the school, their colleagues, the new administration, and their role on the council at the same time that they were trying to make a new governance structure work and define the meaning of SDM. The work was difficult and tensions developed as council members tried to define their roles and responsibilities.

Council members said that on some occasions they were verbally "attacked" during meetings, that some "people on the council have hidden agendas," and that their colleagues were sometimes rude. These tensions are probably traceable to members' role confusions and anxiety over who gained control of the council's activities and direction. One teacher explained that word spread among the faculty that "on the council there are certain people who have more say than others, and they kind of monopolize."

Although some teachers say that power is not an issue at FMS, many teachers believe that it is. What has changed since the early days of SDM is the way FMS teachers now deal with their concerns about the powerful and the power-less. Since the original council was elected, two team leaders have been elected to the council and a council member was elected to a team leader position; teachers seemed to have reconsidered their earlier stand to block teacher leaders from formal leadership positions. The council is working more effectively as a group. Early meetings were tumultuous and some members considered re-signing. Most are glad they stayed to witness the progress the council has made recently. Several members said that the council benefited from the help of a consultant who suggested communication strategies and taught them how to run more effective meetings. Several members also said that the current council facilitator has helped to keep the group on task. Council members believe that it has taken time for them to mature as a group and to understand one another's perspectives. As one council member explained,

> Those of us who attend meetings consistently now understand each oth-er's perspective. [Now] when someone starts taking we don't get angry or offended; we realize where he's coming from, we understand him. I think we're more mature now.

Another power-related issue is the tension between advocates of substantial change and those who are perceived to support the status quo. A noncouncil teacher explained that SDM is really just a power struggle between new teachers and "the old guard power people." Council members tend to frame the issue differently. They see a tension between those who want to restructure the school and those "who will not take a risk." Several council members are frus-trated with those who respond to proposals for change by saying, "We can't do that here," or, "This is the way we've done it in the past and it's always worked for us." The risk takers are eager to push the limits, to propose something really innovative, but say they meet with strong resistance from some teachers. Part of the frustration stems from the belief that the "defenders of the past" are powerful teachers who have a lot of influence with the principal. Without the principal's support, the risk takers believe they will be unable to alter the status quo.

The principal speaks eagerly about wanting to make fundamental changes at FMS. He believes firmly that he is not aligned with any particular teacher or teacher group and genuinely desires input from everyone on the faculty. It al-ways takes time for groups in an organization to reach common understandings, build trust, and learn to work together toward common goals. The council worked to learn that lesson and it appears that the faculty is ready to do the same. Central to that work will be improved communication among FMS faculty and staff. The principal has taken a step in this direction by increasing the number of schoolwide faculty meetings. His plan is to bring teachers together regularly to talk about school improvement. Council members are pleased that the principal is taking this initiative.

Responding to Contextual Problems

Council members recognized that SDM was moving slowly. The union's work-to-the-rule policy shortened SDM meetings. SDM momentum also was stalled by ending the 1990–1991 school year without a clear plan of action for the fall and by not holding summer meetings to gear up for the next year. Low morale and lack of faculty cohesion (due to the contextual factors discussed earlier in this case study) further slowed the SDM effort. Teachers reported they were trying to survive the poor teaching conditions caused by the construction project and to simply get through each day. Some believed they did not have time to give to SDM committee work.

The council has taken several steps to address the momentum problem. First, in January 1992, they decided to meet more often and for longer periods. Second, they organized the shareholders' meetings to rekindle enthusiasm for SDM. Third, they have contacted committee chairpeople to encourage them to hold meetings during the summer so that they will begin the 1992–1993 school year with plans in place.

Another contextual problem is related to teachers' belief that district and state officials do not strongly support SDM. The teachers say that the district and state send mixed messages about SDM. Officials claim to support SDM, but send mandate after mandate to the schools with which schools are expected to comply immediately. Rather than feeling empowered by SDM, teachers who believe their change efforts are neither recognized nor supported feel frustrated and powerless. One teacher said,

> Are they really serious about giving us autonomy? You know, there was a school that wanted to change its schedule to some kind of unusual schedule, and it was bounced back at the state level. And the same thing happens at the district level. The superintendent announced that there will be no middle school specialists next year, regardless of what the individual schools want. So the state and the district still have veto power. A lot of people are very upset and discouraged over this kind of thing.

Since the inception of SDM in the 1989–1990 school year, teachers have become increasingly skeptical about the district's commitment to SDM. Their most recent concern is over the two district SDM coordinator positions that they fear will not be filled or will be amalgamated into other positions.

Negotiating Improved Communications

Some decisions made at Fredericks Middle School during the fall of 1991 spurred a number of teachers to ask, "Who is involved in what decisions and at what point in time?" As mentioned earlier, the name "shared decision making" was interpreted by many teachers to mean that they would have input into all school decisions that affected them. When this did not occur, some teachers complained, "I thought this was supposed to be a shared decision making school."

A number of council members were initially confused about the roles of the SDM Council and the leadership group. Some council members thought that they should have been consulted on issues that the principal took to the leadership group. The principal and a small number of faculty saw the two groups as having distinct responsibilities. During spring 1992, questions about school decision-making responsibilities were addressed by the SDM Council, the leadership group, and the administration. The decision-making responsibilities chart (Figure 3.1) was presented to the faculty to help them understand school processes.

Although communication within the council has over time ranged from poor to good, it was apparent during the fall of 1991 that communication on the council was poor. Although a noncouncil teacher said, "You really don't know what's going on [with SDM] unless you're on the council," it was evident that even council members were not sure what was going on. At that time, council meetings occurred only once a month and lasted for only 30 minutes. In addition, the minutes from council meetings were not always distributed to council members or to the faculty. As a result, council members were not sure of the status of certain committees and of council actions.

Most council members recognize the fall of 1991 as a low point in SDM activity. They attribute this to the contextual factors described earlier in this case study. After the December holidays, the council worked to revive the school's SDM efforts by meeting more often, clarifying roles and purposes, and planning shareholders' meetings.

Communication between the council and the faculty has been a problem. Because there has been a lack of momentum, a perceived lack of support, and a lack of clarity and shared vision, the council has not involved the rest of the faculty in SDM. (The previous principal commented that the steering committee, formed during the early days of the coalition, wrestled with communication problems, too. She said, "We were always looking for ways to communicate better with the rest of the faculty.") As a result of poor council-faculty communication, many teachers do not view SDM as having accomplished anything. Some council members believe that the faculty had little interest in SDM because teachers never heard much about the project.

To this point, the council-faculty pattern of communication has been that each fall there has been little communication and there has seemed to be a lull in SDM activity, and each spring teachers look to the principal for leadership and that he sets the tone for the school. It seems that some teachers want the principal to be the leader who works to make SDM succeed but does not dominate the SDM process itself. They want him to be a powerful advocate of teacher empowerment, school reform, and democratic leadership. The principal wants the teachers to take responsibility for SDM.

The issue of leadership is problematic in an organization attempting to operate democratically. One council member noted that the council has developed a shared-leadership style. Each member has certain strengths that enable him or her to act as a leader in certain situations. This concept of shared leadership may help the council and the faculty decide who will be responsible for various activities at FMS. But there does continue to be some confusion about the role of the principal at FMS. What should be the role of a principal in an SDM school? The faculty and administration might want to deal directly with this question in future faculty meetings.

PERSONAL AND ORGANIZATIONAL LEARNING

Two and a half years into the project, SDM is not well integrated into the life of FMS. However, some of the people who have been involved in SDM have learned significant lessons.

First, SDM demands schoolwide discussion and effective council-faculty communication (Elenbogen & Hiestand, 1989). Council members recognize that noncouncil teachers must be engaged in the SDM conversation. They see that communication is important if teachers are to take ownership of and responsibility for SDM. SDM cannot succeed if the faculty delegates sole responsibility for it to the council. Of course, the council has not deliberately kept the faculty in the dark about SDM. Rather, because council members have been working to define roles and purposes, they were not confident about involving the faculty in what was still a murky area.

SDM also demands time (Cistone, Fernandez, & Tornillo, 1989; Little, 1982). A corollary to the communication lesson learned at FMS is a lesson concerning time. Teachers need time to meet and discuss school concerns and visions for the school's future. Some council members have explained that if restructuring is to happen, teachers must begin to think of themselves as change agents who generate ideas, discuss plans, and implement projects to improve the school. Teachers at FMS have not typically met in large groups to discuss curricular and instructional issues, educational aims, and possibilities for the future. Nor are these topics the focus of team and content-area meetings.

In addition, council members need time to plan for and implement change (Little, 1982). A number of council members recognized that brief monthly meetings did not give them the time they needed to launch SDM at FMS. One council member received a grant that allowed the council some in-school time for planning. However, this was a one-time opportunity. No long-standing solution to the time problem has been found. Teachers must share the work load if change is to take place. Some council members and a few teachers who have been active on SDM committees recognize that more teachers should be involved in school projects. This lesson is related to the communication and time problems described above. When teachers do not see themselves as part of the project and as having some responsibility for its success, they are not likely to volunteer their time. A few teachers have quite a sophisticated understanding of this problem, as illustrated by this teacher's comment: "We have to unite as a faculty if we're going to create the context for change."

Another lesson is that SDM demands micropolitical awareness and a willingness to forge alliances (Ball, 1987; Iannoccone, 1991). A few council members have learned the importance of building bridges between groups of teachers. Some young teachers have explained that they must link themselves with the more experienced, influential teachers and that they must work together to improve the school. One teacher said, "We have to work to engage the influential group in conversation. You have to teach them on an intellectual basis. If you have a strong argument, you can begin a constructive dialogue with them." These novice teachers have developed micropolitical awareness. Rather than fighting teachers who have influence, they hope to establish common goals that enable them to collaborate for the good of the students at FMS.

A final lesson is that the manner in which SDM is introduced to a school shapes its future in the school. As described earlier, when SDM was introduced to FMS, teachers' attention was directed toward the procedural issue of forming the SDM Council. Although some communication improves, meetings are held, goals identified, and action plans drawn up. Then, over the summer, activity stops and, in the fall, SDM gets little attention. It may be that with more faculty meetings and more teacher participation on SDM committees this pattern will be broken. SDM activities could begin during pre-planning and continue into the fall, council-faculty communication and communication about school improvement in general could improve, and SDM could begin to make real progress at FMS.

Redefining Leadership

I have discussed the problem of teachers seeing SDM as the responsibility of the council. Another problem in people's perceptions of responsibility concerns views of SDM leadership. Some council members believe that the principal should make SDM a top priority, actively promote SDM throughout the school, and take steps to solve problems in the SDM project. One teacher expressed this opinion:

> SDM has to be addressed continually by the principal. It has to be put in the spotlight, in the forefront, in order to create an atmosphere of cooperation, to show that we are all working on this together. The principal needs to help us get together and set priorities.

The principal believes that teachers are responsible for SDM progress. He does not believe that he should direct the school's SDM efforts and reminds council members that he is a member of the council, just as they are. The council members point out that people voiced confusion about the responsibilities of this council, discussion centered on how it should be formed and who should be on it. There was no discussion about the meaning of SDM and what purposes it might serve at FMS. As a result, the school is still working to develop a shared definition of SDM. It is not surprising that people at FMS hold different definitions of SDM. What we can learn from their experience is that for progress to take place, the faculty must discuss the purpose of SDM and reach shared meaning.

During the spring of 1992, the council acted on some of these lessons to increase communication about SDM and focus teachers on their responsibility for its success. As a result, the 1991–1992 school year ended with schoolwide optimism about SDM. The challenge facing the Fredericks Middle School community was to maintain momentum and begin the 1992–1993 school year with a strong commitment to SDM, conversation about school restructuring, and specific plans for ensuring ongoing teacher involvement.

Although important lessons have been learned at Fredericks Middle School, these lessons have been learned by individuals rather than by the school as a whole. The lessons have not been institutionalized. The organization as a whole has not learned SDM lessons because the whole organization has not participated in SDM or nurtured its evolution. Until recently, there has been little schoolwide communication about the purposes, procedures, problems, and accomplishments of SDM. However, council members have been working to clarify their roles and the purposes of SDM at FMS. Council members believe that they have learned a lot about SDM and how to get it off the ground. As reported earlier, they recently shared their understanding of SDM with the rest of the faculty and are hopeful that the school will enter a new phase of SDM, one in which all of the teachers see themselves as responsible for working toward change.

NOTE

This case study was developed as part of a larger study of six schools implementing shared decision making in Live Oak County. When Live Oak County initiated the SDM Project in 1989, they contracted with the University of Florida to conduct a formative evaluation of the project. Each researcher on the University of Florida team was assigned to one school. Over the next 2 years, we visited the schools five times, interviewing faculty, staff, and parents on each visit. School participants understood that the researcher's role was to collect data about the progress of the SDM Project at the school and to provide feedback that might help the school improve their efforts and that could be used to develop guidelines for schools that might implement SDM in the future in this district.

This case study is based primarily on interview data from 46 teachers and administrators that was collected over a 3-year period, from February 1990 to May 1992. A total of 135 interviews were conducted during six 2-day visits to the school and by telephone. Each interview was approximately 30 minutes long and was tape recorded. A teacher helped arrange for people to be interviewed, by contacting teachers and administrators who represented the school's various constituencies. I established friendly relationships with the people I interviewed, particularly those I interviewed multiple times. Teachers and administrators were eager to talk about their work and their work context, and they were willing to give up precious planning and lunch periods to do so.

REFERENCES

Ball, S. J. (1987). *The micro-politics of the school: Towards a theory of school organization*. New York: Methuen.

Cistone, P. J., Fernandez, J. A., & Tornillo, O. L. (1989). School-based management/ shared decision making in Dade County (Miami). *Education and Urban Society, 21,* 393–402.

Elenbogen, J. C., & Hiestand, N. I. (1989, April). *Shared decision making in local school planning: An urban school system's experience*. Paper presented at the annual meeting of the American Educational Research Association, Boston.

Iannoccone, L. (1991). Micropolitics of education. *Education and Urban Society, 23,* 465–471.

Little, J. W. (1982). Norms of collegiality and experimentation: Workplace conditions of school success. *American Educational Research Journal, 19,* 325–440.

Chapter 4

Implementing Shared Decision Making at Brooksville Elementary School

Dorene D. Ross
Rodman B. Webb

Brooksville Elementary School, like Fredericks Middle School in the previous case study, is located in Live Oak County and participates in a Shared Decision Making (SDM) Project initiated by the school district in fall 1989. Brooksville's effort to become an SDM school has been difficult, but the school has made impressive progress. Roles and relationships have changed, satisfaction with the status quo has declined, receptivity to change has increased, and innovation has begun. The faculty is surprised and pleased by the relative success of SDM because, at the beginning of the project, many believed it would fail due to a recent history of faculty-administration friction at the school. Faculty morale was low, and all agreed that communication between administration and faculty was poor.

This case study is about power, about the history of power relationships in a school, about the problems in trust and communication that have resulted from power relationships, about a crisis in communication and trust resulting from early efforts at SDM, and about how individuals within an organization change their role definitions and their relationships with one another as they begin to share power. That is, this case study provides insight into the micropolitics of school restructuring within a particular setting (Ball, 1987).

SCHOOL CONTEXT

Brooksville Elementary School is located in a relatively stable neighborhood in the southern part of Live Oak County. It is a small school by county standards, with an enrollment of about 625 students. The pupil population is representative of the county, with the majority of the student population coming from low-income families (but not living in poverty), and with 20% minority students. About half of the student population receives free or reduced-price lunch. The school employs 2 administrators, 38 teachers, and 19 staff members. The majority of the teachers are white females; only 8% are male, and 14% are members of a minority (African American or Hispanic).

Brooksville was built in the mid-1960s and has had only two principals: Mr. Olson, who opened the school and served for 20 years, and Ms. Baker, who was appointed in 1985. Veteran teachers report that Mr. Olson gave them a great deal of autonomy, listened to their concerns, and brought many decisions to the faculty for discussion. They said that, under Mr. Olson, the school was a positive, caring, and nurturing place to work, for children and faculty. They said the school had a "family" atmosphere and that faculty turnover was low.

According to teachers who worked with both principals, Ms. Baker's style of leadership is based on power and authority, whereas Mr. Olson's was based on respect for teachers and their judgment. The teachers believe that Ms. Baker's first priority was to establish authority in the building, a task they think was much harder for a woman than it might have been for a man. They noted that Ms. Baker is hardworking, ambitious, and motivated by high standards for teachers and children. The effect of her actions, however, was to lessen faculty autonomy. She was quick to issue orders and slow to solicit suggestions from her faculty. Before SDM, Ms. Baker occasionally asked for faculty input. However, some teachers believed she had made up her mind before asking for suggestions and structured an "input session" so that faculty would confirm what she had already decided. Many teachers doubted Ms. Baker would ever "give up her power." As one teacher noted, "Sometimes [Ms. Baker] wants you to think teachers have input but we don't really. She decides and then she guides people to make that decision."

During research interviews, many teachers reported that Ms. Baker would answer teacher complaints by saying, "If you aren't happy, go somewhere else," or "As long as the word *principal* is on my door, I make the decisions." When a teacher did something that Ms. Baker believed challenged her authority, she warned, "I don't get mad, I get even." In fact, Ms. Baker did get angry. Many teachers told stories of teachers who left Ms. Baker's office in tears after being "zapped" (harshly criticized) for disagreeing with her. Ms. Baker refused a faculty request to establish a faculty council or to put a suggestion box in the teachers' lounge.

Ms. Baker tells a different story. The "laissez faire" leadership of her predecessor, she argued, provided no direction for the school. Serious problems (such as the alcoholism of one teacher) were ignored, and it fell to Ms. Baker to put the school on a more productive course. As a result, she reports that she had to fire one teacher each year and worked to improve the performance of others. She recognizes that she intimidates some faculty members and that she has a "short fuse." She believes that teacher dissatisfaction is the price she has had to pay for turning the school around. Some faculty members, notably those Ms. Baker hired, share her perspective.

To some in the district, Brooksville seemed a less than optimal choice for a pilot SDM Project. However, the commitment of the principal, Ms. Baker, convinced the district SDM planning group to place a project at Brooksville. Nevertheless, people outside and inside the school openly wondered about its chances for success. Brooksville initiated the SDM Project with significant communication problems, a high level of tension, disagreement over the school's past, and no common vision of the school's future.

Faculty Attitudes

There are two levels of faculty attitudes at Brooksville. On one level are faculty attitudes about teaching at Brooksville. The first level of faculty attitudes, which have to do with teachers' daily interactions with children and with one another, are highly positive. On our first visit to Brooksville in early 1990, we were struck by the friendliness of the faculty. At any given time, we found teachers talking in the lounge, hall, or library about everything from diets to graduate school and staff development experiences. They shared information about individual children and discussed how to improve the school experiences of their students. We found strong evidence of school cohesiveness and spirit. For example, on the day of student government elections, the faculty spoke with pride about the election posters, speeches, and real voting booths. On "school spirit" day, we felt out of place because we were not wearing the school's colors.

Thus, on the level of daily interactions, faculty attitudes at Brooksville are very positive. Teachers respect one another, speak with pride about the school, and call it their "own." They do not want to leave.

However, during later visits to Brooksville, when we began to study the micropolitics of the school, we began to notice hidden tensions. As one faculty member put it, Brooksville is a "schizo place to work." At the beginning of the SDM Project, these tensions fell into two interrelated categories, the first from the SDM Project itself and the second from the teachers' relationships with Ms. Baker.

At the beginning of the project, three groups of teachers had quite different perceptions of Ms. Baker and the potential success of the SDM Project. The first group, with all newly hired teachers, liked the principal and were enthusiastic about SDM. The second group, mostly veteran faculty members, did not trust the principal and believed that SDM would fail. They believed Ms. Baker jealously guarded power and would never allow teachers to make significant decisions in the school. As one faculty member put it, "A zebra can't change its stripes no matter how often it says it wants to be a horse."

The perceptions of the third group were more moderate. The members of this group, like the first, were all hired by the current principal. Ms. Baker listened to these faculty members, and attended to their suggestions and sometimes to their criticisms. Other teachers referred to this group as "the chosen." All of the members of "the chosen" were support (noninstructional) faculty.

Members of "the chosen" acknowledge that the principal's moods run "hot and cold." They respect her educational ideas but say she has poor people skills. They believe Ms. Baker forms quick judgments about people and that her reactions often are based on her initial judgment rather than the quality of a person's present behavior or ideas. The ideas or criticisms Ms. Baker will accept from one of "the chosen" would get another faculty member into trouble. However, even "the chosen" have felt Ms. Baker's temper. They say that she does not realize that her behavior scares teachers, hurts their feelings, and discourages trust. "The chosen" believe that Ms. Baker means well. They point out that when the consequences of her behavior are explained to her, she always apologizes and backs down.

"The chosen" understand that Ms. Baker has very high standards. She wants things done in particular ways but sometimes does not give clear directions. "The chosen" note that Ms. Baker wants the faculty to make decisions but often wants the decisions to be the same as those she would make. The result of the principal's retribution and inconsistency is that many people, even "the chosen," feel insecure.

Despite, or perhaps because of, these problems, teachers and administrators were hopeful that the SDM Project would improve their trust in and communication with each other and would improve the educational experiences of students. The principal began with a sincere desire to make SDM work. And, although many faculty members were skeptical about its chances for success, all seemed sincerely interested in trying to make it work.

POLICY CONTEXT

In fall 1989, Brooksville was selected as one of 10 pilot schools to initiate implementation of the SDM Project in Live Oak County. The project was implemented as a result of policies already reviewed in Chapter 3. At the invitation of the district, Brooksville faculty submitted a written application to be one of the pilot schools. The application was supported by a vote of 88% of the faculty.

Brooksville was selected to be a pilot school by a district-level SDM planning group.

At the beginning of the project, school personnel were told that the purpose of the project was to promote the professionalization of teaching and to increase student achievement. They were directed to develop a plan for the project in their school and told that schools could apply to the district for waivers of district policy. Beyond this, schools were given no guidelines about implementation of the project. However, the district provided several types of support for schools engaged in the pilot effort.

One support was the training provided for the core group that accepted responsibility for initiating the project in the school. A core group team (one administrator and two faculty members) from each school participated in the regular training sessions provided by district staff. Training focused on group-process procedures, school-assessment procedures, trust or team building, and planning. The training lacked the specificity schools desired, but it did emphasize the importance of consensus, collegiality, and cooperation. Training sessions enabled core group members to interact with faculty and administrators from other SDM schools and to "compare notes" about progress and problems. Training sessions helped the Brooksville core group see that their problems were neither unique nor unresolvable and to build enthusiasm and knowledge within the group. In this respect, training was highly successful. In fact, the most common complaint about training sessions was that training was limited to core group members and others felt "cheated."

A second support was the training provided by Southern Bell, a business partner of the district. At the request of the district, Southern Bell personnel provided an intensive 2-day workshop designed to facilitate communication and trust among faculty and administration. Ms. Baker cited this training as of critical importance in her efforts to become more open and communicative with her faculty. It increased her insight about the kind of leader required for shared decision making. Although her faculty thought that Ms. Baker was a heavy-handed administrator, Southern Bell training did help her to moderate her administrative style.

A third support was the provision of external facilitators to help schools resolve problems in SDM implementation. External facilitators were volunteers from the district staff with an interest in the SDM Project. The district provided two external facilitators to assist Brooksville. Because of the significance of their problems with trust and communication, the Brooksville SDM Council asked that a facilitator be assigned to their school. Ms. Hazen volunteered her time. She attended many of the SDM Council meetings and taught the council strategies for increasing faculty input into decision making. Although no one factor was responsible for improving the crisis in communication and trust at Brooksville, many faculty members mentioned the importance of Brenda Hazen. The second facilitator was hired for 2 days in May 1991 to facilitate whole-school planning meetings.

INITIATING THE PROJECT: A DIFFICULT START

SDM did not begin at Brooksville with a clear set of goals. In fact, the story of SDM at Brooksville is the gradual development of coherence in explicit goals and the beginnings of a search for school vision. We emphasize, however, that the school struggled to reach a goal that has never been mentioned as an explicit part of the project, although individuals, at times, have mentioned its importance. This implicit goal, which involves the school's most significant accomplishment, is the faculty's and administration's gradual change in role definition. The gradual development of explicit goals and the emerging importance of roles and relationships within the school become apparent in the sequential development of the project.

Ms. Baker entered this project with enthusiasm and commitment. She recognized that there were problems at the school and hoped that SDM would help resolve them. One of the first SDM activities she suggested was bringing teachers together to share their concerns. She divided the faculty into three equal groups. She held one after-school meeting with each group to explain SDM and discuss past resentment and frustrations. Teachers said Ms. Baker was very open at the meetings and that she endured "a great deal of abuse." The meetings served to bring faculty concerns into the open and helped Ms. Baker understand what faculty thought and felt.

Some faculty members felt that Ms. Baker was courageous to call such meetings and believed they were a good start toward improving communication and trust at Brooksville. Others were more wary. They believed Ms. Baker divided the teachers into groups so that she could control the meetings. Ms. Baker asked teachers not to talk about the meetings with colleagues until all the meetings had been held. She explained that she wanted to ensure that everyone got accurate information. Skeptical teachers believed the real reason for Ms. Baker's secrecy directive was to limit faculty communication and keep herself in control of the information. Despite such skepticism, the meetings had a positive effect and Ms. Baker and her faculty struggled to determine their next steps in the project. The plan-act-reflect-replan pattern established early in the project would be used to guide the school through the first 3 years of shared decision making.

Taking Steps to Define SDM

It is important to remember that the district, in initiating the project, provided few guidelines. The district recommended that individual schools be creative in approaching the SDM Project and allowed each school maximum flexibility. Understandably, the Brooksville faculty was unclear about the meaning of SDM and the processes for implementation. Most of their early efforts were therefore directed at clarifying ambiguities.

At the beginning of the project, faculty members saw increasing teacher involvement in decision making as the principal goal of the project. They hoped that faculty involvement would improve faculty-administration communication, faculty collaboration and teamwork, and children's achievement and attitudes toward school. Guided by high hopes and vague guidelines, the SDM core group and the group of grade chairs (i.e., chairs of teams of faculty organized by grade level) met to determine the composition of the SDM Council, a representative group of stakeholders within the school who would be the school's decision-making body. Within each category identified (i.e., teachers, special class teachers, paraprofessionals, parents), people were invited to volunteer and the first SDM Council was created.

For the first 5 months of the project, Ms. Baker, the SDM Council, and the Brooksville faculty struggled to define operating procedures for the council and goals for the project. By spring 1990, they had developed operating procedures for the council. They established decision making by consensus within the council, distributed SDM Council meeting minutes to foster open communication, and established four SDM goal committees to develop plans to achieve school goals. They determined that the plans developed by committees would be presented at SDM Council meetings for approval and then taken to the faculty for approval by consensus.

Additionally, the council planned a schoolwide needs-assessment meeting at which the entire faculty and staff worked (at a dinner meeting) to define goals for the school. At this meeting, four explicit goals for SDM were identified:

1. To better manage student conduct
2. To better meet the needs of at-risk students who do not qualify for special programs
3. To involve parents in their children's educational progress
4. To make the curriculum more fun and relevant for the students.

School community members had only had 5 months to develop this plan. As a result, few specific strategies for achieving goals were suggested. Instead, the plan indicated that an SDM strategic planning committee would be formed for each goal area. These committees began working in fall 1990.

Almost all of the faculty attended this planning meeting, and most felt that the four goals that emerged were important. However, a few expressed concern that Ms. Baker ran the meeting and "rephrased" people's comments so that some concerns were never addressed. In particular, they were concerned that improvement in communication and trust within the school was not specified as a goal. In spring 1990 the researcher suggested to the school in a status report that a fifth, but as yet implicit, goal for SDM was to establish better communication and trust between teachers and administrators. In interviews, faculty members stressed that addressing the problems in communication and trust was essential if they were to feel free to take the risks necessary to address the four goal areas they had targeted. At issue, from their perspective, was whether Ms. Baker was willing to share decision making or simply wanted to maintain the illusion of an SDM Project at her school.

Thus, the first year of the project included little discussion or evidence of restructuring or innovation. "Sharing decisions" was the primary focus. However, the school made progress: a council had been created, procedures for decision making were in place, explicit goals had been developed, and faculty consensus about goals had been achieved.

Perceptions of Faculty and Administration

By early 1991, Brooksville was experiencing heightened tension, decreased communication among faculty members, and decreased trust of Ms. Baker and "the chosen." Many faculty members were disillusioned, and trust was so low that over one-third of the respondents refused to allow their interviews to be taped for fear of repercussions. Five months of SDM procedures had made things significantly worse.

The group of skeptics in the school was growing larger, and many respondents reported that faculty members, even those on the council, were unwilling to make decisions because they felt "threatened" and "intimidated." They noted that there was a growing split between "the chosen" and most other teachers. Many faculty members believed that SDM was not working and that the school was run by an ad hoc administrative group handpicked by Ms. Baker. Only some decisions were brought to the faculty and the SDM Council, and even these were sometimes overturned by Ms. Baker. Faculty were hesitant to make decisions and felt the project provided only the illusion of SDM. They did not feel free to express alternative viewpoints during council meetings or general faculty meetings. The following quote reflected the view of many faculty members.

I'm disillusioned. Faculty are not willing to make decisions any more because we feel threatened and intimidated. . . . When we do feel comfortable enough to make a comment or try a decision she is very critical if she doesn't like it. A lot of times she just blatantly says, "I won't support that." I don't even speak up at meetings any more. I'd just rather give it back to her and let her do it.

Teachers said the administration did not support risk taking and that faculty morale was low and declining, and, with it, support for the SDM Project. In fact, many speculated that, if a vote were taken, SDM would be voted out of the school.

Ms. Baker's perception was that the SDM Council and the faculty had begun making the decisions necessary to run the school, but that certain decisions she "just made"—in part because of time pressures from the district. She believed that the faculty wanted to make decisions but did not consider the consequences of their decisions or assume responsibility for their implementation.

During this time, external facilitators began working with all SDM schools. Brenda Hazen was the facilitator assigned to Brooksville. Ms. Hazen worked with the council to try to improve communication and decision-making procedures. She also worked with Ms. Baker to help her see how the faculty perceived her actions. She knew Ms. Baker was very committed to SDM and to the school and tried to help her see that some of her outbursts lowered faculty morale and endangered the program.

Despite these problems, most faculty members supported and respected Ms. Baker. Many understood that SDM puts the principal in a difficult position. They noted that teachers want more freedom to experiment and take risks. Yet, they acknowledged that such freedom for faculty might be impossible unless the district provided more freedom for building administrators to take risks. As one teacher said,

> People don't feel they are making decisions but really the principal is still the decision maker. She was trained to make decisions and it is hard to relinquish power especially because if a decision fails it will all fall on her.

The faculty understood and accepted administrative unwillingness to give up certain decisions, given the principal's accountability for the success of the school. However, they did believe that the school had only an illusion of SDM. In talking about the problems in the school, faculty and Ms. Baker were now beginning to talk about necessary role changes for faculty and administration. But their ideas about the nature of those changes were vague, they had no idea how to bring about those changes, and there was no explicit communication among the faculty members about the issues surrounding role change.

Additionally, although teachers believed the school had made progress toward achieving the goals they had set for the project, they believed SDM simply took too much time. Teachers noted that faculty work committees had always existed at this school and they did not believe that SDM had significantly changed faculty levels of involvement. One teacher said,

> It's not that much different than what we had before. We've always had committees that accomplished these kinds of things. We've always had input about the way the school is run, but now there is a decline in morale and communication.

SDM just made them more frustrated because they believed they "should" have more decision-making power. In fact, many reported a desire to return to pre-SDM days. Teachers noted that Ms. Baker had accomplished a lot in a short time. They were willing to accept her making the decisions. They were less willing to maintain the pretense that school decisions were being made by the faculty when, in their view, all decisions were being orchestrated in the front office.

CRISIS RESOLUTION: REUNITING A DIVIDED FACULTY

The February 1991 status report written by the researcher described the tension and lack of communication in the school. When the report was shared with Ms. Baker, the district moved quickly to provide encouragement and support. Brenda Hazen began attending most SDM Council meetings, and the council began to work to clarify problematic issues such as when SDM goal committees act autonomously and when they require approval from the council or from the general faculty, the role of the general faculty in making decisions, whether the council required the approval of the principal for action, and what kinds of decisions the council (as opposed to the grade chairs group or Ms. Baker acting independently) should be making. At the same time, two of the four support faculty (members of "the chosen") began to decrease their involvement in the SDM Project to try to reduce the split between "the chosen" and the rest of the faculty in the school. Through most of the spring, the council grappled with these problems, but the faculty continued to feel left out of the decision-making process.

In May 1991 the school needed to develop their SDM plan for the 1991–1992 academic year. After polling the faculty, the SDM Council decided to hold two lengthy, whole-school, after-school dinner meetings in mid-May to develop the plan. Almost all of the faculty attended at least one of the meetings, which were led by an external facilitator (not Ms. Hazen). These meetings were a turning point for the school.

At the meetings, faculty and staff worked in small groups to identify the problems and issues important for the 1991–1992 academic year. Within the groups, faculty and staff began to talk about the problems that divided the school and threatened the project. Peer support encouraged some individuals to express the concerns of their small groups to the large group, and the "sub-terranean" conflicts were brought to the surface and confronted. Throughout the meeting, faculty insisted that their procedures for governance and communication be made explicit. The external facilitator assigned to lead this meeting tried to focus the group on the "task at hand," setting goals for the 1991–1992 year, but the faculty persisted. On the second day, Ms. Baker "took the meeting back" from the facilitator, stating that her faculty wanted to deal with issues of governance. That action united Ms. Baker and her faculty and set them in a common direction.

Explicit Outcomes

These meetings had positive results. Up until this time, the grade-level chairs had met regularly with Ms. Baker to make instructional decisions. The SDM Council also had responsibility for instructional decisions, and conflicts between the two groups had become problematic. One result of the meetings was the elimination of the grade-chair group. The membership of the council was changed to include grade chairs. Faculty agreed that the small stipend grade chairs had received in the past would now be divided among the members of the SDM Council. This action reduced conflict among competing groups and improved the council's communication with the faculty. Second, responsibilities for various decisions regarding budget, personnel, and students were clarified. Third, faculty members agreed to meet twice a month to improve SDM communication and broaden faculty involvement in school decisions. The SDM Council agreed to post all council agendas in advance of the meetings so that teachers would have a chance to attend meetings when the issues were important to them. The faculty and staff also developed an explicit set of goals and action strategies for the 1991–1992 academic year (see Appendix). As goals or action strategies were developed, all teachers and staff members were asked if they could support or at least "live with" the idea. Thus, all of the goals and action strategies listed in the plan had the unanimous endorsement of faculty, administration, and staff.

Implicit Outcomes: Changing Roles and Relationships

The meetings changed people's perceptions of the long-term goals of the SDM Project. For the first time, teachers began to discuss SDM as a way to improve the education of children at Brooksville. Faculty talked for the first time about restructuring and what school restructuring meant to them. Faculty began to see that restructuring might mean:

- Redefining people's roles
- Developing innovative ways for community, parents, teachers, and administration to work together to improve the school
- Developing more daring and innovative instructional strategies
- Developing nontraditional assessment strategies for students
- Constantly reevaluating their teaching in order to promote change, growth, and improvement

In addition, faculty at Brooksville reported that, through SDM, Brooksville had begun moving toward restructuring. Although many reported that the process was slow and that too little innovation had occurred, almost everyone interviewed indicated that Brooksville was moving toward restructuring and had the potential to increase the pace of change. In talking about first steps toward restructuring, stakeholders mentioned several components of the plan for the 1991–1992 academic year (see Appendix). These included encouraging each teacher to try one innovative strategy, changing the report card to eliminate a letter grade in handwriting, and experimentation with portfolio assessment by second-grade teachers. The latter was cited as a big step toward restructuring because second-grade teachers were moving away from reporting student progress through report cards. Instead, they were collecting data about students in portfolios and reporting progress to parents in conferences where they discussed the portfolio contents together. In addition, faculty noted that Ms. Baker had begun including teachers on committees to make hiring decisions, consulting them about budget decisions such as whether to use supplemental funds to hire an additional teacher or to hire aides, and working with them to develop basic school policies such as a safer method for dismissing students from school. Teachers hoped that first-step success might encourage other faculty members to experiment and that each new success would make the faculty more willing to take bolder steps in the future.

Teachers and Ms. Baker began to talk about changing faculty and administrative roles. Role and relationship changes had just begun, but the school community was thinking about the changes that were in process and others that were needed.

Teachers began to see that SDM principals have to be "objective leaders," a term Ms. Baker used to describe the essential characteristics of an SDM principal. Principals have to treat every idea with respect, hold their own emotions in check, and offer ideas collegially. SDM principals must perform a difficult balancing act. They must trust the SDM process. They must trust that, with support and gentle prodding, teachers will get the job done. The process may take time and the product may not be what the principal (or faculty) initially envisioned. In the end, however, the product will be better and will enjoy faculty support. Teachers noted that administrators must work as SDM advocates at the district level to find ways around procedural regulations so that teachers will be free to innovate.

The role of a faculty member also changes in an SDM school. Respondents noted that teachers must be able and willing to speak their minds, stand up for what they believe, give time to SDM, make collaborative decisions, and accept responsibility for their decisions. And respondents noted that faculty members must be able to step out of the frame of the individual classroom. They must be able to see the whole picture and to view the school as a unit. The following quotes from two different teachers demonstrate teachers' insights about their new roles.

Under SDM you can't be an advocate for just your classroom or your grade level. It has to be global. You have to look at the whole school.

I'm not just a teacher in a classroom but I am a member of an organization, a company that helps to run the school. I'm not just alone in my room. . . . I want to be involved in as much as I can. . . . We are all learning what is going on and trying to develop something better.

These changes in role definition and relationships suggest that by May 1991, faculty and administrators had a much more complex view of SDM. They express the view that SDM means that faculty and administration are collectively responsible for making decisions about running the school, communicating with one another, accepting responsibility for their decisions and actions, and learning to trust and value one another.

GAUGING SUCCESS

The progress made between February and May was dramatic. Faculty attitudes shifted significantly. Every respondent noted that communication had improved and most said trust had improved as well. They said that there was more unity among the faculty members, more empathy for the administration, and that faculty felt much more included in SDM and more comfortable expressing dissenting opinions. Although some teachers still doubted that SDM would ever "really" work at Brooksville, most felt this group was small and less vocal. Most teachers supported SDM and teachers who had been "on the edges" were joining the effort. They were starting to express their ideas and to recognize that they must take action if they wished to influence the future of the school. Although problems in trust and communication were not completely resolved, the following excerpt captures the prevalent faculty view:

People have become aware that they need to get involved or stop grip-
ing. They have the opportunity to go to meetings, to be heard and express their view. They can be as involved as they want. If they don't want
to take time to get involved in the decision making, then they need not
to complain.

Most teachers said that SDM was making enduring changes in the school.
They expected setbacks, but almost everyone believed an important threshold
had been crossed. Faculty members believed their ideas would be considered.
Most believed that severe communication problems would not recur. They said
that teachers had learned to confront one another, to clarify rumors, and to
speak out. They said these changes assured that open communication would
continue. One teacher noted,

> [Communication] is an up and down issue but I can't imagine it going
> back to like it was before. Now we are confronting each other. People
> are speaking up. There really is communication . . . and people are
> seeing everybody's perspective more. More people are trying to make it
> work.

By fall of the 1991–1992 academic year, faculty members unanimously
agreed that SDM processes and procedures were in place and working. They
reported that the climate of the school continued to be positive, task oriented,
and open. Respondents said that they had become more confident that they
could suggest ideas and influence decisions. Teachers noted that some faculty
members will never be able to see "beyond the classroom door," but that most
of their colleagues had changed their roles by developing a more schoolwide
perspective.

Respondents also described some role change on the part of Ms. Baker.
The "I'm the boss" image was still apparent. However, the administration did
solicit more faculty input, and Ms. Baker had begun to allow others to make
decisions, as the following quote indicates.

> I see the principal coming to us more and conferring with us and mak-
> ing it seem as if she wants us to decide together, but there are times
> when it is solely her decision. Sometimes it is a matter of time. I under-
> stand that; it's not a problem. On important issues, we sit down together.

Teachers said that Ms. Baker had become a more "objective" leader, although
a few respondents still believed it was very difficult to suggest or implement
ideas with which Ms. Baker disagreed. By fall 1991, faculty members noted
many accomplishments of SDM. SDM procedures were established. As one re-

spondent noted, "We're into operation instead of laying ground rules." Additionally, stakeholders noted that the previous year's agreements about communication procedures were being kept and that faculty communication with the council had improved. Agendas had been posted prior to meetings, reports about SDM activity had been made at general faculty meetings, many grade-level chairs were reporting SDM activity to their colleagues, and the SDM suggestion box was visible and was being used by faculty and parents. There had been lapses and times when information did not "get out." However, teachers understood. They explained that "[we] are not used to being in an organization and doing things like reports at faculty meetings." Whenever these problems were pointed out, the SDM Council acted to solve them. Thus, the level of trust among faculty and administration improved substantially, though problems remained.

Focusing on Goals

Concern about the long-term goals of the project also began to surface, however, in fall 1991. Several teachers expressed concern that SDM had done little that was truly innovative. Teachers had solved some problems and settled into a routine. Teachers were concerned that SDM would do little more than promote "business as usual" at Brooksville. They worried that impetus for significant change and restructuring might be lost in the day-to-day running of the school. The following quotes represent teachers' concerns.

> It seems like now it has settled into routine meetings. It's almost like grade chair meetings used to be. We just discuss things and move on. It doesn't seem like major things are happening. We're into operation now instead of laying ground rules.

> It would be accurate to say that we are dealing with basic routines now. We are starting to discuss where we are in terms of our goals. . . . We are trying to do too many things. It would be useful to focus on a limited number of things.

> I can't really say that we have accomplished anything except setting up procedures, except the evening meetings where we spent time together and brainstormed. . . . I think the development of mutual respect and getting to know how others feel was broadening.

These concerns were expressed during interviews in November, a time when two factors created a less than optimal context for SDM progress. First, the school had been overenrolled since the beginning of the year. This meant that teachers in several grade levels had class sizes larger than the class size limits specified by the district. Second, a contract dispute between the district and the teachers' union led the union to suggest that teachers do no more than "work to the rules" of their contract. Some teachers chose to comply with this suggestion, others did not, a situation that might have led to considerable conflict and tension among the faculty.

Despite these two factors, SDM was progressing. SDM goal committees had been created and were meeting to develop plans related to the goals (e.g., developing a discipline plan, setting up grade-level teams to develop strategies to meet the needs of at-risk students). Additionally, the second-grade teachers began collecting portfolio data and conducted the first set of parent conferences. The SDM Council made decisions about how to use the supplemental funds provided by the district to alleviate the overcrowding problems, and communication procedures for the council were institutionalized. Because of these accomplishments, almost everyone interviewed indicated that Brooksville had taken some steps toward restructuring. At the same time, teachers were beginning to question whether they had done enough and hoped that SDM would enable them to do significantly more. Thus, faculty concern about the limited scope of innovation can be interpreted as a signal of faculty readiness for more significant restructuring in the future. They saw the development of a school "vision" as the next big task, as reflected in the following quotes.

From what I've gleaned, the creative juices are flowing and we feel now we can really go. . . .

There is more support and encouragement and I think we will see more blossoming of things that are more exciting and risky. We have laid a foundation for more risk taking.

We don't have a vision yet but it isn't necessarily bad not to have a vision. We may be the kind of school that has to see change is possible to create a vision. All schools have the potential for a vision. I don't believe you have to start there.

Factors That Fostered Change

The process of change at Brooksville has been gradual. The history of the school and the nature of faculty-administration relationships at the onset of the project almost seemed to set this school up to fail, and yet the faculty and administration made significant progress. Four factors have been important to SDM progress at Brooksville. First, the commitment of many faculty members and of Ms. Baker and their mutual respect for one another as people and professionals were critical in making change possible. School personnel worked to preserve the "family feeling" that was a part of the school's history and culture. Concern about the school culture pushed faculty and administrators to take risks, to communicate their concerns, and to struggle to understand one another's perspectives. These actions were significant in resolving the communication crisis that threatened the success of the project. The work that these people have done to try to understand one another seems rooted in their definitions of the school as a family. Family members may have their problems, but they are family, and successful families take work.

A second factor was the structure of key planning meetings. It is significant that all school stakeholders were invited to the planning meetings held in spring 1990 and in spring 1991. These inclusive "town meetings" helped people confront their problems, develop common perspectives, and accomplish the tasks set before them. The combination of work, accomplishment, and fun (serving dinner) at the meetings helped them see one another's perspectives and helped noninstructional staff to feel included in the SDM effort. The size of the school made schoolwide planning meetings possible and the commitment of all stakeholders made them productive.

A third factor was the use of structures to support increased communication. Because communication was such a significant issue at Brooksville, the establishment of structures to support communication was essential. One productive structure was the use of small-group process. At the "town meetings," school stakeholders were divided into groups to express concerns and to develop ideas. Within the anonymity of a group, stakeholders were able to take risks and express their viewpoints. A similar structure that enabled stakeholders to express concerns anonymously was the use of an SDM suggestion box. Another key structure was the use of a consensus model that encouraged all to develop commitment to the project's explicit aims and strategies. The establishment of these procedures provided faculty with assurance that communication was important, that their voices would be heard, and that, collectively, they did have the power to confront Ms. Baker. They noted that confrontation was not necessarily easy but they understood that it was both possible and productive on issues of importance to the faculty.

A fourth and final factor can be mentioned as contributing to Brooksville's efforts. In developing this project, the district included an evaluation component. In 1990, when SDM was initiated in 10 schools in Live Oak County, the district contracted with the University of Florida to provide formative evaluation in 6 of the 10. As a part of this evaluation, Brooksville faculty members have participated in interviews and have received five reports and a case study describing the status of their project since its inception. It is impossible to determine exactly what influence the evaluation study has had at Brooksville. How-ever, it certainly had an influence. Indeed, the greatest impact of the study is that it has provided a way for faculty members to express their views about the project. That is, the evaluation study was another structure that supported communication among school stakeholders. The evaluation has increased the faculty's voice and brought to the surface problems and tensions that might otherwise have festered and never been resolved. Several faculty members said that the evaluation helped them understand and remedy the communication and trust problems that had become severe in February 1991.

Barriers That Impeded Progress

Over the course of this study, respondents mentioned three barriers that stood in the way of SDM success. The first is time. Many respondents noted that SDM makes more work for faculty, yet provides no additional time. They ex-pressed concern that they would "burn out" unless they find ways to make SDM less time consuming. A related concern is that some faculty members believe too little has been accomplished for the amount of time they devote to SDM work and meetings. Although these teachers desire change and the school is ready for change, they note that the change process needs to be speeded up to keep the SDM Project from losing momentum.

A second barrier that teachers mentioned is money. Respondents react to funding limitations in different ways. Some lament the lack of supplemental funding for the SDM Project and note that its impact will be lessened because money is so tight. For example, these respondents expressed concern about lack of money to pay substitutes so as to provide faculty with time to generate plans to implement innovative instructional strategies. Similarly, they were concerned about lack of funding for additional instructional or psychological services staff. Other stakeholders noted that funding limitations are a result of a larger eco-nomic downturn and simply must be endured. They added that continued dis-cussions of "impractical" ideas took too much time and limited the impact of the project.

The third and most significant barrier to successful shared decision making at Brooksville has been the nature of the school's teacher-administration rela-tionships and communication patterns. This issue has been a concern in the school since before the initiation of the SDM Project. Although trust and com-munication have substantially improved, many note that the problem has not been solved. Respondents report forward progress but also note that everyone needs to continue their efforts to trust one another and to seek valid informa-tion rather than rely on rumors. They note that the climate in the school re-quires continuous and vigilant attention to maintain present levels of success and make further improvements.

PERSONAL AND ORGANIZATIONAL LEARNING

At Brooksville, personal and organizational learning are fused. Perhaps the essence of organizational learning is the collateral development of individual perspectives that eventually get woven into the fabric of the organization (Foster, 1986). This case study details the 3-year change process that allowed administrators and teachers to significantly alter role definitions and relationships with one another. These changes are not universal, are still in process, and are still fragile. Nevertheless, significant change has occurred. Thus, the dominant learning within this setting has been the development of a sense of collective responsibility and power that is at the heart of the change in role definition.

Through the project, many (but certainly not all) faculty members have learned to take a schoolwide perspective of school improvement. They see the school as a unit and no longer focus exclusively on room-level or grade-level problems. Collaborative work on schoolwide goals helped teachers and administrators build a sense of school community (Lieberman, 1988; Passow, 1989; Wirth, 1983). At Brooksville, teachers and administrators worked collectively to accomplish the tasks associated with the SDM Project. They learned to listen to one another, to look for commonalities among differing perspectives, and to confront real differences of opinion when necessary. Brooksville teachers now speak about being collectively responsible for running the school, about trusting others to make good decisions, and about everyone putting in the time needed to make and implement good decisions. Faculty members have learned that *together* (in large or small groups) they can confront the principal and discuss differences. Though they do not like confrontations, they have learned that they can express themselves, build a case, and successfully work out problems. In this sense, faculty members have become professionally empowered as they redefined their roles.

Ms. Baker, too, has come to accept and value collective responsibility for decision making in the school. Like other SDM administrators (Gomez, 1989; Meadows, 1990), she worried that she would be held accountable for any perceived failure in the school. Nevertheless, she has tried to alter her interactions with her faculty and to become more accepting of faculty ideas and actions. She has worked to become a leader rather than a manager of her faculty (Foster, 1989; Johnson, 1990). The process has been difficult for faculty, but, at times, the change process must have been agonizing for Ms. Baker. She had few allies or confidants to help her through the difficult period of change. Although it may sometimes be hard for Ms. Baker to see, she, too, has been empowered by the SDM Project—empowered to change herself and her interactions with others, and empowered to lead her school toward significant restructuring.

WHAT CAN WE LEARN FROM THIS CASE?

This case is interesting because, in many ways, SDM seemed unlikely to succeed. Yet, to date, the project has succeeded and lessons from this school may help others beginning similar projects or those attempting to understand change processes in schools.

The specific factors that have contributed to Brooksville's success have already been discussed. These factors played an incremental role in the school's restructuring process. That is, without any one of them, Brooksville might not have been able to sustain its change efforts. An additional but undiscussed factor, however, seems equally important. At Brooksville, micropolitical issues were brought to the surface and confronted, and thus work toward resolution was productive.

It has been noted that Brooksville had a turbulent recent past. Prior to Ms. Baker's arrival, the faculty believed that the school was a peaceful and pleasant place to work. Based on their previous interactions with Mr. Olson, teachers had developed expectations about principals and school leadership (Spindler, 1979). However, Ms. Baker did not match their expectations and thus was a catalyst for change. Many acknowledged that she made some good changes in the school. They also believed, however, she had changed the culture of the school in ways that made it less comfortable. Communication and trust had declined, but the conflict remained subterranean (Lacey, 1977) and unconfronted. Older faculty members continued to support one another, to communicate with and trust one another, to operate as a "family," with Ms. Baker as the outsider to be avoided if at all possible. New faculty members essentially acted as a bridge between Ms. Baker and older faculty members. They were accepted into the "family," but they also perceived Ms. Baker more positively and were more accepting of the changes she tried to institute. Although many faculty members talked among themselves about problems in communication and trust in the school, few actively confronted Ms. Baker.

The initiation of SDM provided a second catalyst for this school. Change in an organization inevitably creates conflict (Ball, 1987). SDM was a significant change because SDM is about changing the dynamics of power relationships in a school, and many in this school were unhappy with the existing power relationships. As a result, their fledgling efforts to initiate SDM erupted into a crisis. The problem was so explosive that it would have been difficult to ignore. School personnel began to actively confront problems of power and information control and, in the process, developed strategies to resolve those problems. These strategies were useful in themselves, but they had another, unintended consequence: they led teachers and administrators to begin redefining their roles and altering their role relationships. Active confrontation of micropolitical issues was of critical importance in this school's restructuring effort. It must be noted, however, that successful resolution of conflict required a lot of work and good will from faculty and administrators alike. SDM was a catalyst in this school, but the widespread commitment to make SDM work and to preserve a positive climate at Brooksville brought the crisis to successful resolution.

The story at Brooksville has not ended. Roles and role relationships are still evolving. SDM has been defined and is in place at Brooksville. The work done thus far has taken time, hard work, and extraordinary commitment. The question now is whether stakeholders will settle back, comfortable with the changes they have made, or move on to tackle the next tasks at hand, notably, creating a school vision to guide them through significant restructuring.

APPENDIX: 1991–1992 SDM/FOCUS 2000 GOALS, OBJECTIVES, AND ACTION STRATEGIES

Goal 1: Improve discipline
> *Objective:* Teach students to demonstrate respect for people, property, and rules
>
> *Strategies:* a. Create discipline committee
> b. Stress parent involvement
> c. Do staff development

Goal 2: Improve ability to meet needs of at-risk learners
> *Objective:* Provide interventions so students will experience success and enjoy more positive attitudes toward school
>
> *Strategies:* a. Set up "at-risk" teams by grade level to design interventions (waiver)
> b. Have each teacher use one innovative technique
> c. Establish parent involvement committee to increase parent involvement
> d. Request additional psychological services

Goal 3: Improve trust and communication among staff
> *Objective:* Foster a secure, trust-building environment conducive to open communication and honest feedback
>
> *Strategies:* a. Give a sensitivity training workshop
> b. Set up an orientation committee for new faculty
> c. Hold bimonthly faculty meetings with the agenda posted 2 days in advance
> d. Have SDM Council provide a yearly curriculum calender
> e. Have SDM Council foster communication with open agendas and open meetings
> f. Make minutes from all faculty and SDM meetings available to staff

g. Set up SDM governance committee to clarify roles and responsibilities (waiver)

(Governance plan attached)

Note: In addition to these strategies, which are listed in the Focus 2000 plan, it is our understanding that agendas for bimonthly SDM Council meetings will be posted 2 days in advance and that SDM memos will be color coded for easy identification.

Goal 4: Curriculum restructuring

Objective:	Provide an atmosphere conducive to innovative curriculum restructuring to increase student interest and achievement
Strategies:	a. Develop a proposal to permit discretionary use of Chapter One funds (wavier)
	b. Establish on going, scheduled release time during the school day for professional development activities
	c. Administer needs assessment to determine the interest in and need for staff development
	d. By March 1992, rethink, reevaluate, and restructure schoolwide standardized testing program
	e. By September 1991, rethink, reevaluate, and restructure method of reporting pupil progress (waiver) (portfolio assessment for second grade; same report card waivers for the rest of the grades as last year)

NOTE

The current case is based on 62 interviews conducted with 33 faculty, staff, parents, and administrators at Brooksville Elementary over 3 academic years. Interviewing began in February 1990, and the last set of interviews was conducted in November 1991, just before this report was written. Most of the participants were interviewed twice and key participants three or more times. Fifty-one interviews were conducted at the school; eleven more were conducted by telephone. The interviews lasted from 20 minutes to 1 hour, but most were about 25 minutes long. The interviews were taped and transcribed verbatim, except in six cases when participants requested that the tape-recorder be turned off. These interviews were transcribed on a portable computer as participants talked. This case study grew out of analysis of the 62 interviews and a collection of school and district documents.

REFERENCES

Ball, S. J. (1987). *The micro-politics of the school: Towards a theory of school organization.* New York: Methuen.

Foster, W. (1986). *Paradigms and promises*. Buffalo, NY: Prometheus Books.

Foster, W. (1989). Toward a critical practice of leadership. In J. Smythe (Ed.), *Critical perspectives on educational leadership* (pp. 39–62). London: Falmer Press.

Gomez, J. J. (1989). The path to school-based management isn't smooth, but we're scaling the obstacles one by one. *American School Board Journal, 176*(10), 20–22.

Johnson, S. M. (1990). Teachers, power and school change. In W. H. Clune & J. F. Witte (Eds.), *Choice and control in American education* (Vol. 2, pp. 343–370). London: Falmer Press.

Lacey, C. (1977). *The socialization of teachers*. London: Methuen.

Lieberman, A. (1988). Teachers and principals: Turf, tensions, and new tasks. *Phi Delta Kappan, 69,* 648–653.

Meadows, B. J. (1990). The rewards and risks of shared leadership. *Phi Delta Kappan, 71*(7), 545–548.

Passow, A. H. (1989). Present and future directions in school reform. In T. J. Sergiovanni & J. H. Moore (Eds.), *Schooling for tomorrow* (pp. 13–39). Boston: Allyn & Bacon.

Spindler, G. D. (1979). The role of the school administrator. In R. Barnhardt, J. H. Chilcott, & H. F. Wolcott (Eds.), *Anthropology and educational administration* (pp. 3–38). Tucson, AZ: Impresora Suhara.

Wirth, A. G. (1983). *Productive work in industry and schools: Becoming persons again*. Lanham, MD: University Press of America.

Chapter 5

Restructuring Schools in Hammond, Indiana

Mark A. Smylie
Ute Tuermer

In the early 1980s, the School City of Hammond, Indiana began an evolutionary process of school restructuring. Starting as an experiment in a handful of schools, this process became a districtwide policy and priority. This case study describes the course of school restructuring in the Hammond public schools. It shows how the concurrent development of collaborative labor relations, community support, administrator-board relations, and systems of capacity building have supported restructuring initiatives. This is a case that argues that school restructuring requires long-term, systemic individual and organizational change.

THE CONTEXT OF RESTRUCTURING

Located on the northwestern tip of Indiana between Gary and the Chicago metropolitan area, Hammond is for the most part a middle-income, residential community. Over the past 20 years, Hammond has experienced many of the demographic changes characteristic of the nation's "rust belt." Between 1970 and 1990, its general population declined by almost 22% to 84,236. During this period, the city's population also became more ethnically diverse. The white proportion of the population fell from 95% to 78%, while the African-American and Hispanic proportions rose to 9% and 12% respectively. Steel plant closings and job layoffs nearly halved the available jobs in Hammond and surrounding Lake County (including Gary and East Chicago City). The concentration of available jobs shifted from the industrial manufacturing to the lower-paying retail and service sectors of the economy. These changes were accompanied by increases in unemployment and poverty. Between 1970 and

1980, for example, unemployment rose from 4% to 9%. The number of people below the poverty line rose 23%. In 1980, 13% of all children under the age of 18 lived in poverty.

The Hammond public school district, formally named the "School City of Hammond," is the seventh largest school district in the state. It employs approximately 880 teachers and 70 district and school administrators. The district enrolls students in kindergarten through twelfth grade in 24 elementary, middle, and senior high schools. It also supports the Area Career Center for high school students and adults. The district is governed by a popularly elected, five-member board of school trustees. It is administered by a superintendent and four assistant superintendents for curriculum and instruction, business, personnel, and school improvement and partnership programs. David Dickson has been superintendent since July 1984.

The School City of Hammond enrolls approximately 14,000 students. Between 1970 and the mid-1980s, enrollment declined almost 43%. By the late 1980s, however, it stabilized and began to grow for the first time in almost 20 years. Like the city itself, the district's student population has become more ethnically diverse and poorer. Between 1970 and 1990, for example, the African-American and Hispanic proportions of the enrollment rose from less than 10% combined to almost 15% and 18% respectively. Between 1980 and 1990, the proportion of elementary school students participating in the federal government's school lunch program increased from 30% to almost 45%. Student achievement, as measured by scores on standardized tests, declined during the 1970s. However, in the mid-1980s achievement began to improve. By 1987, no grade level scored below national norms.

Since the 1970s, the district has experienced a deepening financial crisis. The district attributes much of this crisis to the 1973 state legislation that froze school general fund tax levies. Coupled with declines in taxable properties and assessed property values, this freeze severely limited the district's ability to raise local revenues. Between 1971 and 1987, the district's operating debt rose from $3.6 million to over $7 million. During the 1980s, the district administration used a number of strategies to reduce this debt, including postponing payrolls, reducing staff positions through attrition, delaying bill payments, issuing bonds, seeking state approval for transferring monies from categorical to general funds, and actively seeking private sources of funding from the community.

The relationship between the Hammond public schools and the community has been positive and largely stable. Since 1970, there have been few seriously contested school board elections. Referendums and bond issues have been generally successful. No controversies about school matters have divided the community politically or cast it against the district. Broad-based community support has been cultivated proactively by Dickson and his administration. This success is evident in the establishment of the Hammond Education Foundation, a community-led organization founded to provide external funding for instructional innovation, and the Partners in Education Program, which has forged dozens of mutually beneficial projects between schools and local government agencies, universities, businesses and industries, and private citizens.

Hammond teachers are represented by the Hammond Teachers' Federation, Local 394 of the American Federation of Teachers. About 80% of the district's teachers are members. Pat O'Rourke, a teacher at Hammond High School, has served as the union's president since 1974. He has yet to be challenged seriously in a reelection bid. The relationship between the Hammond Teachers' Federation and the school district has been positive and stable. There has been no serious labor unrest or a teachers' strike since the late 1960s.

During the 1980s, the Hammond school district implemented two major school restructuring initiatives. These initiatives, one the outgrowth of the other, were based on participative decision making and school-based management. The district believes that teacher participation in decision making provides crucial information closest to the source of many problems of schooling— the school and classroom. Increased access to and use of this information is thought to improve the quality of such ideas and decisions. Furthermore, decentralizing decision making to the school level permits identification of local issues and development of initiatives best suited to the contexts of individual schools. The district believes that teachers' participation in school-level decision making promotes commitment to new programs and policies and increases the motivation to implement them. Finally, it believes that the enhanced quality of ideas and decisions and increased commitment and motivation expand prospects for improving opportunities for student learning.

These beliefs form the foundation of a vision shared by the district administration, school board, and teachers' union. But of paramount importance to this vision are students' interests. According to Superintendent Dickson:

> We all believe in kids and we work for the benefit of the kids in everything we do. . . . Our acid test, the proof of the pudding, whatever you want to say is whether or not something changes in terms of student learning. If not, we're just playing games to make each other feel better.

THE SCHOOL IMPROVEMENT PROCESS

The first initiative, Hammond's School Improvement Process (SIP), evolved from an experiment at Hammond High School. During the middle and late 1970s, student achievement at that school, formerly among the highest in the state, fell dramatically. Absentee and dropout rates soared, as did racial tension, gang activity, drug use, and vandalism. Teacher morale eroded and hostility and distrust between teachers and administrators simmered. In fall 1981, Elizabeth Ennis, an assistant principal at Hammond High, and Raymond Golarz, an assistant district superintendent, called together a group of teachers, parents, principals, district administrators, and school board members to meet with representatives from the Kettering Foundation and the Lilly Endowment to discuss the school improvement initiatives of the Institute for the Development of Educational Activities (I/D/E/A). This group recommended experimental adoption of the I/D/E/A school-based improvement process at Hammond High School. In spring 1982, the school board approved the project and underwrote its costs.

Hammond High School's experiment began to receive attention from other schools in the district. In fall 1983, Eggers and Spohn Elementary/Middle Schools, two of Hammond High's feeder schools, adopted similar school-based improvement processes. Frank Sanders, then superintendent, formed a task force of teachers, administrators, and parents to consider districtwide adoption of such initiatives. To ensure that each school had an opportunity to participate in the deliberations, the board and superintendent sponsored a day-long "School Improvement Project Awareness Workshop." At least one teacher, parent, and administrator from each school attended the session and virtually every representative supported adoption of the improvement process. In spring 1984, the board endorsed development of a shared decision making, school-based management model for the district.

In 1984–1985, his first year as superintendent, Dickson appointed a districtwide group of teachers, principals, and district administrators to develop a school improvement model. The group met regularly and routinely sought ideas from teachers, school administrators, parents, and community representatives. As the year progressed, the Hammond Teachers' Federation joined and became deeply involved in the planning group. Several union members, including president Pat O'Rourke, participated actively. O'Rourke and other union members were initially concerned about potential conflicts with collective bargaining. However, they began to see that increased collaboration with the administration around issues of school improvement could be very effective in promoting teachers' professional interests as well as enhancing the district's capacity to serve students.

The Model

This planning group developed a model of participative decision making and school-based management that closely resembled the I/D/E/A school improvement process piloted at Hammond High and Eggers and Spohn Elementary/Middle Schools. This model, the School Improvement Process (SIP), created a nested, team-oriented, decision-making structure in each school. At the center was the core team, composed of the building principal, one or two teachers, and a parent. This team was responsible for setting a school improvement agenda and facilitating the work of a larger school-level committee called an SIP team. An SIP team consisted of 9 to 25 teachers and parents, depending on the size of the school, and served as the primary decision-making body for school improvement. The principal could be a member of the SIP team or a consultant to be called for specific information or expertise. However, the principal could not serve as team chair. A majority of the SIP team's members had to be teachers. The model stipulated that the SIP team decisions were subject to review by the district-level program review committee and the school board. This provision was intended to ensure compatibility of SIP team decisions with government regulations and district goals and policies.

To encourage school-based decision making, the model left open several key aspects of core team and SIP team structures. It contained no specific provisions about team composition or how often teams should meet. It did not determine a priori which decisions were to be made by the SIP team and which were to remain the prerogative of the principal or district administration. In addition, the model did not specify how core team or SIP team members should be appointed. The selection process was left to individual schools.

This model incorporated a multistage, "vision-to-action," consensus-based, decision-making process. It specified a system of "pyramiding" for gathering and sharing information. Pyramiding required each SIP team member to interact at each stage of the process with five to seven peers (i.e., teachers with other teachers and parents with other parents), inform them of team deliberations or proposals, and gather feedback. These peers in turn interacted with five to seven other peers, and so on, until most if not all interested and affected members of the school community had been informed and given opportunities for input.

The model also called for SIP teams to create small task groups called "design teams" to develop specific programs and strategies for achieving school-improvement goals. Design teams were also to identify the professional development needs of teachers, administrators, and other members of the school community. They were to monitor and evaluate new programs and strategies. These teams would be ad hoc groups formed to address specific issues. Membership would consist of teachers, administrators, and parents or community representatives with knowledge and skills germane to the teams' tasks. As the tasks changed, memberships would change. To ensure continuity, design team leaders would be chosen from the SIP team. The model specified that before a proposed change could be implemented, it would have to be reviewed and approved by the school's entire faculty. Design teams were intended to broaden teacher and parent participation in SIP beyond the standing committee structure, as well as to tap relevant expertise from all parts of the school community.

District Support

The district provided two forms of technical support. In spring 1985, it held two- and three-day "preimplementation" workshops to help SIP teams understand the model and to help members brainstorm, build consensus, and creatively solve problems. Additional leadership development workshops were held during the implementation for SIP team chairpersons and principals. Both forms of support were planned by the office of the assistant superintendent for school improvement. The primary responsibility for conducting these workshops and facilitating core team and SIP team work at the school level fell to Wayne Pecher, a Hammond High School math teacher who was granted half-time release from teaching, and Jane Kendrick, then principal of Eggers Elementary/Middle School.

Implementation

Implementation varied considerably among schools. In some cases the SIP team functioned sporadically if at all. In others, they met regularly and functioned as primary decision-making bodies in their schools. Some addressed a limited agenda of procedural and management issues. Others engaged a wide range of complex curricular, instructional, and organizational issues. In some schools, the SIP team functioned at the discretion of and under the strict control of the principal. In others, the team provided opportunities for teachers to collaborate with administration and participate actively in decision making.

During the 1985–1986 school year, the first full year of implementation, most schools focused on forming core and SIP teams and setting school-improvement agendas. In very few schools did the teams engage organizational or curricular and instructional issues. In 1986–1987, most SIP teams continued to work on vision and goal statements and to strengthen working relationships among team members and explore parameters of authority. Much like the previous year, few schools went beyond these activities to curricular and instructional innovation.

To promote SIP activity further, the district appointed Thomas Knarr assistant superintendent for school improvement. It also infused the process with additional resources. In 1987, the district received a $66,000 grant from the Federal Mediation and Conciliation Service to provide more release time for teachers to coordinate SIP activities in their schools. The grant also provided resources for SIP team professional development, a newsletter to promote communication among schools, and special SIP-related events, including two labor-management conferences for principals and teachers. In addition, the district developed new procedures by which SIP team teachers could obtain release time from classes beyond that which was supported by external sources.

During 1987–1988, SIP team activity increased markedly. By the end of that year, almost every school in the district had developed some form of school improvement activity. As before, some schools addressed only procedural and management issues. Others addressed a variety of organizational, curricular, and instructional issues. For instance, several SIP teams dissolved academic departments and reorganized their schools around community concepts. Other teams developed plans to enhance communication among teachers, administrators, and parents. Three SIP teams worked with architects to design new school buildings. The teams' curricular and instructional initiatives ranged from new kindergarten and early failure-prevention programs to integrated curricula and computer-assisted instruction.

Several problems emerged from this flurry of activity. In several schools, teachers perceived that their expectations for SIP participation and curricular and instructional change were thwarted by their principals' efforts to politicize the process. In other schools, confusion developed about which decisions SIP teams could make and which decisions remained the prerogative of principals. In some schools, confusion led to conflict. In others, it led to atrophy because teachers and principals were unwilling to risk confrontation over decision-making authority.

As SIP activity increased, so did the demand for professional development and technical assistance. The people who assumed these responsibilities soon became overburdened and unable to meet the growing need to facilitate SIP activity at the school level. Indeed, in 1987–1988, when most SIP activity developed, the district was unable to allocate funds to provide release time for Pecher, the primary SIP staff developer. This increase in demands also revealed a need for an institutional system of ongoing professional support.

Perhaps the most visible and volatile problem concerned the district-level review of school-based decisions. As SIP activity increased, district administrators became concerned that some schools were concentrating on matters peripheral to student learning. They requested written copies of team plans and conveyed more specific expectations for SIP team activity. Several schools had reached decisions without adequate consideration of government regulations and district policies and procedures. Knarr recalled advising SIP teams against implementing specific plans because they conflicted with state regulations. Other SIP teams' decisions were controverted by district administration because they conflicted with district policy and the teams did not seek waivers before they began implementing them.

Tension and confusion at the school level reached a flash point in spring 1988 when the school board reversed the decisions of two SIP teams. One team sought to develop a new foreign language curriculum, the other a new grade-reporting system. While both initiatives had relatively strong faculty support, the board concluded that the teams began implementing their plans without properly following district review and approval procedures. The board's decisions triggered turmoil. Teachers and principals across the district began to question whether the district administration and school board truly supported school-based decision making. The fragile trust that had developed between schools and the district administration was directly challenged. These events suggested to many teachers that the administration and board had given only "token support" and "lip service" to SIP. One teacher argued that the "central office really wasn't willing to give up authority." Another teacher recalled these developments as evidence of the inevitability of SIP failure: "SIP happens."

The district administration moved quickly to address these tensions between school and district authority and between creativity and control. The superintendent and school board established a 25-member strategic planning committee to review SIP and make specific recommendations for improvement. This committee was composed of district administrators, teachers chosen by the teachers' union, principals selected by the superintendent, and parents selected by the district council of the Hammond Parent-Teacher Association. One student from each of the district's four high schools and representatives of the school board and the teachers' union served as advisors. The committee met regularly throughout the 1988–1989 school year. In fall 1989, the district sponsored a series of meetings for the committee to share a draft proposal with other teachers and principals. In March 1990, the committee presented a final proposal to the board.

THE SCHOOL-BASED RESTRUCTURING PROCESS

The proposal that was adopted by the board established a new school-based restructuring process (SBRP) to replace SIP. In many ways, SBRP resembled SIP. It retained SIP's nested structure of core teams, planning teams (formerly SIP teams), design teams, and the district-level program review committee. It also retained SIP's group-building strategies, "vision-to-action" planning, pyramiding, and decision making by consensus. However, SBRP introduced several changes to address specific problems of SIP and to cast SBRP as a fundamentally enhanced process.

Recasting the Reform Agenda

One of the most significant elements introduced by SBRP was conceptual. SBRP shifted SIP's focus from "improvement" or "doing what we do now better" to reconceptualizing and reinventing schools and the role and responsibilities of teachers, administrators, students, and parents. According to the strategic planning committee, this shift was necessary to move teachers and administrators beyond prevailing views to consider more creative ways to organize schools and enhance learning opportunities for students.

In addition, SBRP denoted specific functions and relationships among core teams, planning teams, and design teams. While core teams were directed to continue to develop agendas and facilitate planning team activity, they were also asked to assume responsibility for compliance with SBRP processes, to monitor the use of SBRP funds, and to report the status of SBRP activities to the central administration. These provisions were developed, along with others (described below), to ensure that conflicts with government regulations and district policies would be identified and resolved early on rather than at the end of the school-based decision-making process.

SBRP also described in more detail the areas designated for planning team decision making: (1) educational goals, (2) instructional programs, (3) resource allocation and scheduling, (4) teacher professional development, and (5) organizational restructuring. It incorporated a formal needs assessment and stipulated trial implementation, evaluation, and redesign periods before formal adoption of SBRP initiatives. Unlike SIP, SBRP articulated the principal's role in decision making. Principals were required to serve on both core and planning teams. While they were expected to become part of the consensus required for decision making, SBRP provided principals a veto over planning team decisions. SBRP specified core and planning team member selection procedures to ensure representation among all members of a school community.

Finally, SBRP added new provisions for district-level review of school-level decisions. Core and planning teams were expected to document their activities to ensure input from all stakeholders. To avoid conflicts with government regulations and district policies and procedures, the teams were asked to submit vision statements, goals, and program designs to the assistant superintendent for school improvement. Teams were encouraged to seek advice from the program review committee *during* planning. New procedures were provided to help planning teams obtain waivers to implement SBRP decisions that might differ from district policy. In this respect, SBRP was fundamentally different from SIP because if these provisions for documentation and reporting were met, then unlike under SIP, the school board could not overturn planning team decisions.

District Support

Under SBRP, provision of professional development and technical support services was shifted from individuals (i.e., Pecher and Kendrick) to the Hammond Leadership and Program Development Academy. The academy was created as a joint venture between the school district and the Center for Leadership in School Reform in Louisville, Kentucky. It employed full- and part-time staff who, unlike sip staff developers, underwent intensive preparation before working with teachers and principals. Kendrick resigned her principalship at Eggers to become the academy's director and liaison with the Louisville center. The academy established a "neutral" setting outside central administration for ongoing technical assistance and conflict resolution. It placed professional development at the fore and helped institutionalize efforts to build individual and organizational capacity for change, capacity that was underdeveloped in sip.

The academy offered a structured, 12-month professional development sequence for core and planning teams. The sequence begins with creating an awareness of the need for change and new possibilities for redesigning schools. It proceeds to help members identify, collect, and critique information that might be relevant to their work, including a schoolwide needs assessment. It then prepares teams to draft vision statements, goals, and working agendas. This stage emphasizes group process skills, building trust, and reaching consensus. Finally, as planning teams establish design teams and as design teams develop specific programs, the sequence shifts to technical assistance for monitoring implementation, adaptation, and evaluation.

Implementation

sbrp was greeted with ambivalence. Some teachers were skeptical about how much had changed. The phrase "the same old sip" was heard throughout the district. Some teachers thought that the district would not support sbrp any more than it had supported sip. Several teachers remarked that they felt "burned" and "betrayed" by the way that district administration had "blocked" sip. One teacher mused, "Does Hammond really mean this?"

sbrp implementation began in January 1990, before formal board approval, when four elementary and secondary schools began the professional development sequence at the leadership academy. In June 1990, a second group of eight schools began the sequence. A third and fourth cohort of schools began in October 1990 and January 1991. By May 1991, each school in the district had completed at least the first four stages of the sequence. All of the schools in the district were required to eventually participate in the sequence, although each school could choose when it was to begin.

Coincident with the stages of the professional development sequence, most school-level activity focused on conducting needs assessments, forming vision statements, and establishing goals for change. Some schools tried to enhance communication and working relationships among teachers and administrators. Several schools continued to develop curricular and instructional initiatives begun under sip.

INITIAL OUTCOMES OF RESTRUCTURING

Two key issues in assessing school restructuring are (1) what constitutes appropriate outcomes, and (2) when is it legitimate to look for evidence of those outcomes. The expressed intention of school restructuring in Hammond has been to enhance the learning and development of students. However, teachers and administrators were nearly unanimous in their view that it is premature to measure the success of these initiatives by student outcomes or even by the extent of curricular and instructional innovation. According to Kendrick: "You cannot change systems overnight. It just will not happen. . . . [T]his is a 20- to 25-year process. I don't think we're going to deliver until about 2005 or beyond." Instead of focusing on programmatic innovation and student outcomes, the district argued that progress should be gauged by what the Louisville Leadership Center calls "strategic imperatives." These imperatives are considered organizational antecedents to meaningful, long-term programmatic change and increased student learning.

Evidence exists that significant changes have occurred under SIP and SBRP with respect to six of the seven imperatives recognized by the district: (1) shared vision, (2) participative leadership, (3) results-oriented management, (4) flexibility, (5) culture for innovation and improvement, and (6) systems of support. Because SBRP had been implemented for only 1 year when data were collected for this case, it was too early to find evidence of the seventh imperative—continuity and institutionalization. While it may be too early to identify effects on students, a substantial number of teachers indicated that positive outcomes have begun to accrue.

Overview

Progress toward establishing the strategic imperatives has varied considerably across schools and imperatives. Teachers generally perceived the most progress in establishing participative leadership and a culture for innovation and improvement. They also reported progress on results-oriented management and flexibility—the capacity of their schools to focus on student learning, establish quality control, and respond to the changing needs of students and other members of the school community. Progress on these latter imperatives was concentrated in far fewer schools than was progress on the former two.

The most progress was associated with schools that had been highly active in SIP and that participated in the earliest round of the academy's professional development sequence. This suggests that the longer schools are engaged in restructuring, the more likely they are to have established organizational antecedents for programmatic innovation and improvement in student learning.

This evidence also raises issues of motivation and readiness for change. District administrators and union officials acknowledged that several schools had been inactive in SIP because they simply saw no potential benefit. They also observed that the schools choosing to enter the academy's sequence early on tended to be those most supportive of SBRP. Like the length of time spent in restructuring activity, these factors may explain differences among the schools in establishing these imperatives.

Specific comments of teachers and principals illustrate how these strategic imperatives were achieved and what they mean for school change.

Shared Vision and Participative Leadership

Teachers and administrators from both elementary and secondary schools claimed that SIP and SBRP promoted the development of shared vision in a number of different ways. By involving many members of a school community and providing means for systematic needs assessments, these initiatives also helped develop new ways to think about schools and the future. For example, one elementary teacher remarked that SIP and SBRP helped the principal and faculty "work on goals for the school versus goals for 'my' classroom." "You get the chance," this teacher continued, "to look at the whole picture."

Substantial numbers of teachers and principals agreed that SIP and SBRP affected school leadership. These initiatives created opportunities for teachers, parents, and students to become more involved in school-level decision making. For most, involvement meant increased influence in policy making and program development. In a small number of schools, involvement was more symbolic.

Some teachers and principals reported that participative decision making helped principals become more understanding of teachers, their work, and their ideas for school improvement. Likewise, it helped some teachers become more understanding of principals and their work. In some schools, participative decision making reinforced open communication, sharing, and mutual interest in teacher-administrator relationships. In other schools, however, teachers reported that it did little to improve these relationships. An elementary teacher from one of these schools observed, "This program [SBRP] is a threat to our principal."

In most of the schools that reported progress in establishing participative leadership, teachers and principals observed changes in climate, two-way communication, cooperation, and sharing. Most agreed that these changes laid a foundation for innovation and increased productivity. Some teachers suggested that changes in their relationships with administration had positive consequences for how they viewed their work. As one teacher noted, "We have an opportunity to discuss problems in school in such a way that is nonthreatening to either party. This makes me happier at work and able to form better relationships with the administration." Still other teachers suggested that participative leadership enhanced commitment. According to one high school teacher, SBRP "created new ownership. When students, parents, and teachers have ownership, they have a vested interest in the project, idea, etc. They work harder to make the project or idea succeed."

Results-Oriented Management and Flexibility

Teachers across the district reported that SIP and SBRP created new opportunities to talk with students and other teachers about student needs and accomplishments. For some teachers, learning more about students promoted new conceptions of students as learners. One high school teacher remarked, "It has caused me to view students, ideally, as partners in the educational process rather than as passive learners." Most teachers welcomed these developments. To several, learning more about students was "exciting," "invigorating," and "liberating." Other teachers claimed to have developed a more positive attitude toward students and their work with them.

Increased awareness and new conceptions of students as learners encouraged some teachers to reexamine their classroom practice. As one teacher stated, "I assess my own teaching and involvement in making [my school] the best it can be. I realize more and more the importance of what I do for students' future. I sense a greater impact of my decisions." For many teachers, thinking differently about students led to changes in their classroom practice. Several teachers reported creating new goals for student learning that better reflected students' needs. Others reported experimenting with more hands-on activities, cooperative learning strategies, and small-group work. One teacher aptly summarized how changing views of students influenced classroom practice:

I have refocused my thinking of students and the work I give them. . . .
I have the responsibility of developing worthwhile work for the students.
If they do not "buy" it, they will not learn it. I must examine what I am
doing, not "demand" that they do the work or not succeed.

Culture for Innovation and Improvement

In many ways, changes related to shared vision, participative leadership, results-oriented management, and flexibility are important indicators of a new culture for innovation and improvement in schools. Another dimension of a school culture that relates to innovation and improvement concerns relationships among teachers. Substantial numbers of teachers across the district reported that SIP and SBRP reduced their physical and social isolation. They provided opportunities for teachers to work together, some for the first time. Increased interaction helped some teachers learn more about each other. Increased familiarity promoted understanding and professional respect. Teachers from several schools claimed that SIP and SBRP also provided a focus and a process to make interaction productive. One teacher remarked,

> Many lunchtime and plan period hours are now spent arguing and brainstorming issues about school which natural apathy would have left dormant had SIP and SBRP not generated new energy and motivation to bring the issues to the surface.

These changes in faculty relationships promoted a new sense of community in several schools. The community that developed in some schools incorporated skeptical and previously isolated teachers. A high school teacher observed that opening a dialogue brought teachers closer together and "caused those who are reluctant to be part of the process to see that their input will be listened to and considered." Several teachers drew connections between collegial interaction and risk taking, experimentation, and innovation. According to one teacher, "More relaxed interaction [has led to] more contributions to teaching techniques without the feeling of intimidation or inadequacy."

Although SIP and SBRP generally promoted collaboration, community, and a context supporting innovation and improvement, they also promoted dissension and divisiveness in a small number of schools. Some teachers commented that SBRP's assessment process created conflict not only between teachers and principals but among teachers. One teacher reported that it "hurt some feelings and caused some finger-pointing." Another indicated that SIP and SBRP created divisions between teachers who had taken active roles in these initiatives and those who had not: "We are all at each other's throats." Most teachers who identified such problems implicated their principals for lack of leadership. Principals who reported conflicts generally implicated teachers' self-interests.

Support Systems

Participative leadership and a culture for innovation and improvement are elements of school-level systems that support change. In addition to these elements, teachers and principals identified several components of a larger, district-level support system instrumental to restructuring.

One part of this system is the Hammond Leadership Academy. As several teachers, principals, and district administrators indicated, both SIP and SBRP represented new models of school organization. Both were perceived as risky and ambiguous ventures that required substantial individual and institutional capacity-building. Many teachers and principals pointed to the academy as a source of psychological support, motivation, learning, and technical assistance. Likewise, district administrators and academy staff viewed the Louisville Center for Leadership in School Reform and its director, Phillip Schlechty, as an integral part of this larger support system.

A substantial number of teachers and principals also identified the superintendent and district administration as important sources of support for change. Not all teachers agreed, however. Skepticism and mistrust from experiences with SIP persisted with SBRP. Some teachers continued to believe that district administration did not genuinely support shared decision making and school-based management.

As with district administration, teachers differed in their views of the teachers' union. Most gave substantial credit to the union and its president for supporting change in the district. Several teachers applauded the union for giving them more voice in district and school-level issues. However, other teachers argued that by its advocacy of participative decision making and school-based management, the union had given up its responsibilities to membership. Several teachers accused the union and its president of collusion with district administration, of "selling out," and of abrogating membership protections associated with the collective bargaining process. One claimed, "I feel the [union] is glossing over its responsibilities to the teachers by throwing issues on their backs when the [union] should be tackling them." These criticisms, like those of district administration, were not widely shared among teachers in the district. However, they represented challenges the union and district administration acknowledged must be faced as they continue to restructure schools.

Early Student Outcomes

As argued earlier, it may be premature to assess SIP and SBRP by student outcomes. Nevertheless, some anecdotal evidence exists that students are beginning to benefit. In approximately half of the district's schools, teachers identified some benefit of SIP and SBRP for students. For example, one teacher observed that opening school-level decision making to all members of the school community had increased student participation in curricular and extracurricular activities. This teacher witnessed "more enthusiasm" on the part of students. Teachers from other schools noted that as students expressed their interests and concerns, and as teachers and administrators became more responsive to them, discipline problems declined. As one teacher observed, these students now consider school "a place where they want to be."

Several teachers suggested that the curricular and instructional initiatives developed under SIP and SBRP had begun to affect students as well. One teacher observed that a new program of student recognition had "built self-esteem for our children." A second teacher, commenting about new classroom grouping practices, testified, "My student failure rate has dropped considerably." Another said that instructional strategies developed through SIP and SBRP affected student academic learning positively: "[I'm sending] more 'good news' notes to students for achievement."

FACTORS AFFECTING RESTRUCTURING

A number of different factors have facilitated school restructuring in Hammond. SIP and SBRP were developed and implemented during a period of stability in district leadership. Most of the key actors have been with the district for substantial periods of time. Superintendent Dickson, though appointed nearly 10 years ago, is the relative newcomer. There has been little turnover in school and district administration over the past 20 years. Generally, those administrators who have left the system either retired or resigned under favorable circumstances. This stability is likely to continue. In 1990, the school board renewed Dickson's contract for an unprecedented 7½ years. As stated earlier, Pat O'Rourke, who has been union president for almost 20 years, has yet to see a serious challenge to his reelection.

Stability was enhanced by incorporating school restructuring in teachers' contracts. SIP was first included alongside conventional work rules in a 3-year pact ratified in 1985. That contract was extended twice, with no substantial changes in provisions related to school restructuring. The latest contract, beginning in January 1990 and extending through 2001, incorporates SBRP. These contracts did more than endorse SIP and SBRP. They served to institutionalize restructuring by defining it as part of the teachers' and the board's responsibilities. The contracts also encouraged teacher-administrator collaboration by redefining grievance procedures. They redefined the role of the union and the union's building representatives as school-level bargaining agents. They removed the building representative from between teachers and administrators and forced teachers and administrators to work through problems together during the planning process rather than passing them to building representatives for adversarial resolution after decisions were made and an adversarial situation created.

Restructuring in Hammond was also promoted by the generally positive relationships between the district and its community. The strength of school-community relations came from shared perceptions and values about what schools should be for children. These perceptions and values were proactively cultivated by Dickson and his administration. Dickson admits to being an unabashed "cheerleader" for the district, taking any and every opportunity to tout its successes and challenge its detractors. He and his colleagues have carefully crafted expectations for school restructuring, pointing to intermediate organizational accomplishments while emphasizing the ultimate aim of improved student learning.

Collaboration developed at the school level through SIP and SBRP was recently extended to district-community relations. In 1992, the school board and district administration invited the community for the first time to participate in developing long-term goals for the district. Over 120 people from the community volunteered to serve on district Design Teams to draft goal statements. This initiative not only reflects the district's commitment to community involvement and collaboration, it also attests to the trust that the district has in the community and to the overall strength of school-community relations.

Likewise, restructuring was promoted by the development of positive, collaborative relations between the district administration and the school board. Before Dickson's appointment in 1984, the board was characterized by distrust, animosity, and frustration. Dickson worked closely with the board, involving members in professional development activities and planning reform initiatives. He encouraged ownership and trust. Administration's relationship with the board became more collaborative and productive.

Finally, concurrent development of collaborative labor relations played a significant role in Hammond's school restructuring initiatives. Historically, relations between the teachers' union and the school district were defined by a traditional industrial or adversarial model. Although there had not been substantial unrest or a teachers' strike since the late 1960s, labor relations were formal, conservative, and cautious. Toward the end of Sanders' superintendency, O'Rourke became active with the national American Federation of Teachers and began to explore new collaborative approaches to labor relations. He also studied relationships between labor relations and school reform, focusing particularly on shared decision making and school-based management. Dickson, himself a former high school teacher and union building representative, was attracted to Hammond in large part because of O'Rourke's ideas about collaborative labor relations and the district's early experiments in school restructuring.

Dickson's appointment signaled important shifts in labor relations. These are well illustrated in two stories that are part of Hammond's "organizational saga." The first story was recounted by O'Rourke.

> The first time that I dealt with Dave Dickson . . . the [event] that gave me a clue that there was a whole different possibility [for labor relations], was the first month he was hired. Dave called me in and we talked about a budget problem involving NIPSCO [Northern Indiana Public Service Company]. Sanders had authorized payment of our energy bill and the business manager was going to pay it. Dickson said to me, "What do we do? If we pay this bill, which is $2.5 million, we have to lay off teachers." So we started kicking around the idea of changing the paradigm of pay-

ing the utility and bargaining with teachers. We decided to pay teachers and bargain with NIPSCO. . . . It was not paying the energy bill that convinced me there was a whole new way to operate.

The second story was told by O'Rourke and school board attorney, John Friel. O'Rourke began:

> A year [after our decision to negotiate with NIPSCO] we still had the budget problem, and the administration had prepared a RIF [Reduction-In-Force] list of 50 to 60 teachers. I came in and Dave and I just had a long talk about people. Some had 10 years experience, 12 years, 15, 18, 19, and I said, "You really don't want to do this to these people." And he said, "You're right" and tore up the list. My policy has always been to not protect positions as much as people.

Friel continued:

> It was kind of a classic thing. . . . Pat wasn't defending the size of the bargaining ring. He was defending Sam, who's got 12 years. The school board wasn't out to get Sam. It was strictly dollars and cents. When administration realized that the union would work on the "dollar issue" and the union recognized administration's concern for individual teachers, we came up with all kinds of crazy solutions. One was a massive incentive for early retirement. . . . In one situation we had to RIF six or ten social studies people who were long-term veterans. And we just announced they will get a contract next year at their regular rate. We just didn't know where they'd be teaching. . . . By Thanksgiving we didn't have two who hadn't been permanently placed. When you don't have people shouting at one another from a distance, when you really sit down and get at the gut concern, it's amazing the alternatives that can be found. And that's what is going on.

The development of collaborative labor relations promoted school restructuring in several different ways. Collaborative labor relations at the district level became a model for shared decision making at the school level. And, as described earlier, teacher contracts incorporated and institutionalized SIP and SBRP. They also contained specific provisions to encourage teacher-administrator collaboration.

Contrapuntal to these factors supporting school restructuring were several barriers with which the district had to contend. One was state education policy. In recent years, Indiana developed a statewide testing system and a performance-based school accreditation program that suggested standardized criteria for student learning and school accountability. Although the state made provisions for waivers, school officials in Hammond were concerned that these programs posed potential threats to creativity and innovation in the schools.

A second barrier to restructuring has been the district's financial crisis. Recent reductions in state funding have pressed the district to find new ways to avoid bankruptcy without significant program cuts, salary and benefit reductions, or staff lay-offs. Both Dickson and O'Rourke contend that it is extremely difficult for teachers to assume new roles, work collaboratively, and think more creatively about teaching when their classrooms are cold or when they fear for their jobs.

Fortunately, Hammond's history of school restructuring, collaborative labor relations, and community support has been recognized by the state. In fall 1991, the Indiana School Property Tax Control Board granted the district a $2.5 million loan to cover its 1991–1992 operating debt, and an additional $1.7 million loan for the 1992–1993 school year. These were the largest loans the control board made to any Indiana school district that year. With these loans, Hammond was without an operating debt for the first time since the late 1960s. Under state statute, these loans will be repaid from future tax revenues and will not add to the district's bonded debt.

A final barrier to restructuring was conceptual and psychological. SIP and SBRP fundamentally redefined teacher and administrator work roles and relationships. These changes affected long-standing beliefs and practices in schools. The issue of helping teachers and administrators confront change is illustrated in another story, "Joshua's Box," which was told by Pecher, the Hammond High School math teacher and SIP staff developer.

> There is this square and this character, Joshua, inside the square sitting in a corner moping. He walks around the inside of the square and mopes and mopes. He's very unhappy. And then all of a sudden he looks around and there's an opening in a corner of the square. He walks by it, goes back to his corner, and keeps looking at the opening. Eventually he builds up enough nerve that he sticks his head out and peeks around outside the square. Soon he goes out. He's free and he's dancing around. He's so happy and everything is great. Then all of a sudden he gets scared and goes back and climbs into the square. The corner closes up again. The story ends. The problem is, how to get people out of their squares and help them stay out.

CONCLUSION

Hammond's experiences suggest that school restructuring is a long-term process. It involves much more than developing structures and processes. It involves developing new conceptions of work and renegotiating long-established working relationships. Furthermore, it involves conceptual change and developing a new culture of school and district organization. This case suggests that the long and complicated process of restructuring needs to be acknowledged and planned for.

This case also suggests the importance of reinventing the system as a whole, not merely reordering some of its pieces. Hammond's progress may be attributable only in part to its restructuring model. Its progress is inextricably linked to the concurrent development of other aspects of the school system that complement specific restructuring initiatives. Critically important are strong community support, collaborative labor relations, and positive administration-board relations. Support and collaboration do not just happen. As shown in this case, they must be actively cultivated and nurtured over time. In addition, the stability created by long-term contracts and tenure of key personnel seem to have enhanced the district's progress.

Another lesson of this case is the need to build a broad base of involvement in developing and implementing school restructuring initiatives. Hammond made the most progress when the administration sought to incorporate large numbers of stakeholders. It also made the most progress when the administration was able to reconcile the inevitable tension between central control and school-level creativity and innovation. Equally important in this case is the emphasis the district placed on building the knowledge, conceptual understanding, and skills of teachers and administrators. This suggests that restructuring must be viewed as a problem of capacity-building, of individual and institutional learning and change.

Finally, Hammond teaches us something about aims and priorities. From the very beginning, restructuring in Hammond has been framed as an issue of student learning. SIP and SBRP were initiatives from which teachers and administrators could certainly benefit. They were initiatives that could bring about significant changes in organizational structures and processes. However, they were only considered means to an end, not ends in themselves. The emphasis on students, the "mantra" of the district administration and the teachers union, may have promoted progress by providing a focus that transcends individual and institutional self-interest. This emphasis may have promoted collaboration and the true work of restructuring—improving learning opportunities for students.

NOTE

We wish to acknowledge the Center for Urban Educational Research and Development at the University of Illinois at Chicago for supporting in part the second author's contributions to this chapter.

This chapter is based on a more detailed study of the Hammond school district that was conducted as part of Claremont Project VISION, a project that examines emerging patterns of labor relations, work life, and school organizations. Project VISION was supported by the U.S. Department of Labor and the Carnegie Foundation. For information about the project or the initial Hammond study contact the authors or Charles T. Kerchner, Claremont Graduate School, Claremont, CA 91711–6160.

In addition to the documentary sources listed at the end of the chapter, data for this case were collected through a series of semistructured individual and group interviews and open-ended surveys. Interviews and survey administration took place in winter and spring of 1991. Participation was completely voluntary.

Interview subjects included the superintendent, the assistant superintendent for school improvement, the union president, and the director of the Hammond Leadership Academy. Each was interviewed on at least two separate occasions. Seven principals and eight teachers were also interviewed. These subjects were selected in consultation with district administration and the teachers' union to represent schools that played important roles in the history of SIP and SBRP and to represent a cross-section of opinion regarding these initiatives.

Interview subjects were asked general questions about the development and implementation of SIP and SBRP, labor relations, and district and community contexts. They were asked to recount the key events, accomplishments, and factors that encouraged and constrained school reform at the school and district levels. Interviews usually lasted between 60 and 90 minutes. They were tape recorded and transcribed for analysis.

A larger sampling of teacher and principal opinions was obtained through open-ended surveys. These surveys were distributed to teachers and principals in 18 of the district's 24 schools. Schools were selected in consultation with district administration and the union to represent sites that varied in type and degree of SIP and activity and that participated in early or later stages of SBRP training. The surveys were distributed at a districtwide meeting of principals and union building representatives. Both district administrators and the teachers' union encouraged schools to complete and return them. Several follow-ups were made to obtain as high a return rate as possible. One of the 18 schools did not respond to the survey. Among the other 17 schools, return rates ranged from 30% to almost 80%. Of the approximately 500 teachers to whom surveys were distributed, 213 returned usable responses. This sample represents approximately one-quarter of the district's teachers. While the overall return rate and the variations in return rates by schools pose problems of sample representativeness, responses across schools capture the full range of teacher and principal opinion about reform.

The surveys asked teachers and principals to describe the initiatives and accomplishments at their schools related to SIP and SBRP. They asked how SIP and SBRP may have affected work with students in classrooms. They also asked how these initiatives may have affected relationships among teachers and between teachers and school administrators, teachers' relationships with parents, and teachers' relationships with district administration and the teachers' union. Surveys were keyed so that school-level analyses could be performed. Individual responses were anonymous unless teachers voluntarily identified themselves.

Interview and survey data were analyzed using a constant comparative method of content analysis. Identifying and classifying themes and patterns in the data were guided by the framework of strategic imperatives suggested by the school district. In order to ensure accuracy, findings were shared with a group of district administrators, the union president, principals, and teachers, all of whom had been previously interviewed. Findings were also presented to three university researchers whose areas of expertise include teacher work redesign and school restructuring, labor relations, and the organizational contexts of schools and school districts. Comments, insights, and clarifications were incorporated in the case study.

Data collection for this case lasted approximately 1 year. We attempted to establish a collaborative relationship with key informants at the school and district levels. In many ways, this case was coconstructed by the researchers and district personnel. While some areas of inquiry were determined prior to data collection, we asked district administrators and union officials what they believed were the most relevant questions for understanding restructuring in the district. As data collection progressed at the school level, we allowed the accounts and opinions of teachers and principals to suggest new directions for inquiry. We routinely shared our observations and interpretations with a small "focus" group of district administrators, principals, and teacher union officials to ensure that we were "getting it right." As we sought direction and feedback for our work, the district also sought our insights to help them address issues in the day-to-day work of restructuring. With care not to harm the integrity of data collection and case study construction, nor to violate provisions of individual confidentiality, we offered counsel to the district. By the end of the study, our relationship had become mutually informing and mutually beneficial.

REFERENCES

Bradley, A. (1990, March 7). Hammond, Ind. teachers and district agree to unprecedented 12-year-pact. *Educational Week* p.10.

Casner-Lotto, J. (1988). Expanding the teacher's role: Hammond's school improvement process. *Phi Delta Kappan, 69,* 349–353.

Casner-Lotto, J. (1989). Expanding the teacher's role: School improvement in the Hammond, Indiana school district. In J. M. Rosow, R. Zager, & Associates (Eds.), *Allies in educational reform* (pp. 184–205). San Francisco: Jossey-Bass.

Center for Leadership in School Reform. (1991, January). *Strategic imperatives for restructuring schools.* Louisville, KY: Author.

Cohen, D. L. (1990, December 12). Fiscal forecast expected to shape Indiana reform proposals. *Educational Week,* p. 28.

Hammond Education Foundation. (1987). *Acorn, 1*(1).

Knarr, T. C. (1988). Educational partnerships that work: The Hammond triad. *Indiana School Boards Association Journal, 34*(4), 4–5, 9.

Knarr, T. C. (1991). School-based management second generation. *Indiana School Boards Association Journal, 37*(1), 4–5, 10.

Kobe, L. (1988). *Stages of SIP.* Hammond, IN: Author.

Rauth, M. (1990). Exploring heresy in collective bargaining and school restructuring. *Phi Delta Kappan, 71,* 781–784, 788–790.

School City of Hammond. (n.d.). *An overview of the School City of Hammond School-Based Restructuring Program.* Hammond, IN: Author.

School City of Hammond. (n.d.). *Directory of programs and services.* Hammond, IN: Author.

School City of Hammond. (1985a). *Master contract between the Board of Education of the School City of Hammond, Indiana and the Hammond Teachers' Federation Local 394, August 16, 1985 to August 15, 1988.* Hammond, IN: Author.

School City of Hammond. (1985b). *Spirit of education: A report of the School City of Hammond.* Hammond, IN: Author.

School City of Hammond. (1987–1989). *SIP shorts* (Nos. 1–10). Hammond, IN: Author.

School City of Hammond. (1988a). *Master contract between the Board of Education of the School City of Hammond, Indiana and the Hammond Teachers' Federal Local 394, January 1, 1988 to August 15, 1989.* Hammond, IN: Author.

School City of Hammond. (1988b). *The spirit of education: A report to the public.* Hammond, IN: Author.

School City of Hammond. (1989). *Good news! about Hammond and our schools, Vol. 4, April 1988 through February 1989.* Hammond, IN: Author.

School City of Hammond. (1990a). *A guide for students and parents.* Hammond, IN: Author.

School City of Hammond. (1990b). *Good news! Vol. 5, February 1989-January 1990.* Hammond, IN: Author.

School City of Hammond. (1990c). *Master contract between the Hammond Teachers' Federation, Local 394 and the Board of School Trustees of the School City of Hammond, Indiana, January 1, 1990 to December 31, 2001.* Hammond, IN: Author.

Shanker, A. (1987, October 11). Hammond's management by committee: How "they" became "we." *New York Times,* Section E, p. 9.

U.S. Bureau of the Census. (1971). *County business patterns: 1970, Indiana* (Report No. CBP–70–16). Washington, DC: U.S. Government Printing Office.

U.S. Bureau of the Census. (1973). *Census of population: 1970, Vol. 1, Characteristics of the population, Pt. 16, Indiana.* Washington, DC: U.S. Government Printing Office.

U.S. Bureau of the Census. (1977). *County business patterns: 1975, Indiana* (Report No. CBP–75–16). Washington, DC: U.S. Government Printing Office.

U.S. Bureau of the Census. (1979). *Census of governments: 1977, Vol. 4, Government finances, No. 1, Finances of school districts* (Report No. GC77(4)–1). Washington, DC: U.S. Government Printing Office.

U.S. Bureau of the Census. (1982a). *Census of population: 1980, Vol. 1, Characteristics of the population, Chapter A, Number of inhabitants, Part 16, Indiana* (Report No. PC80–1–A16). Washington, DC: U.S. Government Printing Office.

U.S. Bureau of the Census. (1982b). *County business patterns: 1981, Indiana.* Washington, DC: U.S. Government Printing Office.

U.S. Bureau of the Census. (1984). *Census of governments: 1982, Vol. 4, Governmental finances, No. 1, Finances of public school systems* (Report No. GC82(4)-1). Washington, DC: U.S. Government Printing Office.

U.S. Bureau of the Census. (1988). *County business patterns: 1986, Indiana* (Report No. CBP86–16). Washington, DC: U.S. Government Printing Office.

U.S. Bureau of the Census. (1989). *Census of governments: 1987, Vol. 2, Taxable property values* (Report No. GC87(2)–1). Washington, DC: U.S. Government Printing Office.

U.S. Bureau of the Census. (1990). *Census of governments: 1987, Vol. 4, Government finances, No. 1, Finances of public school systems* (Report No. GC87(4)–1). Washington, DC: U.S. Government Printing Office.

U.S. Bureau of the Census. (1991, February). *1990 census of population and housing, Public Law 94–171 redistricting data, Indiana.* Unpublished raw data.

Chapter 6

School Restructuring
and Teacher Power:
The Case of Keels Elementary

Barnett Berry

Joseph P. Keels Elementary, a K–5 school with 570 students and 35 faculty, allows for a provocative case study of restructuring in progress. In some ways, Keels, located in Columbia, South Carolina, is typical of schools facing the daunting challenge of educating transient student populations, with many students entering school with serious academic, social, and personal disadvantages. More than half of Keels's students are on free or reduced-price lunch (52%); a significant majority are nonwhite (74%). Administrators and teachers alike lament that "too many kids are lost to protective custody" and "so many do not have adequate health care." In other ways, Keels is a very extraordinary school—given the leadership of its teachers and principal (and her predecessor) and the ideas and energy exploding from a myriad of school change efforts.

This case study is about capturing the content, process, and initial outcomes of restructuring at Keels and provides numerous lessons—some are painful reminders of how little policymakers and practitioners have learned from the poignant portraits of school change and improvement drawn by Sarason (1982, 1990), Fullan (1991), Lieberman and Miller (1990, 1991), and Rosenholtz (1989). But, other lessons, I suspect, will shed some new light on what it takes for a school to be restructured. The nucleus of these new lessons from Keels will be *teacher power* as the driving force for change. While restructuring has become a buzzword only over the last several years, teachers at Keels—with the Herculean support of two principals—have been in the process of change and cultural transformation for over a decade. Indeed, an amalgamation of several comments from teachers and administrators best captures this transformation at Keels:

> This case study is certainly about a shift in culture—an underlying belief
> system amongst the principal and teachers that moved from "Oh woe is

us for all the difficult students we have to teach . . . if only we had better students" to "all kids can learn" to "we are so damn good that all kids will learn, think, and do!"

Without question, the teachers and school administrators have extraordinarily high expectations for all their students. But what is so striking about the culture of Keels is not just the intense, high expectations for students, but the intense high expectations that teachers have for themselves as professionals. To tell this restructuring story of Keels—a story of ideas, energy, and professionalism, I will describe the context for restructuring, the emergence of teacher power, the content and process of restructuring, the initial outcomes, the barriers to restructuring, and the lessons for both practice and policy.[1]

THE CONTEXT FOR RESTRUCTURING

Keels is one of 14 public schools located in Richland County School District Two, a suburban district that serves several of Columbia's upper-middle-class enclaves. The district is a relatively "rich" one (spending over $4100 per student) that serves relatively well-to-do students (only 18% on free or reduced-price lunch compared to 43% statewide). Most education observers would consider District Two to be a "have" school district. However, Keels could be considered, or let's say, was considered, to be its "have not" school. Keels's students bring many daunting challenges to the educators who serve them. A significant proportion of the students move frequently, which is not surprising given that the school is near a very large military installation. In fact, 60% of Keels's fourth and fifth graders did not begin their elementary education at Keels. Fifteen years ago, some district administrators thought that Keels "was in such bad shape that it would have to be closed." Several administrators spoke of the shifting demographics that had robbed Keels of its previous community support. A regional shopping mall had opened in the area and residential property values in the school neighborhood had dropped. Commissioned officers from the nearby fort moved to more desirable neighborhoods. Rental property increased and trailer parks flourished. More and more students came from lower socioeconomic strata and were entering school with what most educators would consider to be "huge learning deficits." Teacher morale worsened. The school climate became suffocating.

Today, Keels is considered to have "risen from the ashes" and may be the district's "shining star." For the last 6 years, Keels has won South Carolina's school incentive award—part of a highly visible program created out of South Carolina's omnibus school reform legislation of 1984 (the Education Improvement Act). Based on aggregating schoolwide year-to-year gains on the state's two basic skills achievement tests, Keels has consistently garnered approximately $18,000 a year in incentive money. In addition, the school has also been named Palmetto's Finest (a statewide exemplary school recognition program); is seen as a leader amongst the state's seventy "Associate Schools";[2] has earned state "deregulated" status;[3] just last year secured over $100,000 in competitive grants related to the arts, early intervention, after-school programs, technology, science, and performance assessment; was named as a statewide training site for Reading Recovery; and, most recently, was awarded an *Inviting School Award* by the International Alliance for Invitational Education.

The context for all of the plethora of restructuring efforts is framed by teacher power. To understand teacher power at Keels and its use in restructuring, two factors must be revealed. Perhaps, these factors should be considered *preconditions for change*. First, Keels has become a school filled with educators (teachers and administrators) who are deeply committed to children and their families. Second, the school has benefitted enormously from the evolutionary thought and action of its previous principal, Richard Inabinet, and its current one, Shirley Henderson.

Teacher Commitment to Children and Families

Keels exudes a caring, family atmosphere. When I asked teachers at Keels why their school was changing, there was a consonance of responses—all revolving around their intense responsibility for the students and their futures. Enter the school, and before one gets to the marvelous visual products created by students and displayed on every wall, one is confronted by the proclamation, AT KEELS WE DO STUDENTS RIGHT. Walk down the school's hallways—outlined in the warmth of cheerful, inviting felt banners demarcating the entrance to each classroom—and one feels that the place exudes care and an inordinate capacity for the total development of students. Enter a classroom, and you find an eruption of color, knowledge, reminders, exhibitions, maps, words, math formulae, number lines, symbols, and dates on the walls *and* the ceilings. Listening to teachers, one hears claims about their belief that you "cannot teach children who are not loved and happy." Listening to students, one hears claims about "real understanding teachers who will help you out if you really need help." Teachers buy clothes for needy students. In the middle of my conversations with teachers, students came up and hugged them. The students smile a lot. Teachers make sure students have car rides for after-school programs. Teachers volunteer time in the summer to work with students at the nearby public library. Child care and transportation are offered to increase participation in parent education workshops. And, there is more. Some grade-level teachers (e.g., first grade) are especially forceful with parents, extracting their commitment to and involvement in the school with the very same high expectations that they have for themselves and the students. As one teacher noted, "some of us just demand that parents come to participate . . . and guess what, they do."

These efforts did not unfold in a predetermined way. Instead, the principal, along with a critical mass of teachers, began to collectively decide how they were going to actually make a difference in the lives of their students. For example, Keel is a school, as several teachers noted, "where children enjoy learning" and "they do not mind the hard work." No prepackaged curricular program created this ethos. Instead, everyday, the children actually see teachers and administrators who enjoy learning and do not mind hard work. The challenge to students comes from not only teachers and administrators but also custodians, secretaries, and teaching assistants. Most importantly, students are well in tune with the vision of the school, which focuses on quality education and continuous improvement. In fact, the students interviewed repeatedly talked about quality—as if they had indeed read William Glasser's (1990) *Quality School* or recently attended a Deming seminar. Students noted that their teachers and administrators want them to get "good grades without the pressure" and to "do good, high quality stuff—like our social studies projects and science experiments."

The Evolutionary Thought and Action of the Principals

The interviews revealed the critical role both Richard and Shirley have played in creating the culture for change, and then providing opportunities for teachers to "expand their horizons" and continually broaden their capacities. In many ways, Keels has found a way to balance the ever-present tension between administrative and teacher leadership (Lieberman & Miller, 1990) and, in doing so, has allowed for the principal to emerge as a "cultural leader" who uses authority to obtain ends rather than to dominate teachers (Sergiovani, 1989).

At the nub of Shirley's thoughts and actions (and those of Richard's) is teacher professionalism—even before it became a part of the lexicon of school reform. At the core of the administration's values is a profound respect for teachers' knowledge, both expressed and tacit. To tap into their knowledge, time must be created. At Keels, teachers have a common planning period every day for each team (50 minutes when homeroom students go to art, music, PE, etc.) and an additional 30 minutes of time during lunch. As Shirley quipped, "we do not mandate anything during this period."

Today, Shirley is an "instructional leader," but maybe not in a traditional sense. She does not control instruction. She observes and critiques. One teacher claimed that she is "not seen as a clinical supervisor." Another teacher noted that she does not "negatively judge" teachers. Instead, Shirley is more likely to exert her instructional leadership by, for example, helping a group of teachers incorporate the public library into their curriculum plans. For teachers, she is a "facilitator" and a broker of new ideas who "carries out ideas and plans they generate." She manages the teachers' energy.

A recent statewide teacher survey, replicating the Carnegie Foundation's 1990 working conditions study, provides additional contextual information related to Shirley's leadership. For example, 92% of the Keels teachers rated the effectiveness of the principal as excellent (compared to 15% nationally and 17% statewide). Similarly, 81% of the Keels teachers rated the support of teachers by the principal as excellent (compared to 29% nationally and 28% statewide). The respect Shirley receives at the school (much like the respect that Richard still receives) transforms her into a first among equals. Shirley does what good leaders do, that is, she "gets the stuff out of the way" of the professionals. Even among the few known teachers who resist change, she is viewed as supportive and "respectful of different teaching styles."

An entrepreneur, Shirley won't let anyone or anything stand in the way of getting new ideas and opportunities to teachers. She is known as the "Queen of Grants" because of all the external funding that she has garnered for the school ($100,000 last year). Much of the money has been used to free teachers up to travel and work with each other. But, there is a price to pay for working on grants and being successful. The school has had many outside visitors (other educators, researchers, reporters, etc.) who seek to learn from Shirley and the teachers. Shirley regularly worked 14-hour days this past spring, and, subsequently, she had less time to work directly with teachers.

But this story is not just one of progressive principals transforming a risk free environment for kids into one for teachers and staff. In some ways, it appears the seeds of change at Keels took root right before Richard came, when, as one central office administrator claimed, the district "committed talented teachers to the school" in hopes of saving it. In this vein, the case of restructuring at Keels reveals the emergence of a critical variable—teacher power.

THE EMERGENCE OF TEACHER POWER

There is a critical mass of teachers at Keels who are characterized by the district superintendent as "the most direct group of teachers in South Carolina." Those from outside the school are quick to say that Keels's teachers are "not shy with other adults" and that they have "very strong personalities." As one district administrator commented: "Teachers at Keels are cocky but not to a fault. . . . They provide leadership for other teachers, train each other, and they challenge and critique—both others and themselves." The teachers consider themselves excellent teachers. In fact, teachers told us that "they were damn good." This assertion was not seen as evidence of braggadocio. Instead, given the context of students with such troubled and problematic lives, the teachers learned that they had to be excellent in order to "ensure" student success. On the working conditions survey, 78% of the Keels teachers rated their performance as excellent (compared to 32% nationally and 34% statewide). And, indeed, there is considerable evidence for this assertion. A large number of Keels's teachers have been named District Two teachers of the year. But, perhaps more importantly, there are the increasing requests for Keels's teachers to provide professional development experiences for teachers across the district and the state.

Perhaps this is the root of their power—their ability and willingness to establish, convey, and enforce (at least, informally) norms of excellence. And, this type of power may very well set Keels's teachers apart from other teachers who are empowered by administrators. As Cooper (1988) has noted, if teachers receive a blueprint for professional conduct then the culture (and the power relationships) that unfold will be alien to their setting. But, unlike the concept of teacher empowerment where administrators delegate authority from afar, Keels's teachers took leadership and ownership, refusing to be submissive and dependent, searching instead for their own voice. The interviews revealed that this critical mass of teacher leaders began to coalesce approximately a decade ago when Keels was "in trouble" and many teachers were suffering from the "dictatorial leadership" of certain administrators. It was at this point in time that teachers began to set a course for their own professional destiny, including taking a stand against the state policy system as well as publicly displaying their displeasure with their then-current school leadership. One respondent told this story:

> This district is well known for its teachers giving their principals very nice gifts at Christmas—like framed prints and the like. Well, this group at Keels one Christmas gave their principal at a faculty meeting a t-shirt. . . . On the front of the t-shirt was this—"EVERY SCHOOL NEEDS A DYNAMIC, VISIONARY LEADER" and [on the back of the t-shirt] was "IF YOU CAN FIND ONE LET US KNOW." Then, they gave the assistant principal some jewelry. . . . You see they did not think it was appropriate for her to come to school wearing ornate, expensive gold jewelry, which she always did. The teachers did not think it was the right dress for working with kids, so what they gave her was a box full of cheap K-Mart jewelry. . . . The next thing we knew was the assistant principal changed her dress and the principal resigned.

This story captures how a small group of teachers took a stand on an issue and let their expectations be known to their colleagues in a very public way. This story of the teachers' public dissatisfaction with an administrator carries both the myth and symbolism suggestive of group expectations for professional behavior. This story is important because it frames a set of teacher-developed norms that are at the core of Keels's cultural transformation and restructuring efforts.

This cultural transformation did not take place overnight. In fact, now it appears that teacher power and restructuring began to "really take off" about 3 years ago when first-grade teachers transformed the language arts program, putting in over 2500 hours combined in remaking the curriculum in the best interests of their students. The behavior of the first-grade teachers sets expectations for the second-grade teachers who set expectations for the third-grade teachers, and so on. Now, collaborative work is the norm. Indeed, the working conditions survey revealed that 51% of Keels's teachers claimed they are deeply involved in designing staff development (compared to 11% nationally and 10% statewide), and 91% claimed they are deeply involved in shaping the curriculum (compared to 22% nationally and 14% statewide). Without question, teachers at Keels share and learn from each other much more so than one finds in most other schools. Nevertheless, the interviews revealed that while Keels has made considerable headway in "de-isolating" teachers (a common fact of teachers' organizational life), the teachers still do not have enough opportunity to see each other teach. For example, a few teachers have not been as deeply engaged in restructuring because, as one teacher claimed, "they have *not* seen all the fabulous things going on here." Perhaps, because of the immense strides made in getting teachers together to share and learn from each other, there is now a growing awareness of the need to learn more from direct observations.

While evolving administrative leadership has been extremely critical to the birth and growth of teacher power, a number of other factors contributed to its emergence. Some teachers point to the "right age" of the majority of the staff—an age where familial and childrearing responsibilities do not conflict with the rigorous demands of the teaching and learning workload at Keels. This factor is especially critical in South Carolina, where 85% of the state's elementary teachers are female. Others point to low turnover among teachers as the "greatest factor" related to teacher involvement in school restructuring. Low turnover and staff stability are a well-documented (but seldom dealt with) variable in the school-improvement equation (e.g., see Fullan, 1991; Seashore-Louis & Miles, 1990). But, perhaps most important at Keels, when vacancies do arise, teachers, as one noted, tend to "pick their own." In fact, teachers at Keels prefer to select new teachers who interned (student taught) at their school, so that they have a chance to assess their level of commitment to Keels's students and to "really see them in action."

THE CONTENT AND PROCESS OF RESTRUCTURING

At first glance, Keels's restructuring efforts reveal a myriad of initiatives:

- Participatory decision making
- Self-contained heterogeneous classes

- Reading Recovery, Writing to Read, Math Their Way
- Cooperative learning, parent education (e.g., workshops, home visits, etc.)
- After-school programs (including tutoring, supervised homework sessions, student council, recreational opportunities, and computer lab work)
- Summer enrichment, remediation, and accelerated learning
- Extended day kindergarten for early prevention of school failure

These projects were identified, researched, and created by a wide range of Keels's administrators and teachers over a period of years. However, Keels has avoided the project mentality of school reform by focusing on the continuous improvement of curriculum. In part, "projectitis" was avoided because of the painstaking work of Shirley—who constantly monitored progress and brokered communication among the teachers. Clearly, curriculum has been the core of Keels's restructuring efforts of the last 4 years—which have been fueled by an infusion of technology and changes in assessment. In fact, these curricular and technological changes led to Keels's selection in 1991 by the State Department of Education as one of "12 Schools" to pilot alternative assessments in science that included the development of performance tasks, rubrics, and portfolios. Each is described below.

Curriculum Change

There is wide acceptance among the educators at Keels that curriculum must change. Nevertheless, the current curriculum is an amalgamation of the new and the old. All South Carolina K–12 educators face high-stakes, basic skills achievement tests every year. For almost a decade innumerable policy decisions have been tied to these state tests, including the school incentive program (mentioned previously). Given the numbers of students at Keels, the school has the prospect of winning almost $20,000 a year in incentive money. Thus, teachers can easily resort to traditional teaching practices that are assumed to lead to higher student test scores. Several teachers admitted that since they "had been conditioned for so long to do things one way," change has been difficult. But, teachers appear to be relying on textbooks less and less as the focal point of instruction. With Shirley as a catalyst, more and more teachers are reading research literature, visiting other schools, and attending state and national workshops. Now, teachers read the works of Bob Slavin, Nancy Karweit, Grant Wiggins, and others. Over time, more teachers have been making curricular decisions based on research findings as well as on their professional judgment. It has been these activities that have been the basis of Keels's restructuring.

For example, in the language arts curriculum teachers draw on whole-language philosophies, but still use basals as well as phonics and decoding strategies to teach reading. Teachers, as Shirley noted, "spend a great deal of time on helping children learn how to read a novel . . . what to look for and how to enjoy it." One first-grade teacher described the language arts curriculum:

At the first of school we give them things they can do . . . in fact, the first two words we make sure they can read are "I can" and "we can." We add more words . . . we do drill . . . they go home and say they can read . . . we do a lot with phonics. My kids come back here in the afternoon for extra help. It is a real eclectic approach—we combine whole language, phonics, and old-fashion drill—and lots of reading. Now, with every story from the basal my team made up an additional story with the words. This took a lot of time but it was worth it. With every skill we teach, we use the visual, the auditory, and the kinesthetic. We write words, make up sentences, draw pictures. We push them into being complete readers. One way we do this is by cutting the junk and the fluff out of reading programs—like all the pages in the workbooks.

As one walks around the school and peers in classrooms, it is evident that children are having a good time and working hard. Teachers and students "laugh together" and "read together," and "get into relaxed positions almost like a college seminar." No outsider says to this group of teacher professionals that one approach—for example, whole language—is best. Instead, teacher professionals work together to decide what is best from the "old" and "new" curricula for their particular students.

The math curriculum is also a unique blend of the old and new. While traditional lessons take place, students readily log on to the integrated computer system and apply their skills in measurement, estimation, mental computation, and problem solving. New software and manipulatives are becoming more and more the standard tools of learning. The teachers recognize "the revolution (that is going on) in math" with new approaches as "Math Their Way." One teacher noted that "we had been doing (math) hit and miss, but we have learned that we must go deeper if students did not learn something." For example, when students have difficulty learning, teachers work together to "create games, rhymes, puzzles, and visuals—something they can hang on to."

Teachers recognized the important math curriculum support they have been receiving from the district office. In particular, the district's math consultant is usually the first support person outside the school that teachers mention in their conversation about their math reforms. But, perhaps, much like with language arts curriculum reform, teachers have taken (as well as been given) the opportunity to observe and critique each other's lessons. Considerable time during teacher meetings is spent on defining and articulating good practice.

Technological Change

The faculty at Keels view themselves at the "forefront in implementing computer technology" and have become a showcase for the elementary model. About 5 years ago, the teachers and Shirley decided that technology would be the key to motivate and engage their students in curricular content. Their thinking was not as much about the efficient use of instructional time as about the rich visual and auditory representations computers provided for their largely disadvantaged student population. At the outset, IBM's Writing To Read (WTR) program was initiated for first graders and a computer art program was introduced for all students. With each step of a new program the faculty became more comfortable with technology. With funds from incentive awards and grants, Shirley provided increasing levels of staff development. As one teacher noted, before most teachers had not even "touched a computer," but now, some "always seem to have a computer disc in [their] hand." In 1990, Keels entered into a project with IBM and Jostens Learning Corporation. With 2 computers in every classroom, 11 computers in the media center, a 27-station lab, a take-home computer program for Chapter I students, and an early learning computer program for kindergarten students, Keels clearly has the hardware to be a technologically literate school. Jostens Integrated Learning System of Reading, Math, and Writing; Explorations in Science; Compton's Multi-Media Encyclopedia; IBM's Primary Editor Plus; and Measurement, Time, and Money are all available in classrooms through a computer network. With state incentive funds Keels has now added a computerized circulation system for the media center. This computer system allows the media specialist, as Shirley has noted, to become "more creative in the use of her time" and has been able to support the ongoing costs of "running the system." In fact, with incentive funds generated annually, Keels can readily afford "the yearly costs of WTR, computer discs for all students to store their work, and additional software and computer supplies."

Assessment Change

As a part of the statewide 12-Schools project, Keels has taken on the re-design of its science curriculum. The 12-Schools project was initiated in 1991 by the South Carolina Department of Education (SDE) to pilot alternative assessments in math, science, and language arts and begin the process of reforming the state's student assessment system. Schools were awarded a grant of $12,500 (and were given the option of suspending the state testing program) in return for working on the new assessments. Keels, one of the original 12 schools to work on the assessments, submitted one of the most innovative proposals to the SDE to work on this set of reforms. During the first few months of working on the 12-Schools project, small groups of teachers across five grade levels were involved in developing and implementing performance tasks and rubrics. The rubrics that were initially created were nothing more than a very simple "quality" scale that delineates the number of questions answered correctly. Clearly, the creation of these initial tasks are not quite yet reflective of the new assessments articulated by national experts such as Dennie Wolfe, Grant Wiggins, and Lauren Resnick. While the procedures allowed students to create knowledge, an analysis of the tasks did not yet tap into much of what students were learning. The initial assessments required answers to questions that were fixed. They did not require students to justify their responses, nor did they provide opportunities for students to reveal (or allow their teachers to understand) their intentions. The teachers themselves recognize that their initial efforts have been rudimentary, and they anxiously await continued opportunities to refine their tasks and rubrics. But, to only critique Keels's attempts at assessment change at this level would be to miss the point. In a few short months, teachers as Keels have "geared" their attention to students doing, knowing, appreciating, and communicating science. They learned about and acted on important assessment concepts (e.g., developing a table of specifications) and have begun to plug the development of rubrics into the ongoing curriculum. For this to occur requires a paradigm shift for teachers—especially given that science is one of the more neglected aspects of the elementary school curriculum! And this shift is occurring—and very rapidly. While the assessments they initially developed were "rudimentary," the teachers' transformation of the science curriculum was extraordinary. As one first-grade teacher asserted:

> Before I thought they just needed to know the basics in science. . . . I do not believe this anymore. . . . We are in the first stages of this with the 12-Schools project . . . We are wedding basic science building blocks with major math principles. We are now really using the Windows on Science. Students are learning to sort, graph, weigh, measure, and predict. . . . They are learning about data and constructing hypotheses— all in first grade . . . I did not learn this until high school.

Without question, the quality of Keels's teachers across all five grade levels is a cornerstone of the redesign of the science curriculum. A first-grade teacher, Sandra McLain, is the only elementary school teacher named to the National Committee on Science Education, Standards, and Assessment. But to create conditions for change—even in the technical arena of science reform—takes not only subject matter expertise but also "hugs and encouragement." Perhaps my observations of and reflections on the 12-Schools project in action best capture this pivotal point:

> Walking into the Writing To Read room with Sandra McLain in the middle of 18 children conducting experiments, writing on the computers, illustrating, reading—individually and collectively—I was immediately struck by the passion for learning on the part of all in the room. A sign proclaimed: "This Is A Risk-Free Environment." A kid comes up and hugs Sandra while she begins describing to me what is going on in the room. With the expert skill of a master teacher Sandra deftly handles students' questions as well as mine—without missing a beat. In one corner of the room, a group of students is working a lab experiment where traits of plants were being investigated and students were classifying, sorting, and measuring. These students were finishing up a 3-week unit focused on seeds, stems, and leaves. Above them is a poster board displaying vegetables and their traits—with categories developed by the students, revealing a great deal of what they are learning—very little of which shows up on paper-and-pencil, multiple-choice examinations. These students wore visors with the word "scientist" inscribed on top.
>
> Other students were writing about what they were learning. Those students wore visors with the word "author" inscribed on top. Sandra deftly reads and critiques Constance's work, and says to her in a fast-paced, resonant voice, "You just about have a science book written." Constance joyously responds with a "YES!" Another student rushes up to Sandra (and eyeing me, just another visitor to the lab), shows her essay which concludes with, "We are the most famous school of all thanks to Ms. McLain." Sandra responds to her praise by saying, "Many hands make light work." A student comes to me wearing yet another visor, this one with "illustrator" on top, showing me his picture that went along with his essay about his science experiment. With his dazzling smile, he asks what I think. I tell him it is marvelous, and he offers me his work of art. I graciously accept.
>
> In other corners of the room, a child reads sitting on a bean bag chair and next to him another child "meets an author" on audio-tape. Across the room there are three computers where students brush up on phonemes. Sandra tells me "the more they write the more they learn." I looked around the room and saw—at least it looked like—"50 different personal-learning interactions" going on at one time. I thought, I sure hope this image shows up on any formal evaluation of the 12-Schools project.

INITIAL OUTCOMES

By examining numerous formal and informal measures, one finds that Keels is a successful school. Every visit revealed Keels to be a happy place for children and a professionally rewarding place for teachers. Looking in all of the classrooms, one sees a lot of activity—with significant variations. Kids are working in groups, playing educational games, writing, tackling interesting tasks. Kids laugh and smile a great deal, in the halls they readily stretch out a hand for a "high five." The walls of the hall are literally covered with student work. The floors of the hall are spotless. Some teachers eat lunch with students—even though they are not required to do so.

Teachers and administrators speak of how computer technology has made learning "fun" for students. For example, in writing, students find it "easier to compose and edit" and to "work hard at creating polished copy" using the "Children's Writing and Publishing Center." Also, students are likely to conduct research—"gathering information and ideas through the use of the on-line encyclopedia."

Basic skills test score results have also revealed considerable progress. For example, in 1991 the average number of South Carolina's students meeting standard on the state's elementary school readiness test was 74%, while at Keels, only 47% met this standard. Despite the relatively low level of readiness of Keels's first graders, in 1992, 94% met the standards in reading and 92% met the standards in math on the state's Basic Skills Assessment Program. In addition, in 1992, at least 50% of Keels's students at each of its respective grade levels scored above the fiftieth percentile on the "3R Battery" of the nationally norm-referenced Stanford-8 examination (e.g., 88% at Grade 1; 69% at Grade 2; 59% at Grade 3; 54% at Grade 4; and 50% at Grade 5). Despite the relatively high scores and the fact that 60% of the fourth and fifth graders did not begin their elementary education at Keels, the teachers are not satisfied with these scores.

There are many other indicators of success. Some of these indicators are very straightforward. Others may be viewed more as supposition. First, the interviews revealed a high level of consensus among parents, administrators, teachers, *and students* with regard to Keels's mission. Parent support has been evidenced by the school book sale that generated significant profits ($800) as well as by the PTA meetings that are "standing room only." Additionally, in 1992, 70 families who live outside Keels's school attendance zone have requested that their children attend Keels for the 1992–1993 academic year.

Second, Keels continues to receive affirmation from external referents. For example, over the last several years Keels has received statewide school incentive rewards, garnered numerous competitive grants, received an *Inviting School Award* from the International Alliance for Invitational Education, and has been nominated for the Redbook *America's Best Schools Project*. Most recently, Keels has been nominated as a "blue ribbon" finalist for the U.S. Department of Education elementary school competition. External affirmation also has been evidenced by the high number of visitations (from other schools, newspapers, etc.) to Keels.

Third, Keels's teachers have received significant awards and prestigious state and national committee assignments. Also, teachers have had increasing opportunities to extend their own professional development opportunities (including collaborative planning and critiquing each other's classroom practices), as well as increasing requests to provide professional development experiences for teachers across the district and state. Teachers are relying less on textbooks and more on other curricular resources and their professional judgment.

Finally, students themselves are exercising leadership. Students have been provided considerable opportunities to be involved in making decisions affecting discipline in the school as well as important extracurricular events (e.g., a fifth-grade school dance). The elected student council, 30-odd activity clubs, the safety patrol and perhaps, most importantly, peer teaching, all empower students and bind them closer to their school. In interviews, several students noted that even though their grades are not as high as they were in other schools they attended they "liked Keels more." Students spoke enthusiastically about having opportunities to work with their peers, "fun" social studies projects, writing, and learning about the stock market. As one student claimed, "We do computers art and stuff here . . . at my old school we just had to sit and do work all the time."

These restructuring outcomes only represent some of the accomplishments of the last several years at Keels. However, they are suggestive of what might be considered as a more appropriate indicator system for school restructuring.

BARRIERS TO RESTRUCTURING

Despite Keels's considerable success in its restructuring efforts, several barriers stand in the way. These barriers include: (1) time for teachers to work with students and each other, (2) state testing, and (3) overcoming burnout.

First, teachers want more time with students. Given the constraints in their students' lives, the principal and teachers spoke incessantly about the need for year-round education. Many teachers are at school anyway and see endless possibilities to enhance learning if they only had more instructional time with students. For teachers, year-round education, with its expanded (and perhaps more flexible) calendar, also would provide more opportunities to better serve students with ancillary (health and psychological) services. It is almost as if Keels's teachers have had just enough success with their collaborative planning time that they now know how much more time they really need. Ironically, Keels's teachers cited a lack of time as the major barrier to restructuring even though—compared to most schools—the teachers have garnered far more opportunities to travel to other sites and collaboratively plan as a result of grant money. As one teacher noted:

> We are constrained by the number of hours we have with the children each day . . . We need more time . . . It is unpopular with some teachers, but we need to be spending as much time as the Japanese and the Germans. This is not unpopular at this school. We have so much going on at this school—like the 12-Schools project—that we can't get it all done. We are rushing here and rushing there. We are never done, we never sit down.

Keels's teachers have made considerable progress because of their summer work—some of it compensated at a modest $60 a day, but most of it uncompensated. And, herein lies some of the rub. Keels's younger and single teachers—under pressure to supplement their low salaries during the summer—cannot afford to participate in professional development experiences.

Also, despite the fact that Keels's teachers embrace the state testing program and surely use it to their financial advantage, the multiple-choice, basic skills assessment can be viewed as a barrier. The teachers have struggled to find ways to decrease the amount of instructional time spent on reviewing skills—skills that show up on the test. In fact, in spite of the teachers' continuing quest to go deeper into subject matter, curricular revisions still focus "on covering more content before (spring) testing." Through the state incentive program (described previously) high test scores have generated $107,000 over the last 6 years. Not tending to the scores may be irrational. Despite teachers' openness to change to employing teaching strategies that may not immediately translate into high test scores, curriculum decisions still hone in on ensuring that the year-to-year aggregated gain scores are high. These confident teachers indeed want an external referent to challenge them to do better. As one teacher noted, "The Stanford test helps make us real and can push us to grow." Yet, when asked about the impact of testing on Keels's teaching, one district administrator affirmed that "if the test would change so would the teaching of the teachers at Keels—they are very competitive." This is a reasonable assertion. The teachers are not wedded to testing per se. They are embracing new forms of testing (because of the benefits they have for students) and have responded positively to the "creditability it has given to teacher judgment" in assessment. One wonders what their approach would be if there were no multiple-choice, basic skills assessment. While clearly these teachers would not totally change their teaching, if the tests changed tomorrow, would as much drill and practice prevail?

Third, teacher "burnout"[4] is becoming a problem at Keels. Last year, three teachers left—primarily because, as Shirley suggested, "they are tired . . . (and) could not live up to their own expectations." For example, one teacher left to work in another school with students who were not so difficult to teach. This particular teacher was identified by both administrators and teachers as exemplary. However, the long, intense hours of both teaching and collaborative planning for continuous change left her depleted. Another teacher left for private business. This teacher—recognized as an excellent teacher by her peers—was tired and "got to a point in her life" where she was not willing to work as hard as Keels's educators demanded. To serve the students well requires enormous teacher knowledge, skill, energy, and commitment. Extraordinary efforts are expected, and their effects are not always positive.

LESSONS FOR BOTH PRACTICE AND POLICY

As Lieberman and Miller (1990) have suggested, successful restructuring at Keels has emerged from a blend of influences that have been "present at the same time and over time" and has taken hold due to an extended period of "leadership, a shared mission, school goals, necessary resources, the promotion of colleagueship, and the provision of professional growth opportunities for teachers" (p. 761). As previously described, the school has been involved in an incredible array of change efforts. However, the school avoided the project mentality of school reform by focusing on the continuous improvement of curriculum through altering the relationships between teachers and administrators and teachers and students. However, the center of the transformation has been the emergence of teacher power and the powerful culture of reform. To be sure, this examination of restructuring has been as much about studying a school culture. And, in the effort to adequately attend to Keels's culture (and the norms, expectations, and behavioral regularities embedded within it), I offer the following initial lessons related to both policy and practice. Importantly, these lessons are generated from the perspective of an outside researcher as well as from the perspective of Keels's teachers after they had an opportunity to review an initial draft of the case study.

High Expectations for All Students . . . But There is Much More

Clearly, at the core of Keels's success in restructuring is the deeply held belief by teachers and administrators that all students can learn to be active learners and knowledge producers. Although the staff was not familiar with

Steele's (1992) essay, "Race and the Schooling of Black Americans," it was as though his blueprint for a "wise school" was the cornerstone of their efforts. The development of trust between teacher and student, the challenge and promise of personal fulfillment (not remediation) as a guide for education, the integration of different groups to mitigate vulnerabilities, and the inclusion of different cultures throughout the school curriculum are "the elements of wiseness" (Steele, 1992, p. 77). Keels's curriculum—in most respects—follows this blueprint. The staff has created this atmosphere out of its own unique philosophy and its willingness to embrace this moral dimension of schooling. This is not easy, especially when innumerable policies (for example, state and district gifted and talented directives and resources) provide opportunities to segregate students by so-called ability levels. Keels's staff has consciously chosen to group its gifted and talented students in the least blatant way and has gone to considerable lengths to mitigate any negative effects of academic differences among students. At the same time, the staff does not bury its head in the sand with regard to student differences and deficiencies. They expect a great deal from their students, and the students and parents know it!

But, there is more. Teachers have learned to transform high expectations for students into high expectations for parents, for administrators, and for themselves—as a collective faculty and community. A "simple" lesson from all this is that schools, principals, and teachers can accomplish all this if state and district officials let them. However, the translation of this simple lesson into a reality for all schools is quite complex. In discussing the case study, Keels's teachers spoke about the issue of having a critical mass of teachers who do indeed know what to do, and will do it! Yes, resources were important, and to some degree necessary, but not sufficient. Knowing what to do with available resources was critical and having a principal who promoted the use of teacher power was even more critical. For principals, having supervisors who let them operate in a risk-free environment was paramount for them to let teachers find out and do what is necessary.

More "De-Isolation" of Teachers and Teaching

As a part of the effort to create teacher power, more opportunities must be made to de-isolate teachers and teaching. With the time that grant money has purchased, Keels is breaking up teacher isolation and the longstanding "cellular structure" of the school organization (Lortie, 1975). Teachers are learning from other teachers in planning sessions and from those in other schools during workshops. Yet, they are not even beginning to learn *enough* about pedagogical practices from their colleagues down the hall in their own school. Restructuring will move at a rapid pace where teachers learn from each other during collaborative meeting time and workshops (i.e., the de-isolation of *teachers*) *and* where teachers as a team critique and reflect on their own classroom teaching (i.e., the de-isolation of *teaching*). Keels's teachers have struggled to find the time to do curriculum planning and allow for appropriate professional development in technology, assessment, and curriculum reform. There is a growing thirst for more observations and more critiques of practice. Perhaps because of the immense strides made in getting teachers together to share and learn from each other, at Keels there is now a growing awareness of the need to learn more from direct observations and reflection. More release time for teachers may be necessary, but not sufficient. Increased teacher involvement in the school's personnel evaluation system may serve as an additional lever in this regard. The enhanced use of video technology to observe and critique lessons and continued creative use of teaching assistants may be needed to leverage individual teachers' time for observing each other. Nevertheless, what is clear is that increased observations must not be casual. The increased de-isolation of teaching must be integrated into the routine work of teachers, identified with the successes of those who take part, and associated with the necessary transformation of the school (Little, 1988).

Lack of time is the most critical barrier in de-isolating teachers. Research on school change points to the pivotal variable of teacher time necessary in schools where innovation and reflection are paramount to success (Fullan, 1991; Fullan & Miles, 1992). The ideas that emerged from time away from children and the time that only money allows generate a critical lever for the necessary professional development and teacher power required for restructuring.

Create the Learning Organization . . . and Share the Vision

If policy makers indeed want students to be knowledge producers and group problem solvers then there must be new structures that allow for teachers to be knowledge producers and group problem solvers. This type of adult learning is anathema to the type of learning that we assess and value—both for students (e.g., BSAP and Stanford-8 as well as those proverbial end-of-the-chapter tests) and for teachers (e.g., college-level coursework and assessment, teacher evaluation, one-shot workshops conducted by outside experts, etc.). But, what is a clear lesson from Keels is not just the power of individual learning but also of the creation of the learning organization. Senge (1990) describes the five disciplines of the learning organization—employing systems thinking to see how the parts are connected to the whole, drawing on personal mastery to inspire change, building shared visions, creating mental models of the future, and exploiting team learning. As Senge (1990) has noted:

> At the heart of a learning organization is a shift of mind—from seeing ourselves as separate from the world to connected to the world, from seeing problems caused

by someone or something "out there," to seeing how our own actions create the problems we experience. A learning organization is a place where people are continually discovering how they create their reality. And how they change it. (pp. 12–13)

Indeed, the heart of Keels's teachers' efforts to learn is their belief that they are in charge of their destiny of impacting positively on the education of *all* children. They do not see obstacles in the problems that their children bring to school. Instead, they see challenges in those problems, and opportunities for them to exert their expertise and experience in meeting those challenges. In addition, close to the heart of Keels's teachers' efforts to learn is their willingness to go public with what they know—not only with themselves, but with the many visitors who come to their school. As one teacher noted: "We've had so many people come in . . . we enjoy having people come in. And I think the kids do too because it makes them feel special to have people watch." While the visitors are a drain on the energy and time of the staff, they almost provide a raison d'être for administrators, teachers, and students to develop and articulate clear standards and criteria for success—what they are doing, why they are doing it, and how well they are doing it. When visitors "call," the whole school puts on an exhibition of student and adult learning, with each willing to share not only what they know, but how they have come to know. In some respects, visitors prompt for the school what is akin to Ted Sizer's mastery of exhibition for student graduation from a CES high school. This exposure to the public, in turn, reinforces the school's shared vision and mission. A shared mission does not necessarily mean a posted vision statement on the walls of each classroom or a dictated set of goals that people have memorized. Not at all. In fact, at Keels, administrators, teachers, parents, and students used strikingly different words to describe the same shared vision. What makes for the shared vision at Keels is that it has been developed more out of action than rhetoric. In an attempt to understand the learning organization of Keels, it is clear that there is a grave need to go beyond the proven and noble concept of "teachers teaching teachers" (as practiced by the Bay Area Writing Project and South Carolina's own version, the Writing Improvement Network). The next step is for schools that have learned how to learn as organizations to begin teaching other schools as organizations (not just individuals), how to learn and restructure. The Center for School Leadership, created by the state's 1989 Target 2000 legislation, has been one of the few school-based organizations (the South Carolina Center for Teacher Recruitment being another) that has consciously promoted divergent thinking and acting in K–12 schools. Without question, the center has been a catalyst for learning at Keels. But, Keels would be (and is) a much more powerful catalyst to help other school organizations to learn. Just as teachers are the most effective teachers of other teachers, so are schools the most effective teachers of other schools. Unfortunately, very little of South Carolina's educational policy structure supports schools—as learning organizations—teaching other schools.

State Testing and Accountability Policies Still Loom Large

Teachers, even in the most innovative and inspiring settings, still plan and teach with their heads turned toward discrete learning skill objectives. These objectives are specified by the statewide basic skills testing program and the state's accountability and incentive system, which has a virtual unidimensional focus on year-to-year schoolwide aggregated gain scores. While the status of "deregulation" liberates winning schools, such as Keels, from paperwork and provides honorific status, it does not necessarily emancipate them from the lockstep teaching and learning believed to be consistent with the current basic skills testing programs.

The 12-Schools project provided an opportunity for Keels to suspend all standardized testing. The BSAP was suspended because the teachers saw no use in the information generated from the test. Stanford-8 was continued, primarily because the staff did not want to shun the current accountability system and valued the data that this norm-referenced test provided. While the current testing and accountability policies still loom large, a more powerful form of accountability is emerging at Keels. It is not about test scores. It is about teachers holding themselves responsible for students and then creating opportunities, with help from the principal and district office, for public demonstrations of their work. Site visits from those outside the school provide a powerful vehicle for teachers, administrators, and students to coalesce around a set of values as well as valued outcomes. There is a need to transform parts of this process in order to formally capture the diversity and richness of Keels's restructuring efforts in a multi-indicator, multidimensional accountability system. Large-scale accountability systems should not rely on single instruments, no matter how authentic the instrument or test is. Instead, there might be educational audits of opportunities for students to learn, samples of students' work, and annual reports to the community (Sizer, 1992). Similarly, Darling-Hammond and Ascher (1990) have called for an accountability system that reveals "how much individual students are learning and how well schools are serving them" (p. 2), while Oakes (1989) has recommended that indicator systems must reveal such contextual information as access to knowledge, the press for achievement, and teaching conditions. This means student outcomes must not be divorced from school context. In many ways, the case study of Keels—and the examination of the content, process, and initial outcomes of restructuring—provides considerable substance for this accountability framework developed by Darling-Hammond and Ascher (1990) and Oakes (1989). South Carolina schools and teachers await the implementation of such an accountability framework, and Keels may serve as an important starting point.

Teacher Empowerment Is Not Enough

Teacher empowerment, a concept that implies delegated authority where teacher roles and responsibilities are defined from afar, is not enough. As Cooper (1988) has asserted, "essentially, the current empowerment of teachers in such areas as curriculum, school improvement, and professional development is *received* power, limited by others' decisions and subject to cancellation if extended beyond defined boundaries" (p. 50). Instead, as lessons from Keels reveal, successful restructuring will ultimately require teacher power, that is, the capacity of key teachers to establish and enforce norms of excellence and then spread those norms like a contagion throughout the school culture. This takes time, teacher discretion, and a robust belief in teacher knowledge and efficacy. As Cooper (1988) has claimed, the roots of teacher power are not within status or control mechanisms, but with "the quality and depth of practice and the values of the professional" (p. 48). Thus, the rewards for teacher power emerge from the nature and composition of practice, not vice versa. Indeed, this is what has been transpiring at Keels. Teachers believe that they are not near their capacity in enacting change, they are finding new ways to support and define each other's work, and they exude the self-confidence of the experts that they are. They are, as one district administrator noted, "cocky," but probably no more so than the cardiac surgeon with an M. D. from Duke University. However, unlike some professionals, their power does not lead to dogmatism. The essence of their power is *primarily* in collegiality and collaboration. As Cooper (1988) has described:

> Such roles provide supportive, authoritative assistance, but not direction or determination. They are essentially egalitarian. Semantics aside, were these teachers to be perceived as centers of power (which is the way leaders are perceived), then, very likely, from their colleagues' point of view, they would be a threat. (p. 50)

Like in many schools, Keels's teachers have had to work within an emphatic egalitarian culture (see Lortie, 1975). However, Keels's teachers are pushing at the edges of this particular culture. Unlike in many schools, teachers (and the principal!) comfortably can be first among equals. Individuals and small groups of teachers can be recognized publicly for their efforts and accomplishments—with no apparent cultural fallout. When teachers serve on prestigious committees or are asked to help develop other teachers (outside Keels), their peers respect the recognition they have received. And they expect them to come back and share their knowledge. Administrators who can allow this to happen have to be secure themselves. They have to be willing to redefine their role and become what Schlechty (1990) has labeled, "leaders of leaders;" or better yet, what Keels's teachers have labeled, "traffic engineer." Instructional leadership from principals may be more like—as hypothesized by one Keels teacher—"channeling teachers in the right direction so they do not collide." Principals have to be allowed to be risk takers themselves. In some cases, district officials are far less willing for principals to take risks than principals are willing for teachers to take risks. This has not been the case between District Two officials and Keels administrators. While someone has to steer the bureaucratic ship, key administrators (at both the district and school level) have to take on a variety of new roles themselves—as visionaries, facilitators, head teachers, and strong (but not authoritarian) leaders (Lieberman, Clark, & Wasley, 1990). And, clearly, this will require new graduate and training programs and new district and state policies that virtually allow administrators to fail.

In closing, the process of restructuring a school is very much like the process of human learning. As Cohen (1990) has suggested, teachers cannot simply cast off old ideas and practices like a shabby coat, and slip on something new . . . the past is their path to the future" (p. 323). In fact, some sort of mixed practice appears to be healthy for school change, and an indicator of emerging teacher power. With this amalgamation comes some confusion and ambiguity—which is all the more reason for practitioners to have more time to reflect on what they do and how they do it. In this sense, restructuring takes on a more organic process, with each component of change cultivated by those who *do* reform. Restructuring is not handed down and replicated from site to site. Restructuring is work in progress—continuously. And, in "moving" schools, this belief of continuous work in progress is well accepted and even embraced with a passion.

Concomitantly, restructuring at Keels is moving at a rapid pace because teachers and administrators "do *not* believe they have arrived." In fact, it is in schools like Keels where one does not hear practitioners use the word "restructured." It just is not in their lexicon of reform words. Instead, these practitioners collectively recognize that they must keep changing so that their children can have opportunities to learn for their futures. And it is this collective respect that teachers and administrators have for their children's futures that makes Keels special, a place where restructuring is not just another project but a source of ideas that explode and where teachers have the power.

The case of Keels suggests how teachers have learned to garner and sustain power in the best interest of students. However, Keels is still a school where restructuring is being carried on the backs of extraordinary educators who are exerting extraordinary efforts. Restructuring will be sustained over a large number of schools and districts only when new policies and practices will deeply support more ordinary people doing the extraordinary work of education

(Sykes & Elmore, 1989). Without such new policies and practices both educators and the public will continue to be lulled into the belief that school restructuring, much like it has unfolded at Keels, takes place only with extraordinary people working inordinate numbers of hours and developing an innumerable array of new initiatives. Unfortunately, there are just not enough Shirley Hendersons and Sandra McLains (and *many* other Keels teachers) to spread around the nation's 100,000 schools.

Acknowledgements. Many thanks to Shirley Henderson and the teachers at Keels, who enabled me to learn a great deal about school restructuring. They have great wisdom and offered much support and needed critique of this study. Also, I appreciate the critical assistance of Dr. Rick Ginsberg, who not only collected data and served as external referent, but also critiqued the case study for accuracy and consistency. I also extend deep appreciation to several other readers, including Dr. Dennis Bartels, of the South Carolina State Department of Education, who provided me with substantive feedback.

NOTES

1. I conducted this case study by drawing on an outline provided by the National Center for Restructuring Education, Schools, and Teaching (NCREST) at Teachers College, Columbia University and school evaluation frameworks developed by both McCarthy, Hopfenberg, and Levin (1991) and Seashore-Louis and Miles (1990). In particular, I examined (1) contextual influences in and around the school, (2) the improvement program, (3) the assistance provided, (4) the actual events and processes during implementation, (5) the problems and barriers encountered and how they were mitigated, and (6) the outcomes achieved.

My data sources included interviews with teachers, administrators, students, and parents, as well as document reviews of grant proposals, curriculum guides, student performance assessments, test data, teacher survey data, and observations of key meetings and classroom lessons.

Site visits were conducted over a 4-month period from March 1992 through June 1992. I spent 7 days on site. Assisted by another researcher, I conducted formal interviews in a private conference room. Numerous tours through the school took place, whereby informal observations of student-teacher interactions could take place. Several interviews with parents were conducted on the telephone; other informal conversations took place with parents on site during our visits. Several classes were visited (kindergarten, computer/science lab, first grade, fifth grade) for extended periods of time (more than 50 minutes). In particular, we used snowball sampling techniques to determine which teachers were to be interviewed. We were conscious of the need to interview those who were deeply involved, involved, and not involved in school restructuring.

Data analysis procedures were influenced by those well-known in qualitative research circles (Geertz, 1973; Yin, 1984). I wanted to detail the complexity of the content and processes of restructuring and to analyze the data set (including the survey data) to answer the questions framed by the NCREST study outline. Data analysis was comprised of five explicit segments: (1) becoming familiar with the whole data set through series of reviews (100 pages of field notes), (2) assembling the data by distinctive themes and categories, (3) reorganizing the data set so as to respond to the NCREST study outline, (4) constructing the case study, and (5) having a group of Keels's staff review the case study draft to check for accuracy as well as to embellish the case itself. With regard to the latter, eight teachers (representative of several grade levels and specialty areas), the principal, and the assistant principal met with me over a week-long period to review the case study and contribute to its final section, "Lessons for Policy and Practice." They reviewed the initial draft for accuracy and in several different sessions revealed further understandings and implications for both policy and practice. Overall, Keels's teachers and principal described the first draft as "99% accurate."

2. The Associate Schools program is an effort organized under the auspices of the South Carolina Center for the Advancement of Teaching and School Leadership. This state-funded center assists change-oriented schools with a variety of restructuring initiatives. Annual grants, special workshops, professional literature, and technical assistance is made available to select schools.

3. South Carolina offers deregulated status to schools that consistently perform well on standards defined by the state's basic skills testing program. Deregulation allows for a particular school, if allowed by its school district and board, to waive certain state requirements (e.g., related to class size, teacher certification, instructional time allotted to different core subjects, etc.)

4. Burnout—as suggested in the text—is not used to describe a clinical state of being. Instead, this was a term used by teachers and the administrators to describe the negative (and tiring) effects of restructuring on many teachers.

REFERENCES

Cohen, D. (1990). A revolution in one classroom: The case of Mrs. Oublier. *Educational Evaluation and Policy Analysis, 12*(3), 311–330.

Cooper, M. (1988). Whose culture is it, anyway? In A. Lieberman (Ed.), *Building a professional culture in schools* (pp. 45–54). New York: Teachers College Press.

Darling-Hammond, L., & Ascher, C. (1990). *Creating accountability in big city school systems.* New York: Eric Clearinghouse of Urban Education.

Fullan, M. (1991). *The new meaning of educational change.* New York: Teachers College Press.

Fullan, M., & Miles, M. (1992). Getting reform right: What works and what doesn't. *Kappan, 73*(10), 744–752.

Geertz, C. (1973). *The interpretation of cultures.* New York: Basic Books.

Lieberman, A., Clark, R., & Wasley, P. (1990). *Talks with 21st century educators.* Seattle, WA: University of Washington, Puget Sound Education Consortium.

Lieberman, A., & Miller, L. (1990). Restructuring schools: What matters and what works. *Kappan, 71*(10), 759–764.

Lieberman, A., & Miller, L. (1991). Revisiting the social realities of teaching. In A. Lieberman & L. Miller (Eds.), *Staff development for education in the '90s* (pp. 92–112). New York: Teachers College Press.

Little, J. W. (1986). Seductive images and organizational realities in professional development. In A. Lieberman (Ed.), *Rethinking school improvement* (pp. 26–44). New York: Teachers College Press.

Little, J. W. (1988). Assessing the prospects for teacher leadership. In A. Lieberman (Ed.), *Building a professional culture in schools* (pp. 78–106). New York: Teachers College Press.

Lortie, D. (1975). *Schoolteacher: A sociological study.* Chicago: University of Chicago Press.

McCarthy, J., Hopfenberg, W., & Levin, H. (1991). *Accelerated schools—evolving thoughts on the evaluation of an innovative model.* Paper presented at the annual meeting of the American Educational Research Association, San Francisco.

Oakes, J. (1989). What educational indicators? The case for assessing school context. *Educational Evaluation and Policy Analysis, 11*(2), 181–199.

Rosenholtz, S. (1989). *Teacher's workplace: The social organization of schools.* New York: Longman.

Sarason, S. (1982). *The culture of school and the problem of change.* Boston: Allyn & Bacon.

Sarason, S. (1990). *The predictable failure of school reform.* San Francisco: Jossey-Bass.

Schlechty, P. (1990). *Schools for the 21st century: Leadership imperatives for school reform.* San Francisco: Jossey-Bass.

Seashore-Louis, K., & Miles, M. (1990). *Improving the urban high school: What works and why.* New York: Teachers College Press.

Senge, P. (1990). *The fifth discipline: The art and practice of the learning organization.* New York: Doubleday.

Sergiovani, T. (1989). The theoretical basis for cultural leadership. In L. T. Sheive & M. B. Shoenheit (Eds.), *Leadership: Examining the elusive.* Alexandria, VA: Association for Supervision and Curriculum Development.

Sizer, T. (1992). *Horace's school: Redesigning the American high school.* New York: Houghton Mifflin.

Steele, C. (1992). Race and the schooling of black Americans. *Atlantic Monthly, 269*(5), 68–78.

Sykes, G., & Elmore, R. (1989). Making schools manageable. In J. Hannaway & R. Crowson (Eds.), *The politics of reforming school administration* (pp. 77–94). Bristol, UK: Falmer Press.

Yin, R. K. (1984). *Case study research: Design and method.* Beverly Hills: Sage.

Chapter 7 _____

The Evolution of a
Restructuring School:
The New Suncook Case

Lee Goldsberry
with Alice Holt, Karen Johnson, Gary MacDonald,
Rhonda Poliquin, and Lauren Potter

Change is a process, not an event. This phrase should probably be inscribed in the cornerstone of the New Suncook School because it seems to be repeated each time another venture is undertaken. Our case, a study of events and evolving structures, attempts to capture some of this process of change over the last 7 years or so. Like the process itself, this portrayal is a collaborative effort. We authors are mostly classroom teachers (Johnson, Poliquin, and Potter), though one of us (Holt) is labeled a special educator (actually, we are all special), one of us is called principal (MacDonald), and another is a university type (Goldsberry). That is fitting, too, for our story is one of educators with varying titles and backgrounds working together to make both sense and a success out of this process called change. Moreover, we storytellers represent many other caring educators, both at New Suncook and elsewhere, who have offered their own energies and ideas to making the process work. Our charge is to tell our story as accurately as we can so that you, the reader, can compare it to other such stories to identify themes. We sincerely hope you find it useful.

Tucked away in rural, western Maine, New Suncook School seems an unlikely site for a restructuring school, or for a professional development school. We really did not set out to be either. Before either label gained fashion, the faculty at New Suncook (with ample support and encouragement from our principal) set out to create a school environment that made learning joyful—where critical dialogue about our hopes for the youngsters who attend are connected to the daily experiences they encounter as part of their schooling. While many of us view the spirit with which we pursue our varied emphases and approaches as the center of this change process, most often outsiders focus on the altered structures and the ways in which we changed them. Therefore, after we try to describe the large context in which we operate, including our sense of mission, we will present a chronology of the structural changes which, consistent with our view of change, are still underway.

OUR CONTEXT

Organizationally, we are part of a School Administrative District (SAD # 72) that consists of five elementary schools and a central middle school serving Grades 6 through 8. Like schools everywhere, our school has its own unique story. One of the most important factors in our continuing development is the presence of a building principal whose vision and actions recognize the importance of teachers who think deeply about their educational purposes and who have the courage to act on their ideas. Not only has Gary MacDonald, our principal, encouraged individual teachers to share our dreams, to work with others to stretch our ideas as well as our practices, and to assess our efforts for their consequences for the children we teach, but he has also shielded us from many of the draining demands of bureaucratic life—clearly making the necessary though often tedious job of coordinating our own change efforts with the large school organization his job.

On the other hand, when the questions and tasks involve clarifying our goals or pursuing external resources, Gary has consistently encouraged, even demanded, that we speak for ourselves. Thus, over the past 7 years, many of us have developed meaningful connections with fellow educators in diverse settings that have helped us immensely. While the casual observer might see New Suncook as a typical rural school with a staff as insulated from differing perspectives on educational issues as the school's inhabitants are insulated from Maine's winter, nothing could be less true. Whether the connections are through the rich human resources of the Southern Maine Partnership,[1] through the rewarding involvement in the Department of Education's exemplary innovative grant program, through our discussions of common and uncommon problems with our colleagues in a "restructuring school in California,"[2] or through our formal involvement with graduate education at the University of Southern Maine, we have developed linkages that have both fueled our energies and provoked our thinking. To describe our involvement and our benefits from such connections seems impossible without helping you see the evolution.

THE EVOLUTION

Who really knows exactly when it all began? For each of us there is a unique history of becoming educators, of discovering our own identities as teachers and leaders. But, teachers generally work under conditions of extra-ordinary personal and professional isolation. This naturally promotes a reluc-tance to share ideas, techniques, successes, and especially failures with col-leagues.

In fall 1985, with this problem in mind, there were discussions between Gary and individual staff members about the need for conversation about edu-cational issues. Through these conversations, Gary found a teacher who shared his desire to find a way to deal with the isolation. They developed a proposal for a $2,000 Maine Innovative Educational Grant[3] to provide six teachers an opportunity to study and analyze recent educational research and its implemen-tation in the classroom. Based on Roland Barthes' assertion that "when teachers individually and collectively examine, question, reflect on their ideals, and de-velop new practices that lead toward those ideals, the school and its inhabitants are alive,"[4] the grant established a research into practice (RIP) team with four goals:

1. Obtaining information about current educational issues
2. Getting teachers into one another's classrooms for observation
3. Enabling teachers to talk with one another about instructional matters
4. Creating an environment for teachers to reflect on their teaching

The RIP team was formed in June 1985, with the early summer months used for planning and goal-setting. Prior to the start of school, 2 days of meet-ings involved team-building activities, dissemination of reading materials, de-veloping a time schedule, and discussion of teachers' classroom expectations, as well as conferencing strategies for peer coaching. Meetings were held after school twice a month throughout the school year. Because each of us was con-cerned with doing better that which we were already doing, the RIP team ini-tially focused on such topics as lesson design, time-on-task, and questioning techniques. In addition, each of the six teachers was also provided release time to observe and confer with another team member weekly. New Suncook School staff who were not part of the RIP team were kept informed of new learning and successes and failures through presentations at staff meetings. In addition, a library of materials was created for all of the staff to use. Though initially they met with skepticism, the six teachers of the RIP team (and Gary) formed the critical mass needed for meaningful school change. The modest resources of the grant provided the first structured opportunity for us to step outside of our normal classroom routine to reflect collaboratively on our prac-tices. (It didn't hurt at all that the success of the proposal signaled to us that this innovative practice was deserving of state support.)

Comments from the RIP team membership captured the power of the effort:

I weighed the pros and cons before signing up. I finally decided to go for it because I didn't want to be left out. I thought it would help my weaknesses about being observed. Somewhere about November it dawned on me that the whole thing was a very positive experience—good comments, sharing questions, and nonthreatening suggestions. (A fifth-grade teacher)

Being a member of the RIP team has been the most rewarding learning experience of my teaching career. I feel that the collegiality that has evolved among our team members has created an inner security for me. No matter what problems arise in teaching, I'll never have to face or solve problems alone. . . . My team members have been in my classroom, can relate to my needs, understand what I am dealing with and are always there to help. (Lauren Potter)

During this year of peer observation, I began to realize that by building this into your schedule, it eventually becomes natural. Subtle changes begin to take place. You acquire greater patience with yourself and fellow teachers during the process of change. Change involving human beings takes time. You appreciate the differences in colleagues teaching, and they in yours. You feel as if you're doing the right thing. (A third-grade teacher)

As I become more knowledgeable through the research, I find that it has created a desire and interest to pursue more research. I think the best part of the year has been the exchange of ideas to encourage growth in us all. It is the start of a professional community within the school. Personally, I am more organized, more self-confident, and have enjoyed the responsibility placed on me. It is an avenue that I never thought I'd want to pursue—leadership in any form. (Karen Johnson)

In looking back at this initial step, we realize that Gary was the key figure. Gary's nurturance of us was what helped give us the support to examine our beliefs and question our practices. The teacher who collaborated with Gary on the grant proposal remembers becoming very excited about the idea for the grant and leaving numerous notes to Gary on the subject. She realized that the seeds were planted by him and he watched and waited to see if they would grow. The idea was already part of the vision that he had, and we began to share and take ownership of this vision through his support and encouragement.

As fate would have it, spring 1986 brought the birth of the Southern Maine Partnership (SMP), whose goals seemed remarkably similar to those of our own RIP team. Our involvement in the SMP gave us connections both to its organizer, Paul Heckman, and to a larger cluster of teachers in the region who were eager to explore meaningful educational change. The exposure was timely. All of the teachers in the district were invited to attend smp meetings at the University of Southern Maine's Gorham Campus, and many New Suncook teachers, including the rip team, took advantage of this opportunity. Not everyone who attended partnership meetings came away with the same sense of purpose. As we discussed at various times, not everyone is ready at the same time. This is a point that we are quick to make when we are talking about developmentally appropriate practices for children but are less likely to show understanding of when we talk about adult learners. However, the partnership, and particularly Paul Heckman, acted as the change agent that effectively broke the equilibrium holding an organization place. (Paul Heckman was the original director of the Southern Maine Partnership.)

As Lauren Potter observed,

> In many ways Paul Heckman helped us realize or remember that we, as teachers, are professionals. He gave us an opportunity, through the Southern Maine Partnership, to come together as professionals in a collegiate setting. He challenged us to question why we do what we do in school everyday. He stimulated our thinking and introduced us to the writings of change agents in education. Through our monthly dinner meetings we began to engage in the art of reflective practice. Most importantly, our experiences with Paul Heckman and the Southern Maine Partnership gave us permission to change that which had existed for years in schools. Along with that permission came the knowledge base, confidence, and challenge to take risks, make changes, and face those who question those changes.

Another timely development was the state-funded coalition of Western Maine School Improvement Teams in 1985–1986. The rip team represented New Suncook School as one of seven teams of teachers and administrators in the area who were making meaningful changes in their schools. Our team attended conferences, collecting insights and perspectives from varied speakers to serve as a springboard for discussions among all the teachers at New Suncook. These discussions, which took place during biweekly staff meetings, were the first time all of the teachers at the school had convened in a formal way to discuss educational issues.

The rip team was funded for a second year (in 1986, meeting monthly with some smaller discussion groups) with a subtle, but potent, change in focus. Rather than simply looking for ways to improve present practices, we began to examine the rationale behind our actions. Asking, "What are we doing, and why?" forced us to reconsider our basic beliefs about learners, learning, and subject matter. The revised goals for that year's funding reflect the evolving focus: (1) to make available and create dialogue about current educational research, (2) to provide a format for regular peer observation, and (3) to create a professional climate that promotes risk taking, growth, and collaboration. Taking advantage of some of our new connections, the RIP team expanded to include Paul Heckman of the Southern Maine Partnership and two more teachers (one from another school in our district). We began that second year by generating a list of individual concerns. After much discussion and with Paul's help, we decided to focus on teaching reading as a vehicle that both captured common aims and allowed for each of us to work on individual concerns. This brought us to discuss curriculum not as a bureaucratic guidebook but as a description of what we were actually doing with kids. We focused on two separate but related questions: (1) Are we doing what we say we are doing? and (2) Are we making more work for ourselves with our daily practices? These questions went beyond the safe environment we had created for ourselves, asking us not only to reflect on this private territory but also to share it with others.

> As one of the new teachers coming into this group, it was very exciting. It was really my first experience talking about a big picture. I was always waiting for someone just to ask me why I was doing what I was doing with kids. This was the first real opportunity that arose that invited this type of sharing. It was a very eye-opening yet exciting time to be involved at New Suncook. (Rhonda Poliquin)

Another result of the grant work involved creating a greater sense of camaraderie among many staff members. Often on Friday afternoons, various staff members would get together to socialize. Though the point of these get togethers was social, many issues about children, learning, and school were discussed in an informal manner. Many of these informal gatherings prompted a more formal sense of direction for our own classrooms as well as our school.

Broadening Opportunities

During this time, the staff at New Suncook became very aggressive in seeking out any opportunity that might enhance our efforts to create a norm of inquiry about teaching and learning practices. While attending the second annual Southern Maine Partnership retreat in the summer of 1987, four members of the RIP team (three teachers and Gary MacDonald) were invited to participate in that fall's National Education Association's Symposium on School Based Reform in Minneapolis, which brought together educators from the National Network for School Renewal, from Sizer's Essential Schools project, and from NEA's Mastery Learning project. A focal activity of this symposium had participants engaged in defining what made their school unique—its goals, beliefs, standards, and reform efforts to date. Our representatives brought back a process called the Comprehensive School Reform Exercise, which was developed by the NEA Mastery in Learning project. For a year, our entire staff worked at staff meetings and in committee meetings to respond step-by-step, as our representatives had in Minneapolis, to this exercise. Teachers were asked to respond to statements involving teaching, learning, curriculum, and school culture, individually and then through discussion in dyads. If none of the statements reflected their beliefs, teachers were encouraged to write their own. The statements were then reviewed in the whole group until we reached some degree of consensus. It was torture for some, tedious for others, and exhilarating for a few. Countless revisions of goals and belief statements were presented to the staff and the discussion needed to reach consensus was intense and time consuming. Finally, we achieved a consensus that became our vision statement, a set of shared understandings that would be the basis for our practices. We discovered that building a true consensus can be very frustrating, particularly for those who judge success by a completed product, rather than by a productive, if incomplete, process.

Actually, two groups emerged from this process that we believe are really important for any change process in organizations. One group truly enjoyed grappling with the "big ideas," pondering where we might be in 5 years; the other group was eager to clarify implications for the here and now, so-what-do-we-do-today. Obviously, both emphases are needed for meaningful change, and we came to appreciate the contributions of each group to a balanced evolution. And, a product did emerge. The resulting New Suncook Vision Statement reads:

> Our goal is for children to attain knowledge and understanding that goes beyond school boundaries because learning takes place in any environment. Students and teachers share the responsibility for this learning.
>
> Students use their experiences and expertise and are given the opportunity to make choices within an effective learning environment. The teacher is a model and facilitator of children's learning within that environment.
>
> To create an effective learning environment, time is provided on a daily basis for teachers to collaborate and work individually. The curriculum is organized across integrated subject areas and based on specific student needs and interests. Opportunities are provided for children to learn as individuals or in various sized groups.
>
> Our curriculum provides children with the resources to become lifelong learners. Students apply thinking skills, acquire subject matter content, and develop confidence and positive attitudes toward learning.

Assessment decisions are based on a student's self-evaluation and the teacher's professional judgement.

Teaching decisions are based on a combination of valid and reliable research, common sense, and practical experience. All school staff relate on a professional level, formally and informally, with the continued growth of the school in mind. The responsibility of leadership belongs to all professionals within the school. Teachers and administrators assist each other in their own professional growth and with the education of children and the community. Communication between the home and the school occurs frequently.

The work that went into developing a concise and clearly idealized vision for our school left us both with a sense of satisfaction that we were able to agree on a mission that captured our varying perspectives and with a lingering question: How does our vision statement relate to the daily life in individual classroom, to the professional growth of our staff, and to the school's relationship to the larger community? Each of us was encouraged to explore what we might do to bring New Suncook a bit closer to our ideals. Along with this, it was also important for us to discuss that never are we all at the same stage of the change process. For some there need to be plateaus, for others retrenchment, and for still others these need to be more questions. The tensions that arose among people at various stages helped progress. While it may not have seemed so at the time, this was a good tension.

In 1988, those who were ready to move on applied again for and received support from the Maine Innovative grant program—this time to support the initiation of the MAGIC (multi-age grouping with integrated curriculum) class as a combined kindergarten-first grade program.

The kindergarten teacher (a member of the RIP team) and the first-grade teacher became concerned about district practices that were causing young children to be bussed beyond New Suncook School to the district Early Kindergarten and Transitional First Grade. The goal of the MAGIC class was to provide a developmentally appropriate early childhood program that was flexible enough to meet the individual needs of all children in their neighborhood school. The grant provided a para-educator to help during the first year of the program.

The following year, the program expanded to four classrooms that included a second grade as well as the full integration of special needs primary learners who had previously been served by a segregated composite room. The two additional teachers in the program were members of the RIP team, and one was the teacher who had been serving in the primary composite room. In addition to taking over one of the four K–2 multi-age classes, she continued to consult with colleagues regarding the learning plans and strategies needed to help the former composite-room youngsters succeed in the new hetero-geneous environment.

The multi-age classes were made up of 20 to 25 5- to 8-year-olds. Children were placed in a multi-age class in their kindergarten year and a child would remain in the same classroom and environment with the same teacher until she or he was ready for third grade (usually 3 years, in rare cases 4 years). Children in their kindergarten year would go home after 3 hours.

Mornings in a multi-age classroom, while the kindergartners were present, were spent sharing read-alouds, big books learning centers, concrete math activities, and investigative experiences that focused on an integrated theme of study (i.e., zoology, botany, astronomy). The second half of the day (after the kindergarten children went home) focused on individual literacy activities designed to meet the challenge level of each child. At this time of the day, children also continued working on investigative theme activities in cooperative groups, as well as problem solving and symbolic mathematical challenges. Throughout the day, children were actively engaged in hands-on experiences, movement, language, and cooperative learning.

Drawing from our own personal visions, from readings encountered through the RIP team and Southern Maine Partnership related to the developmental needs of young children, and from the teachers' experiences and values, six assumptions were articulated that lay the foundation for the multi-age classes. They are:

1. Children operate on variable biological and psychological time and not on uniform physical time.
2. Each child is unique with his or her own individual pattern of growth, individual personality, learning style, and family background.
3. All aspects of children's development are integrated—physical, social, emotional, cognitive, and aesthetic.
4. Children's learning is also integrated. They do not distinguish learning by subject area.
5. Primary-age children learn best through active participation with their learning environment.
6. Opportunities to make choices help children to gain independence in thinking, decision making, and problem solving.

These beliefs were presented, though no votes were necessary, to parents, other teachers, other administrators, and the school board. These groups supported the beliefs and were hard-pressed not to support the multi-age program that was the vehicle for putting these beliefs into practice.

Our six assumptions led us to include learners with identified special needs in our multi-age classes. The full inclusion of former resource-room children in the multi-age setting raised overall questions, all focused on the relative merits of such a "mainstreamed" environment for these learners. The reservations of the district's director of special education were an early challenge in this area. If students who were previously in a self-contained special education classroom were spread among four multi-age classrooms (as was our plan), the director wanted to be sure that the services provided by the existing special education teacher and para-educators would meet the identified needs of students. Not only did we have to sell our plan for delivery of services, but we also had to sell our belief that the inclusionary model would be an ideal to work toward for special education services. At this point, the special education staff had no clear vision of how services for students should ideally be provided, largely because the director of special education advocated that special education staff were first members of a school staff. Synthesizing the missions and practices of the six schools in our district made developing a coherent philosophy among the special education staff difficult. We were unsure how she felt about how "inclusive" services should be for special education students. Without the director's consent, this new model for special education services would not be possible in our school.

While at the time the need to work through the special education director appeared to be an obstacle, in reality it was quite productive because it caused us to think about and articulate more clearly what we were planning to do. Part of the problem was that the director was included in the process late—when we were beyond the concept stage and well into planning. Earlier discussions about beliefs of how special education students' needs should be met probably would have eased the tension. Our excitement with this new challenge and our strong belief in what we were doing made it hard for us to be patient with the change process, and to work with colleagues outside of our own school in order to make the change successful.

Another unanticipated resistance was from other special education teachers in the district who were sending children to our school. (Our school was the receiving school for special education students requiring more than 50% of their day receiving special education services.) Some of the concerns were voiced when placement of students was discussed. When a student was recommended for placement outside her or his community school, and then mainstreamed into a multi-age setting at New Suncook, the student entered a learning environment that many teachers perceived as being less structured than what the student was leaving. Some of these students were labeled behaviorally impaired, so how would a perceived less structured environment be appropriate?

Grapevinelike mechanisms where one might hear third- or fourth-hand what was happening in the primary classes were another problem. Attempts to address these "rumors" were made through explaining the plan to all of the staff involved. Again, part of the problem was in not involving them earlier in the process in an attempt to learn where their concerns lay and to build a common understanding before planning the structures. With the growing excitement of those staff members involved in the change at New Suncook, our belief in what we were doing became very strong, sometimes to the detriment of our listening carefully to the concerns of the resisters outside the school. We did realize, however, that though the meetings helped with communication, everyone's satisfaction could not be achieved before changes were made; those closest to the change continued to move forward.

Lauren Potter, one of the multi-age class teachers, examined how the belief system translated into daily life in her classroom as part of her master's degree program and concluded

> that our practices are matching our assumptions . . . although most of those assumptions were probably met in the individual graded classrooms that the teachers of the multi-age classes taught before the restructuring efforts. To justify a multi-age class as the optimum structure for early childhood education, one almost needs to look beyond the original six assumptions to two other factors that have emerged as a result of the study. The first factor is the positive modeling created in a multi-age structure. Children are learning from each other, receiving more support than a single teacher can ever give and reinforcing their knowledge by having so many opportunities to share it with others. The second factor is the cooperative, sharing, and noncompetitive environment that is created by putting children of varying levels together. No longer does being the best become important in a group where it is known from day one that everyone is a different age. Progress and growth become an individual issue rather than a comparative one.

The careful evaluation of the multi-age program did not end with the master's paper. Some time after her master's thesis was done, Lauren and her colleagues identified yet another factor considered important for their learners:

> The third factor is the consistency of the structure where young children work with the same teacher for 3 years, in the same environment for 3 years, and with two-thirds of their classmates remaining the same from year to year. The familiarity of the environment from year to year appears to instill confidence in the returning children and enhance their involvement in helping the younger entering students feel secure in the school setting.

The sentiment that good teaching means adapting to the learning needs of the child was not limited to the primary grades. A fifth-grade teacher commented:

I found my first year at New Suncook filled with a very supportive staff and administration. The school had an environment of academic freedom to do what was best for the students, not just what could be assessed easily. The environment was very close to the ideal school talked about in university education classes.

Alice Holt, another author of this study and a special educator with experience at other sites, verified this impression by reporting relative ease of delivery for special education support services within the regular classroom setting. She noted that teachers seemed willing to adapt to individual needs, simply because it was the right thing to do. Also noted were an increased emphasis on hands-on approaches to learning, as well as an emphasis on consciously developing learning strategies so that learners could take greater responsibility for their own learning.

Coincidental with all this, 1988–1989 was the year for construction on a needed, major expansion of the New Suncook School. Rather than defining as distraction the disruption of routine that construction necessarily entails, the faculty focused the children on learning about the demands of building—with the help of another Innovative Grant from Maine's Department of Education. The result was a whole-school project involving interviews and presentations with architects and various skilled workers, sketches and photographs of work-in-progress, and a publication—"Children, Construction, and Change, written and illustrated by students of the New Suncook Elementary School, copyright 1990."

Increasing the Momentum

The summer of 1989 brought another opportunity for us to consider together some implications of our vision statement in the form of an institute focused on the integrated curriculum. Nine of the twelve teachers of New Suncook's staff were able to take a week away from their summer responsibilities to participate. The institute was sponsored by the University of Maine at Orono and included staff working on integrated curriculum from the Upper Arlington School District in Ohio. Support from within the district came from the district Staff Development Committee. Teachers were able to write plans requesting funds for professional development opportunities that would help to further school goals. Since integrated curriculum was part of our vision statement and three-fourths of our staff was participating in this workshop, the requirement of the Staff Development Committee was easily met. Not only did the institute staff plan workshops sessions that included planning, implementing, and assessing work using an integrated curriculum, but ample time for theme and team planning within individual school teams was also allotted. This time was especially valuable for us because the energy and external attention devoted to the multiage primary effort during the school year had left us with a need to reestablish a sense of camaraderie and togetherness. Indeed, the "busyness" of our change efforts had sometimes had a disturbing, isolating effect, leaving us with the need to "get to know each other again." While the institute helped bring the nine of us a little closer, we again did not build in the time needed to include the teachers who did not attend the institute in the development of theme planning or integrated curriculum. The nine teachers who attended the institute embraced the notion of curriculum integration and developed a plan to pursue such integration. Once again, we had it all ready to go when the concept was presented at the beginning of the school year. And, again, this unintended but real exclusion from planning created some tension among the staff who had not attended the summer workshop. We were able to move ahead because we agreed that people could buy into the integrated theme for the school as much or as little as they wanted. Those who had participated in the summer institute provided individual support for colleagues when asked, and a theme sharing time was incorporated into each staff meeting.

As changes continued within the school, it became apparent that communicating with the larger community was also essential. Understanding that the education of children is necessarily an interactive process that involves the entire community as well as parents and teachers, we sought to develop a community-school partnership to enhance communication and the sense of common purpose, once again aided by Maine's Innovative Grant program. Our first application, in 1988, was not accepted because we needed a clearer focus. Given another year to clarify our goals for involving the community with the school, a second proposal, the Parent Educator Partnership, was accepted in spring 1989. The intent of the partnership was to create a foundation that promoted awareness and understanding between the school and the community.

The five areas targeted for this project included:

1. Assessing community feelings, perceptions, and understandings about schools, in general, and the educational programs at New Suncook, specifically
2. Identifying and communicating the experiences of children that exemplify our mission, and hence drive our practices
3. Eliciting voluntary and cooperative participation from parents and teachers in school-based qualitative research focused on issues of individual concerns
4. Developing methods and vehicles for regularly communicating with the larger community
5. Reassessing community feelings, perceptions, and understanding to determine consequences of our efforts

Under the guidance of a steering committee made up of community and school members, strategies were developed to meet the major goal of this grant: "To inform and utilize community resources to create support in the business and neighborhood communities of our education goals." During the summer of 1989, extensive interviews of randomly selected townspeople (recent graduates, parents, nonparents, retired persons, etc.) were conducted to ascertain their feelings, perceptions, and understandings about the educational programs at New Suncook. These interviews were coded and developed into a report used to help direct other parts of the grant.

A second part of the grant involved parents and teachers as researchers. With the guidance of Dr. Lynne Miller, a group of parents and teachers learned about research design, developed questions about educational practices for individual research, and collected and shared data. The excitement and benefits of parents and teachers sharing data, observations, and findings surpassed any of the participants' expectations.

As a result of information gained from interviews and the Parent/Teacher as Researcher project, a school-based Conference for Parents on educational and child development concerns was planned. The objective was to give parents the opportunity to gain a better understanding of what was happening in contemporary schools. It was held on a Saturday in April 1990 and consisted of Dr. Miller as keynote speaker and 10 choices of workshops related to various parts of school life. All of the teachers in the district were invited to submit proposals to present workshops with a pay enticement from the grant. Only teachers from New Suncook responded to the initial invitation. We then specifically asked some teachers from other schools in the district to present in areas of their expertise. Because of the positive responses from all attendees, a second Conference for Parents was held in November 1990 with some returning participants and many new registrants—this time partly supported by our local community and parents' organization.

Karen Johnson, another author of this study, took a leadership role in the development and evaluation of this school-community partnership project, and concluded that the efforts taken to involve parents were well worth the energy when parents did indeed participate. She concluded:

> We have just hit the tip of the iceberg in our efforts to develop a partnership between partners and educators. Each area targeted was instrumental in establishing a closer relationship with some part of the school community even though the number of people directly touched was small in relation to a district with over 800 children.

Perhaps most heartening about the Parent Educator Partnership effort were the attitudes of the parents who participated. After learning about the challenges of assessing learning and learning environments from Dr. Miller, and after collecting observational data to help assess the qualities of our classrooms, involved parents reported both an increased awareness of and appreciation for the complexities of classroom teaching.

Partnerships, grants, new grouping patterns, parental involvement, and even mission statements fail to capture the evolution. We hope they help convey some of the milestones that mark our journey. Naturally, the evolution is never-ending. Trying to capture and communicate this chronology reminds us that, with all our development and seeming successes, that we are left with the continuing challenge to become better at what we do. And, while we are pleased with the progress we have made, we also see challenges and problems remaining. The struggle we have begun and continue is not without costs. As we look back on the trail of events reported here, we are troubled that such a sequence of events may distort our experience with change—making it seem like a sequential series of steps ever higher on a ladder, rather than the more chaotic spiral that continues to spin a confusing array of peaks, valleys, and tensions. To convey our journey fairly we also need to address some of these tensions.

BARRIERS TO PROGRESS

Napoleon once said, "Go, sir, gallop, and don't forget that the world was made in six days. You can ask me for anything you like, except time." An elementary teacher's job is typically seen as time spent with children. Nearly all of the discussions about needed change, the grant writing, the partnership meetings, and the graduate classes came after school. Once the multi-age classes began, the only time during the school day that we had for planning or reflecting about out teaching, the time when "specials" such as art and music were taught, was devoted to team planning.

As our professional affiliations grew to include such regular evening activities such as Southern Maine Partnership meetings and graduate classes, our "extracurricular" activities like grant writing, data interpretation, presenting our experiences to fellow educators, and even case study writing grew as well. Thankfully, our families were understanding and supportive as our professional activities seemed to demand ever more time. The tension between the personal responsibility we take for the young learners in our classrooms and the need we feel for collaborative planning and reflection time with our colleagues is great. Many of us feel that the extra energy and effort it takes to prepare for a substitute teacher when we are released to plan or present is not justified by the gain. Moreover, we admit to a perhaps irrational sense of guilt when we "take off" for professional development. We have not yet resolved the tension between needing and wanting to spend time planning, and that of learning together as teachers. Collaboration takes time. Sometimes we feel that we have so much to do that some things are done poorly. Our "busyness" had definitely increased.

A second barrier arises as "insiders" and "outsiders" emerge. As we were successful in getting grants and making changes, notoriety followed. We had heard how some "school-within-a-school" programs had polarized faculties, and we met often as a faculty so that no one would feel excluded within our small elementary school. Perhaps, then, we should not have been surprised when some teachers from other elementary schools in the district referred to us as the "country club" school. While we did not see ourselves as very different from our colleagues throughout the district, the evidence of our activity—the grants and local publicity—seemed to set us apart, to distance us from colleagues in other schools. Perhaps because of our insider's perspective we did not realize that our norms had changed, that we were indeed "different." Somehow, "different" seemed to suggest to some others that we had become "superior" or "arrogant."

Adding new teachers to our faculty helped us to realize that our norms were unusual. Over the course of the past 7 years, we have added several new faculty members in the normal cycle of job turnover. Some have transferred to New Suncook from other district schools, while others have come to us from outside the district, but all were interviewed by our teachers and principal and all were aware of our renewal efforts before taking the job. With one exception, all have fit in well and contributed much to our collective development. We have tried to help orient each new teacher to our school, including conscientiously providing the focused attention of a support team of experienced teachers during the first 2 years (as Maine's induction procedure requires). However, even with such deliberate attention to orientation (or perhaps because of it), one of our new teachers was having serious difficulty with the time commitments set by the program and with the pressure to be collaborative. The time commitment issue involved preparation time and a daily schedule that had been developed before she arrived. In short, she decided not to come back after her first year, reporting: "It's just too much work. I can't do that." Apparently, some teachers who were not part of our development do not see the need that we do for the attention to, and communication about, the reasons for and consequences of our teaching practices—or, if they do, they feel that such expectations are too much to ask. As one teacher put it: "In reality, not many want to do the extra work all this 'involvement' takes."

While some new teachers have adjusted and added much to our school, even they (inevitably) lack the common history that has formed the conceptual foundation and the colleagueship of the veterans. We are forced to recognize that "growing together" does form some common understandings and bonds that contribute to the "insider" label. While we have taken active steps to involve other teachers and newcomers so as to diminish even the appearance of being "exclusionary," we have not always succeeded. The tension remains. The challenge to maintain our collegial support system remains.

Visitors to the school represent another type of "outsider." Individuals and the school as a whole welcome visitors. We are proud and eager to share. We thrive on sharing. But we have a stream of visitors from schools around the state, and, occasionally, even farther away. Contacts with other educators have evolved from our participation in the grant process, exposure through work-shops, and participation in a staff development video series. Many of these people want to see our program firsthand. Visits occur on average twice a week, with visitors often staying all day. Generally we are congenial but facets of these visits grate on us after a while. They take time and attention away from the children. Some visitors seem oblivious to the problem and appear to think nothing of asking for attention or copies of materials in the midst of what is obviously work time. Our responsibilities to our learners sometimes collide with our genuine desire to be cordial hosts.

Another barrier clearly related to the insider/outsider tension is the difference between our perceptions of our accomplishments and challenges and the perceptions of those who visit us. Because we were so involved in the grad-ual evolution of our change process and have shared decision making along the way, our changes are truly "ours." When others talk about what we have done, the focus always seems to be on the visible consequences, the evolving products, and not on the exploration and discussion process that brought us here. Visitors seem to see multi-age classrooms, or parent involvement, or theme-focused learning without grasping the process of self-scrutiny and gradual change that led to them. We worry that they want to transplant the product but will over-look the process. We see the process, as slow and sometimes frustrating as it can be, as the soil that nourishes the varied products that grow here. We believe that attempting to transplant any of our projects into a school that has not bro-ken ground with self-examination and deliberate mission setting is unlikely to succeed.

Alas, we do realize the difficulty—as previously discussed—in making time for creating structured opportunities for the collective self-scrutiny and collaborative team building that we believe is vital for continued development. Some of our visitors may see us as cold or unreceptive because (as we see it) we are often too busy to chat, too rushed to be hospitable. Indeed, we ourselves find little time to engage in the kinds of general discussions that characterized some of our earlier meetings because current meetings are often focused on current projects. We see a need now for a retreat, to create a time and structure for us to regroup and reconsider. Though we see and talk about the need, we have not yet scheduled such a retreat. Even when one recognizes the necessity of the process, one does not always act on the recognition. To be sure, tensions remain for us. We suspect they will always be here. So far, we feel fortunate that we maintain the collective energy to face these tensions and take on new challenges. In retrospect, we believe there are some keys to our ability to maintain this energy.

PERSONAL AND ORGANIZATIONAL LEARNING

The strength of our leadership has been crucial for our change process. Gary MacDonald, our building principal for the past 8 years, has been a tremendous asset for us. He seems to view leadership as a commodity to be exercised by every conscientious citizen. He expects teachers to lead, and he expects teachers to help younger learners to learn to lead. He leads by example. He raises important questions, persists in seeking solutions, puts the best interest of the kids first, models respect in disagreement, and actively and visibly considers perspectives and opinions other than his own. He does not walk on water, but his efforts have been recognized by the National Association of Elementary School Principals, which named him Maine's Distinguished Principal of the Year for 1991. His leadership has both prompted our careful examination of our ideals and our practices, and provided us with encouragement and latitude to follow our ideals with well-considered steps and experiments.

Gary has maintained the difficult balance between knowing when and how hard to push in different areas. This balance became very apparent when he assumed the supervision of a second school after a budget cut. The staff there assumed that he would come with a preconceived agenda that would force their school into being a replica of New Suncook. His first and only year there was spent in developing in the staff the necessary confidence in themselves as professionals to ask themselves the questions: "What are we doing?" and "Why?" Although to an outside observer dynamic change may not have been apparent, the groundwork for establishing a trusting environment was being set.

Another indication of Gary's leadership is the subtle yet powerful shift in the focus of staff meetings. The norm of predominantly administratively oriented staff meetings shifted to meetings concerned primarily with learning issues. It's hard to know how influential the seeds of shared ideas were in our evolution, but the focus on children's learning certainly seemed pervasive.

While we honor Gary for his unique and invaluable contribution, we recognize that no one person could provide complete "leadership" for a group of independent thinkers. We equate leadership with assuming responsibility for getting things done, and we have all done that. Moreover, we hope that our view of a learning environment as expressed in our vision statement fairly captures this view of leadership as a function of shared responsibility and of conscientious self-evaluation. We think it does. The challenge for all of us is to model our convictions about leadership as well as Gary does.

Often and unfairly overlooked is the role of the superintendent. Our development began when Dick Card, an administrator with a clear emphasis on educational renewal, was our superintendent. He hired Gary, and clearly established a priority for professional development. When he left the district in 1987 to work with Maine's Department of Education, Rufus Ansley, an administrator who sees his function as more managerial, succeeded him as superintendent. While the change in emphasis did not disrupt the growth we had begun, it did alter Gary's function of linking the school's direction and activities to that of the larger district. Gary's commitment to professional renewal helped assure the consistency of support through what otherwise might have been a more disconcerting change of district leadership. If the change of superintendents had resulted in less support than Mr. Ansley has shown for our efforts, or if the building principal had lacked Gary's ability to adjust to the change in administration, we may well have been frustrated in our development.

The sense of community among our staff has been another key in our story. Although there is always tension between autonomy and coordination, we recognize that until we find the one "right" way to do things (which most of us suspect is akin to discovering the Holy Grail on the playground), each of us will teach differently. As long as each of us evaluates her or his own efforts in terms of both the expected and unexpected consequences for the learners we serve, we respect differences in approach. This focus on learner benefits coupled with respect for varying approaches provides common purpose, which is the foundation for our community of learners. We surely disagree on "how" things should be done, but we try to view these disagreements as opportunities for us to experiment and learn. As we try to model respectful communication of differing perceptions and opinions, we hope to lead by example.

So involved in your own ideas, it's hard to hear others. . . was common when we started and is still there. Personality or personal investment is the new—Where are you in the change process?

Finally, our growth has both led to and been aided by outside affiliations. Whether through our interactions with the Southern Maine Partnership or the Western Maine School Improvement Project, through various graduate courses and professional workshops, or just through professional reading, we have found the ideas and perspectives of educators in other settings invaluable. They enable us to clarify and refine our own ideas, not just because we have found other educators' ideas worthy but also because there is an energizing effect in the sharing of enthusiasm and hope among caring teachers.

Our course for the future can be plotted by exploring several questions that form the puzzles we are currently exploring. For instance, how can we better assess and document the benefits of our "growth" for our young learners? We all "sense" that things are better. How do we know this? Whether we believe that youngsters are happier, or better problem solvers, or more cooperative, or just that they read more, how do we justify our belief? We need to improve our documentation of meaningful learning gains, if for no other reason than to help each learner recognize and take legitimate pride in his or her accomplishments.

What can we do to minimize the "insider/outsider" tension within the school district? So far most of our energies have been focused on New Suncook School. While we have invited teachers from other schools to participate in several of our efforts, such as the Parent Educator Partnership, and have been contributing to regular districtwide committees, we want to and see the need to expand our professional community to include teachers in other schools. Our district has volunteered to serve as a professional development site for the University of Southern Maine's Extended Teacher Education Program, and we will collaborate in the preparation of new teachers next year. We hope this will provide the opportunity for more cross-district interaction.

How do we better orient new teachers (or a new principal) to our "evolved" state? We have not yet solved how to orient new teachers who have not had the luxury of developing along with us veterans, and wonder how a new principal might affect our momentum. Clearly we need to develop better ways of initiating newcomers.

Finally, how can we make time for keeping in touch with each other? As suggested earlier, we have become so busy that it is difficult to make time to discuss our ideas and problems with one another. In what seems to be a cruel paradox, we began by sharing ideas and convictions, which brought us closer together and spurred us to try some things which, in turn, led us to try other things. All of these things succeeded at least well enough to lead us to try still other things. Trying all these new ideas has taken so much time that we seldom discuss and collectively reflect—and, consequently, we suspect we are growing apart. However, if organizational change is like an inchworm, which after stretching needs to contract and bring itself together before stretching again, then perhaps we are stretched as far as we can go and need to collect ourselves before trying to go further. Indeed, coming together to write this case study has provided us with the structure for discovering the commonly perceived needs prompting these questions about next steps. Perhaps making the time to discuss and draft our story should become a regular part of our process. Remember, we strongly believe that change is a process, not an event.

NOTES

1. The Southern Maine Partnership is a consortium of 26 school districts, the Maine College of Education, and the University of Southern Maine. New Suncook School was active in the inception of the partnership in 1986.

2. In the winter of 1988, New Suncook School was involved in a Teacher Exchange Project with the F. B. Miller School in La Palma, California. This connection enabled us to observe, experience, and discuss the common and uncommon problems of educational change in schools that are actively pursuing the notion of school renewal. We exchanged policies, curriculum, and teaching strategies in a partnership that crossed wide geographic differences and found that there were many similarities.

3. One of the initiatives of Maine's Educational Reform Act of 1984 was the Innovative Educational Grants Program. This program encouraged teachers to work with their colleagues to plan new strategies for improving curriculum and instructional practices in Maine schools. Innovative grants were available on a competitive basis to teachers, schools, and school systems. Classroom-based grants were awarded for proposals submitted by individual teachers. School-based grants were awarded on a matching funds basis to schools or school systems. In the first 4 years of funding, grants were awarded in excess of $4 million. Sadly, Maine's fiscal woes have taken their toll on this program that we found so helpful. While the grant program still exists, its present funding is less than 25% of what it was in the 1980s.

4. Barth, R. (1980). *Run School Run* (p. 147). Cambridge, MA: Harvard University Press.

Chapter 8

Policy for Restructuring

Linda Darling-Hammond

The work of school restructuring has changed and deepened over the last 10 years, as these case studies illustrate. A decade ago, schools were immersed in the "higher standards" rhetoric of *A Nation at Risk,* which was translated into a plethora of curriculum and testing mandates aimed at doing better what has been done for over 80 years in our industrial-age schools (Darling-Hammond 1990, 1993). Now, however, rather than just "trying harder," schools are re-inventing teaching and learning, roles and responsibilities, and relationships with parents and communities, so that they can help a greater range of students learn more powerfully and productively.

The school(s) described in this volume are in the business of transforming schooling and teaching in important ways. They are focusing on more challenging and exciting kinds of learning than last decade's "back to the basics" classrooms allowed, helping students to actively construct, use, and generate their own knowledge. And they are finding new ways to reach diverse learners more effectively, creating structures and strategies to meet students on their own terms with a wide range of approaches to support their success—strategies ranging from multi-age grouping to multi-year team-teaching arrangements to pedagogy aimed at the development of multiple intelligences.

If they are to survive and deepen, these changes in schooling and teaching also require new approaches to policy, including new methods for evaluating learning, greater supports for teacher knowledge, and more responsive and learner-centered school organizations. In contrast to the bureaucratic accountability mechanisms used for many decades to enforce standardization of schooling procedures, policies will need to support individually appropriate teaching strategies and responsive forms of school organization that can produce success for diverse learners. Reallocations of educational resources are also needed so that adequate learning opportunities are available for adults as well as children, and resources are directed to where they are most needed—the front lines of teaching and learning.

All of these issues surface in the case studies. In particular, the case studies help us understand the kinds of policy supports needed to encourage the participation, learning, and risk taking that are essential for stimulating and sustaining learner-centered teaching and schooling. The case studies also illuminate the existing obstacles posed by some state and district policies, while they suggest how new negotiations of responsibility and approaches to accountability may be developed. Finally, they illustrate how schools can become learning organizations, committed to and capable of continued improvement on behalf of their students.

POLICY SUPPORTS FOR RESTRUCTURING

Among this decade's changes are early efforts to create supportive state and local policies that facilitate rather than obstruct the invention of learner-centered schools. Though these have emerged at glacier speed, the case studies describe several ways in which state and local policies were able to provide some concrete supports for school restructuring.

Most of these would be classified as capacity-building policies. For example, Maine's Innovative Educational Grants Program, which invites locally designed proposals for revising classroom and school practices, helped to establish the "research into practice (RIP) team at New Suncook School (Chapter 7). When the team received a second year of funding from the state, it was able to deepen its inquiry, asking "what are we doing and why?" by examining educational research, launching regular peer observation, and convening professional conversations throughout the school. A third-year proposal was also funded. This one supported the initiation of multi-age classes using integrated curriculum. This policy strategy acknowledges the importance of continuing support for work that derives from local needs and ideas. It is an approach that builds on the understanding that engaging faculties in inquiry about their own practice is the most promising approach for stimulating deep and lasting change (Darling-Hammond & Ancess, 1994; Lieberman & Miller, 1990; Little, 1993).

Maine also funds coalitions of educators around the state to work collectively to make meaningful changes in their schools. The Western Maine School Improvement Team included six teachers, the principal, and the superintendent from New Suncook, who joined teachers and administrators from other districts in conferences and other learning opportunities aimed at thinking through change. This was yet another stimulus for establishing what the staff called a "norm of inquiry" about teaching and learning practices. Out of these activities grew efforts to conceive and begin working on a vision of a learning environment that includes shared student and teacher responsibility for developing active, integrated learning experiences connected to student needs and interests.

District-level policies in support of shared decision making—especially as these helped deepen staff learning and incentives for participation—were important backdrops for several of the other schools. Brooksville Elementary (Chapter 4) undertook its reforms in the context of a districtwide shared decision making project. Though the project was guided by "high hopes and vague guidelines," which were layered on a somewhat troubled school context, progress was made because of the capacity-building initiatives the district also provided. These included core group training in shared decision making for school-based teams, as well as the provision of two facilitators to assist Brooksville staff in learning how to communicate and reach consensus. These were critical elements in transforming old habits and patterns of behavior and helping to build new ways of working and communicating among staff. An additional support was the formative evaluation funded by the district for several schools. By surfacing concerns and problems so that they could be addressed, the evaluation process enabled greater understanding and growth for those undertaking tough changes.

District-supported team training was a key element in Hammond, Indiana (Chapter 5), and the Wheeler School in Jefferson County, Kentucky (Chapter 2), as well. In both places, district-funded professional development academies had been created to provide new avenues for problem-oriented, staff-led, and school-based learning and inquiry. The Hammond Leadership and Professional Development Academy offered a structured, 12-month professional development program for school-based teams. This program walked them through a process of considering reasons and possibilities for change, school-based assessment of needs, development of vision and consensus, and, finally, assistance for program development.

Hammond undertook other fundamental policy shifts in governance and authority, negotiating new allocations of responsibility between schools and the central office, between administrators and teachers, and among members of the school community at each site. These are so extensive and so important to an understanding of how districts must restructure themselves to support learner-centered schools that they are treated in a separate section below.

Like Hammond, the changes at Wheeler School were supported by district-level policies aimed at both capacity-building and system-changing. In Jefferson County, the district's creation of the Gheens Professional Development Academy in the mid-1980s stimulated a number of school-based change efforts. One of these, an ongoing seminar for a consortium of educators from 24 schools across the county, was aimed at developing professional development schools. Their investigations into educational research, reform ideas, current practices, and barriers also led to an effort to create consensus on a vision for schooling, learning, and professional practice. This vision was differently enacted in each of the 24 schools, but supported in all cases by the professional development resources and network of the Gheens Academy, which extend in a variety of ways to all schools in the district.

Whitford notes that the early sessions offered by the academy "emphasized the need for those expected to implement educational change to be involved in its design." She also notes that because this expectation from the Gheens leadership was contrary to the normal top-down mandates of the past, it was initially uncomfortable and confusing for many school faculties. Nonetheless, it was because of this uncomfortable insistence on local design that the Gheens professional development efforts ultimately produced much greater commitment and capacity for change in local schools.

This is a critical issue for the development of policy in support of restructuring, and one that is difficult for many policy makers as well. The tendency of educational policy makers over recent decades has been to assume little knowledge, capacity, or ethical commitment on the part of school faculties, and to prescribe practices accordingly—to specify precisely what schools should do and how they should do it. Although many of these prescriptions conflict with one another and are frequently grounded in misunderstandings about how students learn well and how good teaching occurs, the top-down approach is comforting to policy makers because it preserves the illusion of control and provides a pretense of accountability.

The problems of such top-down prescriptions for practice are now more fully appreciated (Darling-Hammond, 1990a, 1993; Elmore, 1983; McLaughlin, 1987; Shulman, 1983). In addition to the fallacy of hierarchical intelligence—the flawed presumption that policies made at higher levels in the system will be "smarter" or better informed than those made at other sites for decision making (Darling-Hammond, 1994)—there is also the irreducible problem that the complex, contextually different determinants of good practice and of strategies for change cannot be accounted for in the monolithic approach standardizing policies require.

Instead, policies must find ways to build the capacity of local actors to make good decisions on behalf of their unique students and communities—to support their development of knowledge about good practices, their ability to analyze and respond to problems and needs, and their incentives for being collectively responsive and responsible to the children and communities they serve. This is precisely what the capacity-building policies in these districts, along with the state of Maine, are accomplishing. By creating new places for and forms of professional development that support "bottom-up" learning—and by doing it in a way that creates lasting institutions that can be counted on to continue this work—these policy makers have begun to build a new paradigm for stimulating and supporting school change.

Furthermore, by focusing professional development on inquiry into teaching and learning (rather than the transmission of canned techniques or the implementation of newly prescribed texts, tests, or management and governance structures), they have helped to focus attention on the outcomes of real changes for children and their learning. This also turns out to be a key lesson for supporting productive, long-lasting, and ultimately transformative work on school change.

THE IMPORTANCE OF A LEARNER-CENTERED FOCUS FOR RESTRUCTURING

A subtext illustrated by the case studies is how important a clear focus on learners and learning is for real progress to occur in the difficult work of restructuring. It has become fashionable recently, as it inevitably does with all reforms, to claim that, with respect to restructuring, "everyone's doing it" but "nobody knows what it is." The reason for this recurring reform confusion is that as ideas spread they become adopted and translated in ways that dilute a clear understanding of purpose as it is connected to strategy. As complex, interconnected notions often become oversimplified, schools are often asked to adopt techniques without reference to their goals and to use the ideas of others without reference to their own ideas and felt needs. Without a connection to local goals and needs, efforts at change are necessarily superficial, failing to reach far enough into the organization's workings and deeply enough into the understandings of participants to really transform thinking and practice.

One thing is clear: serious restructuring depends on knowing *why* you're seeking change and what it is supposed to mean for children and their learning. The "why" is initially much more important than the "what" or "how," as it guides and motivates collective efforts so that they remain authentic and focused on learners, rather than becoming subsumed by gimmicks or techniques that eventually lose the force of moral commitment. In fact, the "triumph of technique over purpose" is a frequent refrain in school reform efforts across the ages. When this occurs—when menus of reform tactics overwhelm authentic inquiry aimed at finding contextually useful ways to serve students well—lots of schools get engaged in trying new organizational or teaching technologies that lose coherence, that focus on implementation rather than problem solving and invention, and that consequently fail to transform teaching, learning, and schooling.

At Fredericks Middle School (Chapter 3), Bondy suggests that some of the initial difficulty in making progress on a serious restructuring agenda may have been due to the initial focus of the county's shared decision making program on *procedures* rather than *purpose*. This early focus, according to Bondy, "denied people the opportunity to consider the purposes of the project." It also focused attention on the divisive questions of who would be allowed to make which decisions, rather than on what people in the school wanted to do that could be facilitated by a governance group or team. Starting with governance procedures alone is not a sufficient basis for transforming teaching and learning (Lieberman, Darling-Hammond, & Zuckerman, 1991). If turf struggles among adults absorb the faculty's attention, a candid look at what's working for kids does not soon emerge.

By contrast, schools that started by examining teaching and learning, inquiring into good practice, and questioning how their practices were working for students were able to make serious inroads into positive changes for learners much more quickly. The inquiry-based work at New Suncook School in Maine has transformed teaching, learning, and student success in remarkable ways in a remarkably short time. Indicators of similar transformations are suggested by the statements of teachers at Keels Elementary (Chapter 6), Wheeler School, and in Hammond, Indiana, where a focus on school and classroom work aimed at heightening student success is apparent. As Smylie and Tuermer note, "From the very beginning, restructuring in Hammond has been framed as an issue of student learning. . . . The emphasis on students, the 'mantra' of the district administration, and the teachers' union may have promoted progress by providing a focus that transcends individuals and institutional self-interests."

The nature of the mandate for change as well as the nature of the process for change are both important. Wheeler's learner-centered focus on "expecting the best, producing success," for example, has shaped a radically different learning environment—where students are now deeply engaged in and excited about learning and teachers feel they can create success for each of their students. This is supported by the learning-centered vision statement staff initially worked through for their school, and by the internal ownership of the change process the school has been able to develop. Educators have the flexibility, the authority, and the intrinsic motivation to make change; consequently, the focus of their work is on making changes to improve their success with students, not to satisfy a state or district procedural mandate. Two remarks from staff are most telling:

> Change doesn't come naturally. You've got to work very hard. You've got to change virtually everything you used to do. In going to a reform situation, it's going to test all your abilities, all your resources, but most of the pressure comes from inside you. It's the pressure you put on yourself to make a better program, rather than from the outside.

> I think the reason Wheeler teachers may have difficulty talking about barriers is that they've immediately changed something that hasn't worked.

If something's a barrier they discarded it and try something else. Things that don't work aren't kept around long enough to be barriers.

Policies that enable this kind of local ownership to take hold, and that stay out of the way of student-centered decision making so that barriers can be discarded, are what is needed. Unfortunately, many policies, even well-intentioned efforts that march under the banner of school restructuring or reform, continue to create roadblocks to good practice and school development by misunderstanding the process of change and the critical importance of local engagement.

POLICY OBSTACLES TO RESTRUCTURING

With the exception of New Suncook in Maine (a state which has historically had little top-down regulation of schools), each of the schools described in this book continues to struggle with the effects of unhelpful state policies that slow or distort their efforts and prevent a complete transformation of practice. Some of these are familiar, such as the state standardized testing policies that continue to deflect time and attention from more authentic forms of learning. Berry notes of Keels Elementary in South Carolina, "In spite of the teachers' continuing quest to go deeper into subject matter, curricular revisions still focus 'on covering more content before (spring) testing.'" The state's testing program, linked to monetary incentives for schools, has slowed curriculum transformations aimed at helping students acquire deeper understanding of ideas. The incentives in fact operate to continue traditional forms of teaching that emphasize superficial understanding and rote learning rather than higher order thinking and performance skills. In Hammond, too, state education policy is viewed as a barrier. The statewide standardized testing system, linked both to student progress reporting and to school accreditation, has "posed potential threats to creativity and innovation at the school level."

Nearly all of the schools described in this volume have begun to educate students not only in more exciting and intellectually challenging ways but in more heterogeneous groupings as well. Their faculties' growing ability to find entry points into the intelligences of all children is part of their success at building energetic, socially democratic learning communities. However, some policies continue to work in the other direction. State and district directives for gifted and talented education, for example, are a problem for Keels Elementary School in South Carolina. In the face of incentives and requirements to "segregate students by so-called ability levels," Berry reports, "Keels's staff has consciously chosen to group its gifted and talented students in the least blatant way and has gone to considerable length to mitigate any negative effects of academic differences amongst students." Though working around such policies is to some extent possible, policy makers continue to send mixed messages about whether all children can learn challenging material and whether only some deserve an enriched curriculum as a vehicle to that material.

Kentucky has begun a process of overhauling its standardized testing system, moving to a system of performance-oriented assessments that is intended to support more meaningful and challenging forms of teaching and learning. This is a mixed blessing because the state's approach is substantially top-down and will soon be tied to high stakes for students and schools, with little room for adaptations to meet the real needs of nonstandardized students (Darling-Hammond & Ancess, 1994).

Though the Kentucky Education Reform Act (KERA) has created a climate for change in the state, it was not the stimulus for change at Wheeler, which began earlier. Although some of KERA's emphasis is compatible with Wheeler's already-launched changes, a number of the state's mandates have created obstacles rather than supports to school-based changes aimed at the needs of students. One of these is a state mandate requiring mixed-age primary programs, an example of a well-intentioned but overzealous and ultimately counterproductive policy that takes what is viewed as an often-beneficial practice and prescribes it in ways that immediately become problematic for the very children it seeks to serve. In some schools across the state, the policy has wreaked havoc with schools where faculty and parents are not ready to work with or send students to such heterogeneous groups, leading to failed practice and flight to private schools in some places. At Wheeler, the basic precept of mixed-age grouping is not problematic. Such efforts had already begun and commitment and knowledge about how to practice in this way was being built. However, the state mandate requires including kindergartners in the primary program, a policy about which many thoughtful early childhood educators could reasonably disagree, given the developmental needs of young children below the age of 6 or 7. Whitford capsulizes these concerns:

> Wheeler is complying but not without concerns. Some believe that 5-year-olds need more play time than their older primary classmates. Others express concern over the fact that the state currently only funds kindergarten for a half-day program. Under these circumstances, including 5-year-olds with older children in the primary program who attend all day further confounds teachers' planning problems. Bush says, "It's a Solomon-like decision that must be made. Either leave the child with the mother or put them in school all day."

Though some concerns are typically dismissed by policy makers as signs of local "resistance," they are really signs of educators taking seriously their professional responsibility to do what is best for children. This example is just one of hundreds that could be cited that reveal the problems created for children and parents by people very far from their lives and local schools who cannot appreciate the nuances of fashioning good educational environments for children who differ in their needs.

Kentucky came late to the recognition that supports for learning are more important for real improvement than are directives for changes that, though more ostensibly learner-centered, are nonetheless prescriptions that ignore the variability in local contexts and student needs. In the early years of implementing KERA, there was no systematic attempt to invest in teacher knowledge or in school development. Virtually all of the state's energy was devoted to implementing new mandates. As a consequence, many educators still do not know how to do well what the legislation would have them undertake, and the prospect of new mandates as a response to problems in the field is ever-heightened. This misunderstanding is one that continues to create more policy obstacles to restructuring than there are yet supports.

It's worth taking time to understand this problem as it is one common to "old paradigm" policy making, and it poses a dilemma that must be resolved differently in policies of the future. Though the policy seeks a presumably "modern" approach to education, it uses old tools—a top-down prescription for practice—to achieve its result. The dilemma is that this policy strategy prevents local educators from making decisions that may be more developmentally, contextually, or individually appropriate, and locks everyone into a "one best system" solution that invariably turns out not to work ideally in many cases, sometimes undermining its own goals. In addition, this approach does not build the capacity of local educators to deepen their knowledge, so that they can engage new practices and design new programs effectively. Indeed, in the past, such mandates have often had to be repealed when problems in the field led to the conclusion that "we tried that and it didn't work." This adds to the cynicism of educators and the public about school reform.

What would be an alternative to this kind of policy making? If Kentucky were to invest in initial preparation and ongoing professional development programs that, for example, taught teachers how to engage in multiage teaching and enabled them to examine firsthand a range of successful program strategies, practice would begin to build in ways that would ultimately be more successful, more skillful and responsive to students, and more capable of local adaptation than a simplistic mandate allows. If school accreditation processes also encouraged such practice, schools would have incentives to develop it. Successfully building teacher and school capacity is a strong long-range alternative to the prescriptive policy mandate, which at its best can serve as "an axe but not a scalpel" (Green, 1983) for reform.

Similar problems surfaced in many of the other schools, where states and districts have with one hand given schools the authority for rethinking practice, while holding tight to existing mandates with the other. Florida, long a state that has highly regulated policy for education, is caught in the contradiction. As a consequence, teachers at Fredericks Middle School believe that state and district officials do not really support the shared decision making (SDM) process they have launched. Bondy notes that "officials claim to support SDM but send mandate after mandate to the schools with which schools are expected to comply immediately. Rather than feeling empowered by SDM, teachers who believe their change efforts are neither recognized nor supported feel frustrated and powerless." When efforts to implement new school schedules or staffing arrangements are bounced up to the district and often the state and then vetoed, cynicism and a decline in motivation are inevitable.

It is clear that policy makers have as much need to revise their practice as educators have to rethink theirs. As we develop new possibilities for policy, it will be important to create strategies that build strong guarantees of knowledge and competence among educators so that policy makers feel comfortable that they can be entrusted with greater decision-making authority. In addition, it will be important to replace prescriptions for practice with negotiated responsibility for practice—defining new vehicles for accountability that keep everyone's "eyes on the child" (Jervis, in press), rather than on rules and procedures.

RENEGOTIATING RESPONSIBILITY

One of the fundamental problems of school restructuring is how to reconfigure who is responsible—and ultimately accountable—for what. There is wide agreement, theoretically at least, that restructuring schools for more responsive practice requires that decisions about the uses of many school resources must be made by faculty, principals, and parents to ensure that these address community needs and local problems. At the same time, there are legitimate concerns about safety, legality, and equity in student treatment that must be attended to, alongside the administration of dozens of federal, state, and local programs, each with its own rules and regulations. Districts have some obligations to fulfill, though there is plenty of room to delegate responsibility and authority. Obviously, for all of these concerns to be fully managed at the school level, care must be taken to ensure that the capacity exists in schools to attend to the various ramifications of individual and collective decisions.

The nature of the problem to be solved is increasingly clear. In large school bureaucracies, authority for decisions and responsibility for practice have become widely separated, usually by many layers of hierarchy. Boards and top-level administrators make decisions; teachers, principals, and students are responsible for carrying them out. This makes accountability for results hard to achieve. When the desired outcomes of hierarchically imposed policies are not realized, policy makers blame the school people responsible for implementation; practitioners blame their inability to devise or pursue better solutions on the constraints of policy. No one can be fully responsible for the results of practice when authority and responsibility are disconnected from one another. When authority is removed from the school, so is accountability for learning.

Furthermore, when authority for decision making is far removed from practitioners and is regulatory in nature, change comes slowly. The negative consequences for students cannot be quickly remedied while edicts hang on, immune from the realities of school life and protected by the forces of inertia, lobbies, and constituencies both inside and outside the bureaucracy. The amount of effort and influence required to change a school system policy is so great that most teachers, principals, and parents find it impossible to deflect their energies from their primary jobs to the arduous and often unrewarding task of moving the behemoth. They sigh and strive to cope, looking for loopholes that might allow unobtrusive alternatives to grow.

Thus, adjustments in programs, course requirements, schedules, staffing, and materials to meet the needs of students are difficult to make; the knowledge of school staff about more productive alternatives is not used; and time is deflected from teaching to paperwork, monitoring, and reporting systems. Even where flexibility might exist, the pressures for conformity are so strong that principals and teachers are often afraid to test the limits of the regulatory structure. The end result is that when problems are identified, practitioners feel they cannot challenge the status quo. Eventually a general acceptance of the failings of the system comes to prevail, and cynicism overwhelms problem-solving initiatives by principals, teachers, and parents.

It is this situation that shared decision making and site-based management seek to change. However, as schools begin to make decisions, problems of regulation and dilemmas of responsibility necessarily arise. These were noted in almost all the case studies in this volume and were most prominent in Hammond, Indiana, probably because site-based decision making had made the most progress there and thus began to get at core issues of schooling. Hammond's problems and the system's response are instructive because they point toward the kinds of changes in district governance and management needed to support school restructuring.

In Hammond, initial concerns arose when schools developed plans that seemed to conflict with state or district regulations for which waivers had not been sought. Guidelines and procedures were tightened. The flash point came when the school board overturned the decisions of two local school teams that the district viewed as having committed the greatest bureaucratic sin of all—a failure to follow procedures. These schools' efforts to develop a new foreign language curriculum in one case and a new grade-reporting system in the other had strong faculty support and did not violate regulations. However, as Smylie and Tuermer note, "the board concluded that the teams began implementation without properly following district review and approval procedures."

Clearly, the board's rejection of school plans at that juncture and for such nonsubstantive reasons was deeply troubling to teachers and administrators. The crisis of confidence that ensued led to their very productive rethinking of the process and the relationships among various actors in the district. The result was a new plan for school-based restructuring that renegotiated responsibility at each level of the system. The new plan enabled and obligated schools to institute their own accountability processes for planning and implementing change, thus they would not have to rely solely on the district to decide whether rules would be followed. The Core Team at the school assumed responsibility for ensuring compliance with planning processes, monitoring the use of funds, and reporting on activities in a way that would allow early identification of potential regulatory conflicts so that they could be resolved.

Meanwhile, the plan placed the central office in the role of supporter and coplanner rather than overseer and potential spoilsport. Based on documentation submitted by core teams and conversations with schools *during* planning, central staff could provide general advice, identify regulatory conflicts, and help teams obtain waivers. The relationship between the two levels of governance was fashioned as more collegial and less hierarchical. In addition, the plan provided that if these provisions were carried out, the school board could not overturn local school planning decisions. The plan enabled legitimate responsibilities to be attended to in two ways: by more clearly delegating substantial responsibility to schools for careful planning and monitoring of their own work and by creating mechanisms that allowed central office staff to ensure that their own responsibilities could be carried out *as collaborators with schools* rather than as adversaries.

Finally, stability was enhanced by incorporating school restructuring into teachers' contracts. The contract running from 1990 through 2001 institutionalized restructuring by defining it as part of the teachers' and the board's responsibilities. It also reinforced the notions of collegial responsibility built into the new shared decision making plan by removing the union's building representative from between teachers and administrators, forcing "teachers and administrators to work through problems together during the planning process rather than passing them to building representatives for adversarial resolution after decisions were made." The focus of restructuring work has turned to collective problem solving rather than relying so heavily on the more rigid, traditional systems of adversarial checks and balances.

Other states and districts could profit from this strategy. The problems that initially occurred in Hammond are not at all unusual. All across the country, schools seeking to restructure—often at the rhetorical urging of states or districts—find themselves constrained by the fact that the bureaucracies above them have not themselves restructured. Denials of waivers, often with little or no rationale, and the continuation of regulatory business as usual threaten to strangle useful innovation, while breeding cynicism about the intentions of "higher up" policy makers. Findings ways to renegotiate responsibility so that schools, districts, and states are colleagues in reform will be a critical task over the next decade.

STRUCTURING SUPPORTS FOR PARTICIPATION, LEARNING, AND INQUIRY

The work in Hammond, Indiana illustrates something else: It's one thing to engender enthusiasm, good intentions, and even action around school restructuring, it's another to actually build new structures that allow those good intentions to take root and flourish over the long haul. If policies are the scaffolding upon which schools are built, they must begin to actively enable the kinds of ongoing opportunities for shared work, learning, and continual inquiry that restructuring requires.

Structuring Participation for Ownership.

The model for participation required for school restructuring is a democratic one rather than the representative model traditionally used. In the representative approach, a small number of teachers or parents may sit on a committee for selecting textbooks or reviewing policy or making decisions. Then those decisions are "handed down" to everyone else in the district or school who has not had a chance to participate in the process. In the past, analysts have sometimes noted that those to whom such representatively constructed policies are sent often feel they did not have a voice, and have not "bought in" to the outcome. However, little effort has yet been made to figure out other approaches to structuring decision making and participation. Most existing policies for shared decision making continue the idea of a small, representative committee making decisions for the school, without anticipating the need for broader participation in the committee's work both during and after decisions are made.

Those who have examined restructuring note this phenomenon all the more: those in the "insider group" who make the initial decisions find that they have to take on the additional task of informing and involving others in conversation and planning, so that the end product actually does represent the thinking and ownership of the many rather than the few, and so that insider/outsider divisions do not occur (Lieberman, Darling-Hammond, & Zuckerman, 1991). We see this in these case studies as well. The faculty at New Suncook learned that restructuring is a constructivist process that must be nurtured for each additional group of faculty members as they newly encounter the set of ideas a smaller group has been working on. The process at Keels Elementary also suggests the development of ever-expanding concentric circles of collaboration and conversation about change, so that an insider/outsider divide does not develop between initial planners and later participants.

Similarly, in order for parents, students, and community members to be true partners, schools must enable them to participate in real conversations about children, teaching, and learning. Schools must find ways to allow parents and others to be engaged in fully understanding and participating in an educational dialogue about what's important, how the school community is trying to accomplish its goals, and what changes may be considered and undertaken. Parents must have genuine opportunities to participate in decisions about their own children and about their schooling experience more generally.

This means that parent participation, like that of teachers, must extend beyond the representation of a few on a committee, whether it is a shared decision making committee or the PTA board. Understanding this, the faculty at Wheeler "gave parents copies of everything [they] were reading about primary programs" as they planned for change. As a result of keeping parents informed, they became advocates rather than barriers to change:

> We kept them informed and asked their input, so they didn't say, "Oh this is just one of those silly radical things." They understood what we expected to achieve from the change. It's amazing how far they'll go for you when they believe in you.

Similarly, a Hammond high school teacher reports, "When students, parents, and teachers have ownership, they have a vested interest in the project, idea, etc. They work harder to make the project or idea succeed."

A goal for new policy is to help schools find ways to remove bureaucratic structures that get in the way of serious dialogue and joint problem solving. In addition to revising decision making structures and processes, a critical aspect of this agenda is to help schools organize themselves on a small enough scale that a sense of community can develop and allow for collaborative work. Policy for smaller schools and school units can help nurture the kinds of personalized, collaborative, democratic communities described here and elsewhere (Darling-Hammond, Ancess, & Falk, in press; Fine, 1994; Lee, Bryk, & Smith, 1993). These are critical for creating circumstances in which parents, students, teachers, and other educators can come to know each other, trust each other, and hold to common goals.

Policy supports for creating participative learning communities can be developed by eliminating current incentives for building large warehouse schools and spending excessive resources on administrative superstructures to manage them. These incentives are embedded in policies governing school construction, school approval and registration, categorical program requirements, and other regulations specifying program and personnel inputs. Policy supports for restructuring school operations can be developed by changing requirements that bureaucratize and depersonalize relations between and among adults and students in schools, as well as by proactive incentives for ensuring time for teachers to work collaboratively with one another and with parents and for creating smaller, more personalized school units.

Structuring Learning and Inquiry.

Some of the supportive policies described earlier provide initial inroads in the long-range task of structuring opportunities for learning in schools. These include school-based structures for peer coaching, teacher research, and team planning and teaching, as well as district initiatives such as the professional development academies in Jefferson County and Hammond. Within several schools, efforts to restructure the school day to allow for more shared time for teacher planning and learning were secured through creative invention and, sometimes, waivers. This restructuring of time, schedules, and groupings of adults and children turns out to be critical for advances in practice.

The role of intentional networks for learning and change is also important. These schools were clearly helped by their associations with such networks as the Coalition of Essential Schools, the National Network for Educational Renewal, the National Education Association's Mastery in Learning project, and the Southern Maine Partnership. Local networks of schools nurtured by the professional development academies served a similar purpose of providing opportunities for schools and teachers to learn from each other both within and across school settings.

Yet, for the most part, these kinds of opportunities are exceptional and ad hoc, secured with special grants or extraordinary efforts, and requiring departures from the status quo. If learner-centered and learning-centered schools are to become the norm, policies must reconfigure the ways in which time in schools is organized and resources on education are spent.

Over and over again throughout the course of school reform initiatives, the lack of time and opportunities for teachers to learn about new practices, to plan together, and to discuss and attend to student needs is noted. This is a specifically American problem created by the adoption decades ago of the assembly line model for organizing teacher work. The vision of teaching work as it has been implemented in American schools over the last century is one where the teacher's job is to instruct large groups of students for most of the working day. The other tasks of teaching—preparation, planning, curriculum development, tutoring those in need of additional help, consulting with other professionals, seeking answers to student or classroom problems, working with parents—are deemed so unimportant that little or no time is made available for these activities. With the exception of most teachers' daily "prep period," usually spent filling out forms and trying to get access to the Xerox machine, teachers have virtually no planned time to consult with their colleagues. Because practices have traditionally been prescribed outside the school setting, policy makers envisioned no need and little use for professional consultation or knowledge-building. Thus, separated by their classrooms and packed teaching schedules, teachers rarely work or talk together about teaching practices.

Other countries, including Japan, China, France, Switzerland, England, and Germany, structure teaching much differently, providing much more time for teacher learning and collaboration at roughly the same overall cost. A typical high school teacher, for example, teaches standard-sized groups of students approximately 15 to 20 hours out of a 40 to 45 hour school week. The remainder of that time is used for preparation and joint curriculum planning; tutoring of individuals or small groups; and consultations with parents, students, and colleagues. This is made possible, in part, because virtually all school professionals are classroom teachers, in contrast with the bureaucratized system in the U.S. in which over half of school professionals work outside the classroom as supervisors, administrators, or "support personnel." In addition, because schools are smaller and more humanely organized in other countries, expenditures on security officers, truant officers, attendance officers, and others needed to treat the negative outcomes of large, depersonalized institutions are not needed, and can be spent on teachers and teaching instead.

Under conditions such as those in other countries, teachers can work collegially to design programs, to shape appropriate learning experiences for students, and to develop shared standards of professional practice. They can evaluate their work and make the decisions that are needed to continually improve schooling. There are many ways such restructuring can be accomplished if policy makers are willing to abandon preconceptions of how schools ought to look and work. New uses of teacher time are possible when teaching responsibilities are shared and emphasis is placed on personalizing teacher-student relationships rather than processing students through fragmented courses and grade levels. The Coalition of Essential Schools has created a number of productive teaching arrangements within existing per pupil resource limits. Many others are possible.

Equal emphasis must be placed on regularized opportunities for teachers to share what they know, to consult about problems of practice, and to observe one another teaching. This means adjusting schedules to provide shared time and adjusting expectations about the use of time in faculty meetings, inservice sessions, and other shared settings.

Staff development should be conceived as ongoing and embedded in the process of developing and evaluating curriculum, instruction, and assessment. As teachers consult with one another in collectively developing, analyzing, and evaluating student work; embedding assessment in their regular teaching practice; restructuring their school day; and transforming classrooms and schools into learner-centered communities, a powerful form of learning occurs. An important part of staff development, then, should include time—along with the resources of research, information, and expertise—for teachers to work together on the development and implementation of school changes. Making time in the school schedule for this kind of teacher collaboration aimed at improving teaching and learning will be a powerful incentive for faculties to engage in the kinds of changes necessary to provide all students with the opportunities to learn more challenging material in more authentic ways.

To accomplish this, states, districts, and schools should be considering how to reallocate resources in ways that put more educational money into classroom teachers and teaching than into administration and peripheral programs. Policies should seek to create more personalized environments with high-quality teaching in the first instance so that students are prevented from failing, rather than investing primarily in the Band-Aids that follow when the system has failed. They should invest more directly in teachers' capacity for teaching diverse learners well—in teacher education and ongoing professional development, rather than in supervisory and inspection systems designed to compensate for the lack of investment in teachers.

State and local policies should allow deregulation and rethinking of staffing patterns that sometimes require or fund certain kinds of non-classroom personnel and thus reduce funds for directly supporting the work of classroom teachers. They should provide concrete incentives for restructuring the school day to ensure time for teachers to share work and planning, as well as for less fragmentation of learning for students. Funders should seek to ensure that a sufficient amount of professional development money is directed to the school level so that schools can allocate the time necessary to make certain that teachers have opportunities for continual learning. And schools should have some authority to decide how to spend those professional development resources, including underwriting their participation in powerful cross-school networks for learning and change, using energy from outside the system to help imagine new ways to transform the system.

Ultimately, policies must be reinvented to support the learning, critical inquiry, and ownership that create serious professional commitments to student learning. Teachers involved in restructuring schools speak most eloquently on this score:

> Customizing teaching to each child's level, believe me, is time consuming. But once you try it and see how it works and how much more you enjoy teaching, you just accept it. You start thinking of teaching as a career and not just a job.

> I have refocused my thinking about students and the work I give them. . . . I have the responsibility of developing worthwhile work for the students. If they do not "buy" it, they will not learn it. I must examine what I am doing, not "demand" that they do the work or not succeed.

> I assess my own teaching and involvement in making [my school] the best it can be. I realize more and more the importance of what I do for students' futures. I sense a greater impact of my decisions.

Creating schools that enable teachers and students to succeed in these ways together is the most important goal of educational policy for the twenty-first century.

REFERENCES

Darling-Hammond, L. (1990a). Instructional policy into practice: "The power of the bottom over the top." *Educational Evaluation and Policy Analysis, 12* (3), 233–241.

Darling-Hammond, L. (1990b). Achieving our goals: Superficial or structural reforms. *Phi Delta Kappan, 72*(4), 286–295.

Darling-Hammond, L. (1993). Reframing the school reform agenda: Developing capacity for school transformation. *Phi Delta Kappan, 74*(10), 752–761.

Darling-Hammond, L. (1994). National standards and assessments: Will they improve education? *American Journal of Education,* August 1994.

Darling-Hammond, L., & Ancess, J. (1994). *Authentic assessment and school development.* New York: Teachers College, Columbia University, National Center for Restructuring Education, Schools, and Teaching.

Darling-Hammond, L., Ancess, J., & Falk, B. (in press). *Authentic assessment in action: Studies of schools and students at work.* New York: Teachers College Press.

Elmore, R. F. (1983). Complexity and control: What legislators and administrators can do about implementing public policy. In L. S. Shulman & G. Sykes (Eds.), *Handbook of teaching and policy.* New York: Longman.

Fine, M. (1994). *Chartering urban school reform.* New York: Teachers College, Columbia University, National Center for Restructuring Education, Schools, and Teaching.

Green, T. (1983). Excellence, equity, and equality. In L. S. Shulman & G. Sykes (Eds.), *Handbook of teaching and policy* (pp. 318–341). New York: Longman.

Jervis, K. (in press). *Eyes on the child: Three portfolio stories.* New York: Teachers College, Columbia University, National Center for Restructuring Education, Schools, and Teaching.

Lee, V., Bryk, A., & Smith, M. (1993). The organization of effective secondary schools. In L. Darling-Hammond (Ed.), Review of research in education (Vol. 19, pp. 171–267). Washington, DC: American Educational Research Association.

Lieberman, A., Darling-Hammond, L., & Zuckerman, D. (1991). *Early lessons in school restructuring.* New York: Teachers College, Columbia University, National Center for Restructuring Education, Schools, and Teaching.

Lieberman, A., & Miller, L. (1990). Teacher development in professional practice schools. *Teachers College Record, 92*(1), 105–122.

Little, J. W. (1993). *Teachers' professional development in a climate of educational reform.* New York: Teachers College, Columbia University, National Center for Restructuring Education, Schools, and Teaching.

McLaughlin, M. W. (1987). Learning from experience: Lessons from policy implementation. *Educational Evaluation and Policy Analysis, 9*(2), 171–178.

National Commission on Excellence in Education. (1983). *A Nation at Risk.* Washington, DC: NCEE.

Shulman, L. (1983). Autonomy and obligation: The remote control of teaching. In L. Shulman & G. Sykes (Eds.), *Handbook of teaching and policy* (pp. 484–504). New York: Longman.

About the Editor and the Contributors

Ann Lieberman, Editor, is Professor and Co-Director of the National Center for Restructuring Education, Schools and Teaching (NCREST) at Teachers College, Columbia University. She received her M.A. degree from California State College at Northridge and her Ed.D. at the University of California at Los Angeles (UCLA). She has previously held many positions on national boards and has also served as (AERA) president in 1992. Her research interests have been and continue to be in the areas of collaboration, teacher learning and development, and, more recently, the understanding of networks and school-university partnerships. She has written on all of these topics. Her most recent work includes: *The Work of Restructuring Schools: Building From the Ground Up* and *Building a Professional Culture in Schools.* She is currently working on a second edition of *Teachers: "Restructuring" Their World and Their Work* with Lynne Miller.

Barnett Berry is Associate Professor of Educational Leadership at the University of South Carolina in Columbia. He received his M.A. degree from the University of South Carolina and his Ed.D. from the University of North Carolina. His work primarily focuses on school change, educational policy, and teacher professionalism. A recent foray included work for the Edna McConnell Clark Foundation in creating new images of the school-change process by combining the best of case study research and journalism. Beyond teaching graduate courses, giving workshops for policymakers, directing dissertations, ad infinitum, Barnett has been working hard trying to ensure that his oldest child, Joe, has a good, quality middle school education.

Elizabeth Bondy is Assistant Professor in the Department of Instruction and Curriculum at the University of Florida in Gainesville. She obtained her M.Ed. and Ph.D. degrees in Curriculum and Instruction at the University of Florida. Dr. Bondy served as the first Book Review Editor for the *International Journal of Qualitative Studies in Education.* In addition to her work in school restructuring, Dr. Bondy works in two grant-funded projects in the area of preparing teachers to accommodate diverse students. Dr. Bondy's book, *Reflective Teaching in the*

Elementary School (with Dorene Ross and Diane Kyle), was recently published by Macmillan.

Donna Gaus is a Ph.D. candidate at the University of Louisville in Kentucky. She also holds A.B. and M.A.T. degrees from the University of Louisville. Her research interests have included school-university collaboration, gender equity issues, school restructuring, and student engagement in learning. She recently coauthored her first publication, "Teachers' Work and the Need for Invention," for the journal *Equity and Excellence in Education*. She is currently doing educational consulting half-time while raising her two children, ages 1 and 3.

Lee Goldsberry is Associate Professor of Education at the University of Southern Maine. After completing his D.Ed. at the University of Illinois–Urbana, he worked for several years in the Division of Curriculum and Instruction at Pennsylvania State University. His writings and research focus on teacher involvement in continuing professional development, especially through in-class observation and conferral. His most significant accomplishments are embodied in his two children, Kimberly and Kirk.

Linda Darling-Hammond is Professor of Education and Co-director of the National Center for Restructuring Education, Schools and Teaching (NCREST) at Teachers College, Columbia University. She has worked as a public school teacher and curriculum developer, a senior social scientist and Education Program Director at RAND Corporation, and member of numerous education boards and commissions at the national, state, and local levels. She is current editor of the *Review of Research in Education* and co-editor of the *New Handbook of Teacher Evaluation*. Her research has focused on issues of teaching quality and educational equity.

Alice Holt is Special Education Resource Teacher at New Suncook School. She received her B.S. in Speech Pathology and Audiology from Boston University and her M.S. in Learning Disabilities and Emotional Disturbances from Lesley College in Cambridge, Massachusetts. For over 20 years, she has worked in New England as an educator of students with special needs in public schools and residential placement. Having contracted polio at the age of 6, she possesses a personal and professional interest in education as a shared responsibility with individual learners, not the system, as the focus for decision making. This is her first major publication.

Karen Johnson has been teaching at New Suncook School in a multiage K–2 classroom for the past 5 years. She received her B.S. in Early Children Education from Wheelock College, Boston, and her M.S. in Instructional Leadership from the University of Southern Maine in Portland. Her prior experience includes 10 years of teaching, all but 3 at New Suncook School. She is currently involved in presenting workshops in New Hampshire and Maine on multi-aging, assessment, and integrated curriculum. Her research interests include the reflective practices of teachers, the development of alternative assessment in elementary schools, and site-based teacher education.

Gary MacDonald has been in education as a teacher and administrator for 21 years. He received his B.A. from Marietta College in Ohio, his M.S. from the University of Southern Maine in Portland, and his C.A.S. from the University of Maine, Gorham. Since 1982, he has been Principal of New Suncook School. In 1991, he was recognized as Maine's Principal of the Year. During a 1992–1993 leave of absence, he served as Executive Director of New Hampshire's Alliance for Effective Schools and its School Improvement Program.

Rhonda Poliquin received her B.S. in Special/Elementary Education at the University of Delaware in Newark. Since graduating, she has taken courses at the University of Southern Maine. Currently, she is an intermediate grade teacher at New Suncook School. Her experience also includes providing services for children in resource and self-contained special education programs. She has actively participated in the restructuring efforts at New Suncook School.

Lauren Potter received her B.S. Ed. from Northeastern University in Boston and her M.Ed. from the University of Southern Maine in Portland in the Instructional Leadership Program. She has worked in the field of early childhood education for 18 years. Her research interests have focused on classroom practices, including children's choice-making in schools and the multiage structure. Her writings have included contributions to literature on multiage settings, mainstreaming special needs students, and alternative methods of assessment. She is currently employed as a K–2 multiage teacher at New Suncook School.

Dorene Ross is Professor and Co-coordinator of Elementary Programs in the Department of Instruction and Curriculum at the University of Florida in Gainesville. She earned her M.Ed. in Elementary Education from the College of William and Mary in Williamsburg and her Ed.D. in Early Childhood/Curriculum from the University of Virginia in Charlottesville. In addition to her work in school restructuring, Dr. Ross has published numerous articles and book chapters in the area of preservice and inservice teacher education. She has worked on two funded projects in teacher education, one focusing on the development of professional knowledge in teachers and the other focusing on preparing teachers to accommodate diverse learners. Dr. Ross's book *Reflective*

Teaching in the Elementary School (with Elizabeth Bondy and Diane Kyle) was recently published by Macmillan.

Mark A. Smylie is Associate Professor of Education at the University of Illinois at Chicago. He received his B.A. and M.Ed. degrees from Duke University in Durham, North Carolina and his Ph.D. from Vanderbilt University in Nashville. His research interests concern school organization, leadership, and change; coordinated children's services; teachers' work and work redesign; and teachers' professional learning and development. His recent publications include "Redesigning teachers' work: Connections to the classroom," in the *Review of Research in Education;* "The principal and community-school connections in Chicago's radical reform," in *Educational Administration Quarterly;* "Principal assessment under restructured governance," in the *Peabody Journal of Education;* and "Teacher participation in decision making: Assessing willingness to participate," in *Educational Evaluation and Policy Analysis.* He was a 1992 National Academy of Education Spencer Fellow.

Ute Tuermer is a Ph.D. candidate in the College of Education at the University of Illinois at Chicago, where she also received her B.A. and M.Ed. degrees. She is a Graduate Fellow in the University's Center for Urban Educational Research and Development. Her primary research interests include early childhood education and children's social and moral development.

Rodman Webb is Director of the Research and Development Center for School Improvement at the University of Florida in Gainesville. He received his B.A. degree from the University of Hawaii and his Ed.D. from Rutgers University. His books include *The Presence of the Past, Making a Difference* (with Patricia Ashton), *Qualitative Research in Education* (edited with Robert Sherman), and *Schooling and Society* (with Robert Sherman). His research interests include school restructuring, shared governance, institutional change, teacher careers, professional development, the micropolitics of schools, and the education of hard-to-reach children. He has published numerous articles on these and other topics in recent years.

Betty Lou Whitford is Professor of Secondary Education in the School of Education at the University of Louisville in Kentucky. Her research and writing focus on the relationships among school organization, professional development, and educational change—work that grows out of her extensive experience with school-university collaboration as a teacher, researcher, and professor. She holds A.B., M.A.T., and Ph.D. degrees from the University of North Carolina at Chapel Hill. With Dick Corbett, she is currently coediting a book series on restructuring and school change for the State University of New York Press.

Index